the song of the soul

The authorised Martin Stephenson biography

the song of the soul
The authorised Martin Stephenson biography

Richard Cundill
and Mark Bradley

First published in 2009 by

Ardra Press
PO Box 243
Beverley
HU17 6AX
United Kingdom
www.ardrapress.co.uk

ISBN: 9780954867867

British Library Cataloguing in Publication Data
A CIP record for this book can be obtained from the British Library

Designed and typeset by Julie Martin

Printed and bound by TJ International Ltd, Padstow, Cornwall

Cover art by Kieran Fitzpatrick: kieran_fitzpatrick@yahoo.co.uk

Contents

Introduction

To begin to understand fully the music of Martin George Stephenson, its inspirations and influences and equally its impact on people, involves setting out on a global journey. From Washington, Tyne & Wear to Durham, North Carolina via Newcastle, New South Wales – the blindingly obvious links in the place names cunningly disguise the fact that this is a trip not just covering many miles but many years as well. The music journalist who, back in 1988, described the second album of Daintees songs as '...building bridges between love and hate, between cradle and grave, between folk and pop, between the past and the present' had, unwittingly in one wonderful sentence, set the agenda that this book is based on.

On reading that description at an early stage of my research, I was struck by the possibility that the words had been written already and thus I questioned my motives and reasoning for writing the book at all. However, I was equally aware of the complete lack of any deeper analysis of Martin's music and I very soon began to understand the number of different themes, links and bridges (that word again) that inhabit the songs, stories and life of this very complex man. Add all that to the fact that I knew the journey would be nothing if not intoxicating – sod it, a real scream – and I didn't need any more justification for spending the next few years immersed in the world of a be-hatted, forty-something, gangly, guitar-playing Geordie singer-songwriter.

The 'journey' metaphor could not be more appropriate. The miles I have travelled in the process of putting this biography together; the miles put in by Martin, Joe Guillan and The Daintees in that same period; the miles travelled by fans such as Cyril and Nadya Povyshev, John Meadows and Andy Semple; the miles and years that the music has encompassed covering the country blues of Blind Blake, the bluegrass of Merle Travis, the folk of Bob Dylan, the punk of Richard Hell, the indie pop of Aztec

Camera. Yes, that journey metaphor is perfect – in fact if Gypsy Dave Smith hadn't beaten me to it then *The Dreamer's Road* would have been a glorious title.

That mention of musical influences is not meant in any way to undermine the originality of Martin Stephenson's work. He himself is so aware of tradition and history and the need to communicate songs, playing-styles and values to the next generation, that he would be a traitor to his own beliefs if he didn't reflect those from previous generations – *The Oral Tradition* in fact; thus went another prospective title. No, the originality in Stephenson's work comes from something much deeper than chords and notes and lyrics: it is essentially about a belief in music as a healing device, as a power for good, and as a tonic for emotional trauma – *The Song of the Soul* – yes, that will do nicely.

RC – January 2009

Chapter 1

Youth and Young Manhood
[1961 to 1985]

Date: 3 December 2008; location: The New Roscoe, Bristol Street, Leeds. Martin George Stephenson is playing a three-quarter-size acoustic guitar, backed by percussionist Finn McArdle. Between them they have utterly delighted a small audience of varied ages and musical persuasions during the course of the last two and a half hours or so. One of this book's co-authors and its publisher are present along with an old school friend and early musical associate of Martin's, Tim Reid and his wife. Manning the CD and book sales table are Mick and June Whitfield, two dedicated fans who attend pretty much every Martin Stephenson gig in the northern parts of England.

The New Roscoe is run by John Keenan, a legendary music promoter in Leeds who made his name running the F Club punk venue in the late 70s and curated the Futurama festivals in Leeds in 1979 and 1980 at the Queens Hall (the 1979 version entitled The World's First Science Fiction Music Festival), which featured some of the earliest noises of post-punk bands such as Joy Division, U2, PIL, Echo and the Bunnymen and Siouxsie and the Banshees.

As Martin engages John (who, he points out, bears an uncanny resemblance to a 'late period' Jim Morrison) in some typical on-stage vs off-stage banter, it emerges that John has put Martin up in the same B&B in which he housed The Sex Pistols back in the day. One immediately imagines the rock 'n' roll mayhem inflicted by Johnny, Steve, Glen and Paul on the poor Polish landlady's property, and compares it to the havoc our man will cause tonight as he puts the kettle on for a third cup of coffee to help him wind down after the gig.

The repartee between songster and faithful promoter quite succinctly covers the entire period of Martin Stephenson's musical journey from teenage punk rock fan to 40-something musical troubadour. Despite all the changes in the wider world, the musical world and Martin Stephenson's world, in a way nothing has changed. The point being that Martin is still playing music on his terms, purely because he loves it. You can see it in his eyes. He is just as enthused by picking out a tune from one of his more recent musical inspirations Charlie Poole (who admittedly is from the 1920s) as he was learning the chords to 'Pretty Vacant' when he was 16.

After asking the sound man to provide some dub-esque echo and reverb, Martin guides Finn into a song with a reggae skank called 'I'm in Love for the First Time'. A song which at this point has yet to be recorded and released for posterity, it had been written back in the 1980s by a recent musical collaborator of Martin's. It provides a clue to another link back in time.

Date: 17 September 2008; location: Borders Coffee Shop, Charing Cross Road, London. I am meeting up with former Chefs and Helen and The Horns singer/guitarist Helen McCookerybook for an interview about Martin and his music. Helen is a petite lady in the middle-age of life whose face lights up once I have mopped up the spilt coffee (I'm a clumsy so-and-so) and we start talking about music. Helen talks about how she grew up in Newcastle in the late 70s and couldn't wait to get away from the dark, grim city. Hence she enrolled at Brighton Art College. As a musician she became involved in Brighton's own independent label Attrix Records with her band The Chefs but admired from afar the sounds emerging from the equivalent labels like Zoo in Liverpool and Postcard in Glasgow. She was hugely annoyed when Kitchenware Records of Newcastle put its name on the indie map as she felt she should have been a part of it. She was very much aware of The Daintees' music and especially intrigued by Martin's appearance in *NME*'s 'Portrait of the Artist as a Consumer' article published in 1983. Not only did she think that Martin looked and sounded, from his catalogue of 'tastes', like he could be a Chef, but he also listed their '24 Hours' single as one of his favourite songs. Despite living in similar musical circles Martin and Helen never did meet back then – however in

1988 Helen made a note to write to him at some point but didn't get round to it.

In the interim Helen put her musical life on hold as career and family life became her priority. Her experiences with the 'music industry' had very much mirrored those of Martin's – 'I have known a lot of nice people who have gone into music and ended up as very nasty people.'

However in the early 2000s as her daughters became teenagers, Helen's desire to become involved in music again prompted her to write a book under her pen name Helen Reddington, entitled *The Lost Women of Rock Music: Female Musicians of the Punk Era* – an academic exploration of the world of Poly Styrene, The Slits and The Raincoats et al. Next up was an album of songs entitled *Suburban Pastoral*, released in 2006.

Helen's eyes continue smiling as she regales me with tales of meeting Ari Up and Poly Styrene, legends of the punk world to this writer.

The strangest thing she tells me, though, relates to her first meeting with Martin just a couple of years ago at a What's Cookin' gig in Leytonstone. Expecting a dour, serious singer-song-writer dulled by all the years of trekking around the UK, what she found was a man who she described as 'a male version of me!' – eyes smiling, engaging the audience like a teenager playing their first gig. Even odder, while tidying out some 'stuff' recently Helen found the note she had made for herself in 1988 to write to Martin.

After being aware of each other doing similar things at opposite ends of the country over 25 years ago, their eventual meeting signified a start of a musical and personal relationship; Martin singing Helen's song 'I'm in Love for the First Time' in Leeds may just sum it all up.

From being inspired by the same punk rock heroes in the 1970s to playing, writing and talking about music for the love of it in 2008, you can see it in their eyes. These people mean it, maaan!

*

Washington is a town in the North East of England, a short drive from both Sunderland and Newcastle. Currently with a population of around 60,000, Washington was designated a new town in 1964 and expanded dramatically by the creation of new villages and the absorption of areas of Chester-le-Street to house overspill population from surrounding cities.

William de Wessyngton built Washington Old Hall on the site of an old Anglo-Saxon hall. He was a forebear of George Washington, the first President of the United States, and thus the area has given its name to the U.S. capital and many other places in the United States. Washington Old Hall was the family home, and the present structure incorporates small parts of the medieval home in which George Washington's ancestors lived. American Independence Day is marked each year in a ceremony at Washington Old Hall.

Historically, Washington was heavily involved in the coal industry with a number of pits. One of these in the Albany district of Washington is preserved as the F Pit Museum (pits in Washington were named alphabetically). A number of the old communities of Washington grew up around the pits, e.g. the modern area of Usworth partly developed around the Usworth mine and the area was known as Usworth Colliery (and still is to some of the older generation). In support of the mines there was a series of wagonways and later railway lines to transport the coal. The wagonways took coal to staithes on the River Wear where it could be loaded onto barges to be taken to the ocean-going vessels in Sunderland.

But never mind all that Wikipedia stuff. The weirdest thing by far about Washington is how it is laid out. Washington is divided into small, self-sufficient 'villages' named after towns in the United States. It was originally also divided into 15 numbered districts. These numbered districts have gradually been removed and now road signs indicate the villages' names instead of district numbers.

Whatever, it has proved to be incredibly confusing for me in the past, having had reason to visit for my 'day job' many a time. It is perhaps no wonder that the subject of this biography became a seasoned traveller around the UK who very rarely gets lost. Coming from Washington, navigating pretty much anywhere else must have been a doddle even before the days of Sat Nav.

Martin George Stephenson's particular 'village' was Columbia, but back then, pre-new town, it was known as Brady Square. Specifically, Gainsborough Avenue was where he would spend his formative years after being born at Dryburn Hospital, Durham on 27 July 1961 to mother Frances Ann and father Alfred (Alfie) George. Martin has a sister, Janet, who was three years old when he came into the world.

The Stephensons were very much an archetypal working-class, North East family of the era. Frances and Alfie's families were predominantly miners. 'My Dad had a chance to go to university when he left school,' says Martin, 'but opted to go down the pit with his mates instead. He also worked as a bus driver and a bus conductor. A typical working man who loved his wife and his family. He took his wages and gave them to my Mum every week.'

Frances worked all her life in the Plessey telecoms factory in Sunderland. In short, they were seemingly a fairly standard working-class family. However later in life Martin hinted at some recognizable family traits: 'My Dad had a brother who died when he was 17. He was a special kid, very gifted musically – my Dad's in his 70s and he's still grieving for him, which is weird. But the first time I ever saw anybody connecting with people and making them laugh was when my Dad had a travelling shop, driving round the council estates. He was good at working the people, I think I clocked that.

'I had a very loving upbringing. My grandparents came to live with us when they got old. My Mum had a much more nurturing type of childhood, I guess, as she was an only child whereas my Dad was very much expected to look after himself as he came from a much bigger family. So when he met my Mum's parents they kinda became his parents really; he was very close to my Mum's parents.'

Martin was particularly fond of his maternal grandfather Matthew Carlton, whom he would later write about in the song 'Me & Matthew'. 'He was a great character. He was an epileptic and he spoke very slowly, but watched everything that went on. When I got The Toe Rags together, I was very fond of Gordon, the drummer, because he very much reminded me of my Grandad as he spoke slowly as well.

'When I was about 15 and had my first girlfriend, called Kim,

I brought her back for tea one Sunday and we were having a game of darts in the back kitchen. Kim's Mum came to pick her up about seven o'clock after tea time and I noticed my Dad went really quiet and he sat at the back out the way. It turned out that Kim's Mum was the girl he ditched when he met my Mum and took her to the pictures. It was strange at the time because when you are a kid you think your Mum and Dad have been together forever.'

Bryan Ferry's family lived just a few houses down from the Stephensons, which provides the imagination with some peculiar possibilities – Martin as a pre-pubescent, glitter-clad, Eno-esque Moog player etc – but sadly their paths never crossed as Ferry is 15 years older than Martin and had left town for London by the time Martin might have been aware of his existence.

Martin attended Washington's St Joseph's Roman Catholic junior school followed by St Robert of Newminster senior school – both strong RC seats of learning. 'At junior school I was really ahead of all the other kids in the first couple of years but then felt there was something wrong with that. I felt uneasy and preferred to fit in with the other less bright kids. I think as a working-class kid I felt uncomfortable standing out in that environment. I think you're either the type of person who really thrives on the other kids not liking you or you want to fit in, and I wanted to fit in. In the first years at senior school I went from being in class 1A down to 3S and felt like I'd achieved something. There seemed like a lot of humour in that class and the kids seemed happier and had a lot more individuality about them. Real characters.'

This wouldn't be the last time that Martin would purposely self-sabotage his progression in life when he realised he wasn't comfortable with what had been foisted upon him.

Despite the 'class downsizing' making him feel more comfortable with school life, Martin was bullied at senior school by one lad in particular. 'Not really physical stuff, although he was a right hard case. He would make me go to the shop with him after school so I would be late home and get into trouble from my parents. Or he would borrow my watch and not let me have it back. Last I heard he was in prison.'

At the age of 12 Martin met a man who would be his first major adult influence outside of his immediate family, an influence that would continue throughout most of his teenage years. 'My friend Colin Ingleby was trying to persuade me to join the Boy Scouts but I thought it was all a bit soppy, so instead we went and joined a youth club run by Jim Sixsmith.'

Jim organised sports activities for the 1st Washington Scouts and Washington Youth Club and became an 'uncle' to Martin, whom he recalled in 2000: 'He was a skinny stick of a kid. He was bullied at school, because with his slight stature and long hair he looked like a girl. He was also very young-looking for his age. At 14 he looked 11 and at 18 he looked 15.'

Under Jim's guidance Martin developed a real aptitude for table tennis and football and helped the youth club to win league titles at both sports for three years running. Not bad for a skinny asthmatic. It was at the youth club with Jim and his mates where Martin really felt like he became his own person as a teenager. As well as encouraging him to further his talents at table tennis and football, Jim, as a keen music 'head', introduced Martin and the other kids under his tutelage to music that was outside of the usual chart stuff they were listening to. They now got to hear Frank Zappa, Santana, The Doors and Captain Beefheart, and this clearly enthused Martin: 'I remember Jim lending me Santana's *Greatest Hits* and being amazed at the sounds coming from it.'

After leaving the youth club Martin would continue to seek Jim's advice on many things – songs, lyrics, poems etc – even after Jim moved south to Kent in 1982.

This early teen period of Martin's life was clearly a key time in terms of his development as a music fan and gradually as a musician. His cousin Jamie Harwood, the son of Alfie's younger sister Thomasina, became one of his earliest musical collaborators as they began to learn to play the guitar and make music together. Something which, as it developed, didn't go down too well with Martin's Dad. Jim sums it up: 'Martin was, and still is, very much his mother's son. When you've seen one, you've seen the other. There was always friction between him and his Dad – nothing major, just that Martin's artistic streak didn't fit with Alfie's idea of what a son should be.' Martin agrees: 'My Dad was the typical alpha male. And I guess as I started to grow into a man I was supposed to lock horns with him. But I never did. I would slide down the stairs past him and try and keep out of the way. My sister on the other hand has a more fiery temperament which meant she would take him on!'

*

I got my first guitar in 1978 aged 16 with some Jack Willcock home teaching tapes. The guitar was an Antoria Telecaster costing £79 from Jeavors in Newcastle; my lifetime companion and cousin Jamie Harwood got one too, and we decided to start writing songs together.

Jamie got a job working for Maurice Somerfield, a guitar trader and jazz fan. Jamie worked in his factory setting up guitars. The factory distributed mainly Guild guitars and there were some good players working there who got Jamie into Ragtime guitar. He was 17 at the time and brought a Carl Kress & George Barnes LP home called *Guitar Duets* (which featured 'All I Do Is Dream'). He also brought Scott Joplin's *The Entertainer*, a book full of his rags, so Jamie really set me off on the thumb pick and songwriting path.

But punk was the overriding influence at the time. [LB][1]

For anyone who didn't experience it, it is difficult to comprehend the step-change in music that took place during the fabled Punk Revolution of 1976/77. For a serious chunk of a generation's worth of music fans, it meant exactly what the clichés said. Out with the boring old farts of Prog Rock, Heavy Rock, AOR/MOR, Jazz Rock, Pub Rock and all the various sub-groups of naffness that predominated, and in with the angry young men and women of Punk. The fashion side of it was a minor consideration, providing shock value only, outside of the trendy London art college scenes. In Manchester, Newcastle, Leeds, Glasgow and numerous small towns in between, it was predominantly about musical attitude. For a whole bunch of 15/16-year-olds who were becoming politically aware for the first time, it was also a time when you thought anything could be achieved. Forming a band was the easy bit – three chords and a fuzz box and all the energy and imagination that puberty-into-adulthood brings and you were away. Most importantly you had the chance to communicate.

---

[1] Sections labelled *LB* are from a piece written by Martin in 1987 entitled *Looking Back*.

The basic punk sounds heard on the early releases such as 'New Rose' by The Damned, 'Anarchy In The UK' by the Sex Pistols and any of a number of Ramones songs were gradually being taken and twisted and subverted by exciting young bands like Buzzcocks, Wire and Siouxsie and The Banshees. By late 77/early 78 there didn't seem to be any rules at all anymore. Pre-punk, avant-garde bands like Cabaret Voltaire and Throbbing Gristle were sharing the same bill as the 'new wave' bands, as they were becoming known, and the left field noises of The Fall, Gang Of Four and The Pop Group were being played on late-night Radio 1 and being featured in glowing reviews in the music press.

Numerous new bands were being formed daily all over the country, and they weren't just interested in copying Johnny Rotten and co. They were listening to the real message of punk (not the *Great Rock & Roll Swindle* one): 'Demand The Impossible', as a Sex T-shirt of the time implored – create new sounds out of chaos, and then keep creating.

In Washington Jamie and I quickly found a collaboration: a weirdo called Tommy Watson (drummer in a Pistols style), Roy Errington[2] (bass) and Paul Thompson, nicknamed Prof, who had a Vox Continental organ and a wasp synthesizer. Prof, Tommy and Roy were all aged about 20; Jamie and I were about 16/17. We called ourselves The Next – ha!

We rehearsed in a local hall called the Playbarn throughout 1978 doing covers of 'Pretty Vacant', 'Blank Generation' (Richard Hell) and 'Another Girl, Another Planet' (The Only Ones): all our favourite records, that is, as we couldn't write very good songs at the time. I think we had two of our own: one was called 'Prisoner' and the other was called 'White Machine', about a white Rickenbacker guitar that Jamie was lusting after.

The main band in Washington, without a doubt, during 77/78 were Murder The Disturbed, consisting of Steve Minto (guitar and songwriting), John Farrer (vocals), Chris Mordey (bass) and Foster Nevans (drums).

---

[2] Roy Errington, later immortalised in the song 'Running Water' – 'It was a replica Roy cooked up in his room.'

The Disturbed, as they were known locally, were very different from punk, much more geared towards Bill Nelson and Punishment Of Luxury – robotoid music, I think they called it. Minto's words were very clever at the time for writing songs about the Antichrist and the Cosmos, spiritual topics, demonic subjects very like what John Foxx did a lot later. Yes, Minto was very talented and was the first song-writer I had come into contact with.

When The Disturbed played live it was more like a theatre than a gig, and because of the way they dressed up they would get attacked a lot because anything a bit different then was punk.

These little subtleties were happening in probably every village and town from Glasgow to Brighton, a post-punk new wave I would have called it. I don't think I would have been playing if it were not for the likes of McLaren and the Pistols.

Anyway, The Next were total fans of The Disturbed who actually only released one single,[3] which was reviewed in *Sounds*. I think the review said that it should be melted or something.

The Next would borrow amps from The Disturbed and go watch them rehearse, and play The Clash's 'Tommy Gun' for them on their gear after they finished. Everyone followed The Disturbed who was into music in Washington, Peter Macadam (now a poet) and Adrian Ellis too.

Jamie and myself left The Next after bass player Roy Errington decided to leave. I remember crying when he left but finally we teamed up with 14-year-old drummer Adam Lynham. We called ourselves The Death and continued to rehearse at the Playbarn and follow The Disturbed. Jamie decided to go into the RAF as a gunner so we did a gig at a youth club to say goodbye. I remember doing a Brian James & The Brains cover. We used a wheelbarrow to transport the gear. Adam and I carried on with The Death with only distorted guitar and drums, very influenced at the time by Red Crayola, Pere Ubu and the Nuggets album (13th Floor Elevators, The Seeds etc). We also did a version of 'Come On Now' by The Kinks and 'Lucifer Sam' by Pink Floyd.

I still never wrote many lyrics and if there were any they would be hidden under the bed. Jamie did six weeks' basic training and

---

[3] Murder the Disturbed's single was the 'Genetic Disruption' EP (Small Wonder SMALL-17. Tracks: 1. DNA; 2. Walking Corpses; 3. The Ultimate System)

came out of the RAF (he couldn't handle it) and rejoined The Death, which was great.

The Death carried on for a few months but didn't really know what to do or where to go so I decided to get on my own and practise to be a good guitar player – as that was what I really wanted to be. It hadn't dawned on me yet about songwriting.

Early 1979 – Murder The Disturbed had by this time split up and Adam joined with Steve Minto, the best songwriter in Washington, and Chris Mordey on bass to form Strange Relations.

I was so bloody jealous of Adam joining the ex-Disturbed that I started really hanging around and pestering them until finally Steve let me join and gave me a tape of their set to work out guitar parts for.

This was the happiest time of my life as I had finally packed in table tennis and had gotten a new guitar, which took two years to pay for by the way. It was an Anniversary Fender Stratocaster, silver with a maple neck.

Throughout '79 we played lots of gigs in Durham such as Fowler's Yard and the Coach and Eight; we'd play Le Metro in Sunderland and all the youth clubs in Washington and Balmbras in Newcastle too. Our most successful gig was at the Speedwell in Darlington, which was the furthest we had travelled. I was totally overawed by the thing, playing guitar in a band with Steve and Chris who had actually made a record – we even had plans to start our own record label (Corned Beef Records, if I recall correctly), but that never evolved.

Through me acting so giddy and daft and being so young and stupid I started getting on Steve's tits, so around Christmas '79 he decided to sack me. That was the worst blow imaginable for my immature ego and I had a really depressing Christmas and New Year. I tried playing guitar with The MPs, who consisted of Tommy Watson once again – with a new drum machine after giving drums up – Tim Reid, Strangler (John Evans, that is) and David Reid. The MPs were a little like Joy Division and their claim to fame was supporting Pink Military and Wah! Heat in Newcastle. [*LB*]

Tim Reid, member of the MPs and a friend of Martin's from their teenage years, is still in close touch with his musical buddy. He shares his memories of their early collaborations:

I got to know Martin having been at the same school (St Robert's). I was in the same class as his sister. I had recently moved to the North East from Salford, where I'd grown up – so I was a pretty exotic creature in the middle of all those Geordies. I had just started to play around with a guitar when punk exploded, so I swiftly got my hair cut short, improvised some DIY punk clothes and started my first band – Raw – playing in the school hall and local gigs. Martin's sister told me that he was doing the same thing and was writing a lot of lyrics – she showed me some examples but it struck me as too poetic and certainly didn't have the edge I was interested in at the time.

In 1977/8, we had become a bit more focussed, changed our name to the MPs and were playing as many gigs as we could – though it wasn't easy to get pub gigs as a punk band in the North East. The forerunners of Martin's first band were Murder the Disturbed and they were getting a bit of coverage in the area. Their main man was Steve Minto – a good guitarist with a talent for well written pop songs. He was much too talented for our punk ethic and had a mop of blonde hair which didn't suggest a leaning towards anarchy either, but he was a nice local lad so when he formed a new band Strange Relations, we offered them a gig supporting us at the Coach and Eight pub in Durham. We had played our first paid live gig there a while before – the manageress had paid us off with £13 ten minutes into our second set when she realised we were playing the same songs she hadn't liked the first time. So we were expecting a rough ride.

Strange Relations went on first – they all looked a little nervous. Their second guitarist (Martin) looked not only nervous but barely old enough to be out late – I guess he was about 16 but looked 12! They played well and were well received by the friends they had brought all the way from Washington, but less so by the Durham locals who, ironically, by this time had started to want a bit more aggression from bands. Afterwards I found Martin (who I am sure was wearing eye make-up – not a good move in Durham, punk or not!) with tears in his eyes:

'What's the matter, Martin?' I asked assuming something dreadful had happened.

'The audience didn't like us – they didn't listen and they didn't like our songs,' he sobbed.

'We're punks, man ... they're not supposed to like us!' From the look on his face I knew he wasn't convinced and that he wasn't cut out to be a punk!

A while later my intuition was confirmed. I was living in a flat in the west end of Newcastle – very exotic! Martin called round – he was a bit mixed up, I think. He was pleased because he had bought a new Fender Stratocaster (which he had lusted over for a while) but he had fallen out with Steve Minto and they had parted ways. Anyway we plugged our guitars in and played a few bits and pieces. Two things struck me: first, Martin was impressed by the fact that I wrote my own stuff and wasn't bothered about it being too clever – the sound and the feeling was all that mattered really; he clearly wanted to do his own thing and just needed to be a bit more confident. Second, his playing was really very good – much more musical than my DIY punk style. He played a little rockabilly riff that was fantastic and when I asked how he did it he said it was something he'd heard on the radio and just picked it up – he was genuinely gifted.

As the MPs we managed to blag a gig supporting Wah! Heat, a fantastic band led by Pete Wylie. Martin came along to see us and I think that finally made him realise that the stage was the place for him – I don't think we were that good, so maybe he thought 'if they can do it, so can I' ... but I think it inspired him and the rest (as they say) is history...

Martin takes up the story:

Anyway my heart was still with the last band, Strange Relations, who had by this time become Let Them Eat Cake, turned totally futuristic and Steve Minto had pretentiously turned his name to Jason Quest which he later changed to Steve Zodiac.

Being so young I was full of bitterness towards them and was determined to show them, so I wrote a couple of terrible songs which I truly believed were out and out classics and started a futurist band called Vutura Goya with Jamie and a small drum machine (what a couple of prats!).

The set list would be 'Dance', 'Midnight', 'Surfin' USA', 'Mystery Game', 'Femme Fatale' and 'Blue in Heroes'. Let's face it the only good songs in that set list were the Beach Boys cover and The Velvets' 'Femme Fatale' – which was all the more infuriating as whenever we played people would only remark on the covers.

I had a long black fringe, Jamie had spiky hair and we both thought we were futuristic people – more like a couple of teenage jackasses, I would say!

We did our first gig in Annabel's, Sunderland and the DJ did nothing but take the piss. The funny thing is we turned up with our amp and guitars at 11.00am, hung around all day on the stage and the PA didn't turn up till 9.00pm. We were so naïve and stupid that we helped the bloke up the stairs with all the speakers. It was the first time I had sung through a microphone and, needless to say, I made an absolute pillock of myself. Jimmy Kelly and Wib, who later became good friends, were the only ones who enjoyed it along with some gay bloke who enjoyed the Velvets cover 'I'll Be Your Mirror'. I decided to give up being a lead singer two weeks later after going down like a bag of shit in Heroes, Sunderland and losing an important support gig at Lumley Youth Centre supporting The Moondogs. Guess what: Let Them Eat Cake stole the gig from us – the bastards!

After knocking Vutura Goya on the head I started going out getting pissed a lot as I had a job as a carpet fitter and did some work at Joplings in John Street, Sunderland, some DIY sales and then settled at being a van driver's mate humping fridges around Ashington and Sunderland. [*LB*]

Martin's time as a carpet fitter has since taken on a somewhat legendary status, perhaps more due to the stunning normality of the job than anything else. Martin's 'career' did not pass without incident, though, as he explains in the following story, 'Repossession 1979':

The guy I worked for contracted himself out to the big carpet warehouses. I would go round to his house first thing every morning and have to wait while he finished doing whatever he was doing with his lass upstairs. He seemed a real hard-faced bastard but one time his humanity really showed through. It was just before Christmas 1979 and he told me that morning that we were doing a Repo Job. He explained that this woman hadn't kept up the payments on her carpet and we had to go and take it up and return it to the shop. When we arrived at the house the woman opened the door and she had a dressing where her nose should have been. Earlier that month there had been a story in the local paper about a man who had bitten his wife's nose off in a domestic fight – he'd been put away for it. This was obviously the house where it had happened. The living room was all decorated for Christmas and we had to move the tree out of the way to get the carpet up. A little baby was asleep on the settee and we had to lift it carefully out of the way as well. The woman was in tears about the carpet, saying how miserable the bairn's Christmas was going to be. We slung the carpet in the back of the van and I felt really terrible as we drove off. The carpet fitter started to head back to the shop but then changed direction and went back to his house. In his garage he had loads of spare carpet, remnants and stuff. He picked a really expensive piece of Wilton and I gave him a hand to put it in the van. We drove back to the woman's house and to her utter delight carpeted the living room, the hall, the stairs, the bathroom – even the side of the bath! Her face was a picture!

Meanwhile...

I made friends with a boy called Jimmy Kelly who was a really sharp and popular character and we started having beach parties, loads of fun. This was 1980, and through Jimmy Kelly I met Anthony Dunn at a party. He was playing fifties songs on an acoustic – he said he played double bass too – and we had great fun just passing the guitar to each other singing rockabilly songs. [LB]

Anth was born in Sunderland on 20/6/1961, one of five children: brothers Gary (more about him later) and Keith (later a sound engineer for Teenage Fanclub), and sisters Lesley and Claire (another future Daintee). After attending St Aidan's Roman Catholic School he left at 16 in 1977 to become an apprentice engineer, following in his father's footsteps. However after 3 years he packed in his apprenticeship to concentrate on his chosen path of bass-playing – something he'd begun at 14. Martin recalls:

At the time there was a very strong influence from the 50s in England by people like the Stray Cats and Matchbox and everyone was getting short back and sides and big semi-acoustic guitars. Double basses were very credible. Anyway Anth and myself did a gig together the following week at a place called the Springboard.

He brought his double bass and I brought my acoustic and we did some country songs, 'Ball Of Fire', 'Hold Me' and some Hank Williams ones too. These were songs that I picked up from my driving instructor, Bob, who was also a professional musician, playing Shadows-style guitar in a band in local working men's clubs. He gave me a pile of sheet music, with loads of great songs. The driving lessons were going so well, we'd often just sit and talk about music and guitarists we admired, or sag off for a game of pool.

Marty Yule was at that gig playing in a punk band called I Breathe First. Sunderland was the place, it was thriving, the people from The Bunker keeping punk alive and the likes of Jimmy Kelly and Wib more like American college boys, widening their tastes in music all the way through the spectrum.

Fossy, Ray Callaghan, Frog, John Kelly, Keith Dunn, Simon/Mick Thompson, Anth Dunn – we all used to drink regularly together.

Anth Dunn played bass for his uncle John Alpen, a 50s singer, and I finally joined to learn 50s guitar and jazz. We only played the clubs in between the bingo but it was great fun and Anth and I developed a rapport with each other. We did a gig with Charlie Gracie, an original rockabilly singer, and that was the pinnacle of our achievements! That band was called The Blue Moon Boys but split after about six months as Anth's uncle planned to emigrate to Australia and we didn't want to go.

We were getting into the English band scene and were getting more into doing our own thing than the 50s stuff, although it still had a strong influence.

By late 1980 I had developed songs like 'Roll On Summertime' and 'Smile on the Sunnyside' so Anth and I decided to form our own band called The Caramels.

It consisted of me on vocals and guitar, Anth on double bass, Anth's 10-year-old sister Claire on vocals and a 13-year-old drummer called Terry MacNally. It was a bit weird but Claire was a great singer and Terry could really hit that snare drum. It was really raw, primal rock 'n' roll.

We started playing student parties, busking, any pubs we could sneak the two younger members into. The Caramels changed their name to The Daintees as suggested by Michael Hedley, who made the name up in 1981. Michael was a vegan who didn't drink, but he was a close friend of myself and Graham Anderson and we all used to meet on a Sunday morning and watch jazz at the City Vaults. The songs were influenced from the 1930s to the American college mid-60s, nothing hippy. On the other hand there were melodic English influences such as The Chefs and Young Marble Giants etc. I called them melodic John Peel bands at the time.

I split up with Anth and the rest of the band and joined up with Graham Anderson, whose father was a jazz trombonist. We used to sit in with the old jazz players, which was a great education. We did a short spell of gigs as The Daintees too, consisting of Graham on double bass, me vocals and guitar and a real character called Sid 'RAC Man' Simkins, who played jazz drums. He was by far the best drummer I had met so far. We were a really sharp little trio and did a residency at the Brewer's Arms, Gilesgate, Durham leading up to the summer of 1981.

The name Daintees was becoming a label for a collective of musicians and friends to play my songs. There were no rules and no sense of musical direction, which I thought was evolving nicely as I was becoming more conscious of being a songwriter and singer too. I still needed a lot more confidence though.

So I changed the line-up once again, reverting back to Steve Minto but keeping the name The Daintees with Chris Mordey on bass and Adam Lynham on drums. Steve had hit a low ebb at the time and a lot had changed. He preferred my songs and I his so we collaborated more on an even par this time and worked on a strong set list of songs we had already accumulated. Adam and Chris had a lot more confidence in me now and I felt that in myself I had earned their respect through very hard work and a lot of pain which we all decided to wash under the bridge and put down to inexperience.

Throughout '81 there was a very mellow, laid-back orientation in English music, e.g. wimp rock as so called by the music press, but I think this was a natural wash against all the aggression of the punk era. A very still period and very melodic as bands like Orange Juice and Aztec Camera were emerging – Go-Betweens, Bluebells etc. [*LB*]

Two prime movers in the development of this new wave of post-punk pop were Alan Horne and Edwyn Collins. They formed the Postcard Records label in Glasgow in 1979 primarily as a vehicle to enable Collins' band Orange Juice to release their first single 'Falling And Laughing' – still to this day recognised as a reference point in the development of what became 'indie', with its jangly guitars and cheesy, off the wall vocal. Messrs Steven Morrissey and Johnny Marr surely used this as a blueprint for arguably the most successful 'indie' band of all time, The Smiths. Later Postcard Records became a vibrant independent venture in its own right with a roster that would include Aztec Camera, Josef K and The Go-Betweens. Horne dubbed the label 'The Sound Of Young Scotland' in a direct echo of Berry Gordy's Tamla Motown.

> We were too small a band to do a big tour so we decided to do a lot of busking, but more with electric guitars and bass, so Steve wired up an old 50s record player and we plugged our guitars in that, along with a microphone, and Steve and I would share the singing.
> We stayed together in this format all the way through '81 and into '82. Steve used to make really good posters with The Daintees on and this attracted a young man called Keith Armstrong in the early summer of '82. He invited us to play in his shop as he was the manager of HMV in Newcastle – so we jumped at it! He said he loved the songs which were 90% mine as Steve was rapidly losing his confidence in writing. But that was OK, for Steve sang very well and played good guitar too. [LB]

Frustrated by the lack of an adventurous live venue in Newcastle, Keith Armstrong, Phil Mitchell and Paul Ludford had opened the Soul Kitchen at Newcastle's Casablanca Club in the summer of '81. The first group they booked were The Fire Engines, with Keith personally leafleting every pub and bar in the locality. Subsequent shows by Orange Juice, Josef K, The Jazzateers, New Order and Blue Rondo established the Soul Kitchen as something special and gave an ailing local scene a sorely needed shot of adrenaline. The club also branched out beyond the usual confines of a live show by incorporating slides, videos and photographic exhibitions into an evening's entertainment. A press release from November 1981 described it thus:

> The Soul Kitchen opened as an occasional club to bring back/create some sparkle in a Newcastle drowning in its own musical constraints. The idea was to create a venue for inspirational new groups, to play

records otherwise unheard due to a lazy national radio network and to support live entertainment by other media. To a large extent its ideas were fulfilled. At a time when London was glorifying cocktails and salsa the Soul Kitchen was delighting to the strains of Fire Engines, Jazzateers, New Order and Aztec Camera; 'Severance' by Mark Lucas, 'Young Love' by Derek Ridgers, slide shows and great dance.

Dave Brewis of The Kane Gang recalls: 'My first contact with Keith Armstrong was via Paddy McAloon of Prefab Sprout. They had released their first single on their own Candle label, 'Lions In My Own Garden (Exit Someone)', and I understood that Keith was starting his own label, Kitchenware. As my band were about to release our first single also on Candle we had to find out who was taking over our plans for stardom. Keith had formed Kitchenware with his partners on the idea that if Postcard could be successful as a label in Glasgow, why couldn't a similar thing work in Newcastle? Searching all the local gigs didn't turn up much of the local talent, as everyone with any ideas generally avoided playing in pubs etc as it was a bit too rocky and old-fashioned. Why not just rehearse endlessly in freezing conditions and not have to worry until your chance at a proper club night came along? We had all played bars and nightclubs but there was no really suitable venue until Keith decided to have one. This was The Soul Kitchen, a movable event.'

When the Soul Kitchen closed exactly one year later in August '82, the next steps were blindingly obvious to Armstrong and co. The venue had acted as a magnet for local unsigned bands all desperate to be heard and to make records; indeed the last two shows had featured The Bluebells and Aztec Camera supported by Hurrah! and The Daintees respectively – hence the idea of Kitchenware Records was born.

The new label trumpeted a brand of loud, passionate optimism – Armstrong was just as inspired by the same black soul music as Alan Horne had been in Glasgow three years earlier – however Kitchenware was positioning itself somewhat differently.

A Kitchenware Records press release showed the impatience and energy within: 'It took three years for daytime radio to discover the Bunnymen, Orange Juice and New Order; let's see how

long it takes you this time. OK you've got three years, starting ...
NOW!'

Another press release introduced the characters behind the
label in typically tongue-in-cheek style:

> Keith Armstrong – a 'Cult'ivator, a dreamer with his feet firmly on
> the ground. The ultimate enthusiast of everything/anything good.
> Hatches more ideas than a battery hen lays eggs.
>
> Paul Ludford – a sort of Chancellor of the Exchequer. Someone
> who thinks, cares and worries (sometimes too much). A schemer, if
> something's bad, he tells you; if he says it's good then it must be good.
>
> Jenny & Anita – the women behind the Men behind the Men
> behind the music (phew!). Proof that a woman's place IS in the
> 'Kitchen'!

'We don't adhere to the inverted snobbery of the independent
scene,' said Armstrong in 1983. 'At the same time we don't fall in
with the bland requirements of the major record companies. Thus
we can take the best of both worlds and provide an antidote to the
blandness that currently pervades the music scene.'

Proof of this different approach was provided by the differing
methods of distribution for the roster of bands, which grew to
include The Kane Gang and Prefab Sprout. Whilst the first
Daintees and Hurrah! singles would be distributed via the independent network known as The Cartel, Kitchenware secured
early major distribution deals with London Records for The Kane
Gang and CBS for the Sprouts. This ability to follow the right
approach based on his bands' different needs showed an unusual
maturity in the 24-year-old Armstrong, who had moved up to
Newcastle after managing HMV's Derby branch, where he was
the company's youngest ever manager. 'All the bands are
there for a different reason. But between the four of them,
you've got all the qualities that you look for in music. Hurrah!
are the big conscience, the Daintees are the big fun, Sprout
are the big songwriting talent and The Kane Gang are the
toughness.'

Meanwhile back to the summer of '82 ...

He had one band he liked at the time called Hurrah! (formerly known as the Green Eyed Children), whose song 'The Sun Shines Here' he was going to use his money to record, and wondered if we would be interested in coming down to the recording session and if there was any spare time maybe we could nip in and bang our best song down. And that's what we did as we recorded 'Roll On Summertime', our first single on the Kitchenware label, in ten minutes. It became the single of the week in *Sounds*, reviewed by non other than Dave McCullough. I remember hitting the last chord of the song and Keith running in the door during recording and saying 'I am your manager!' I shall never forget that as long as I live. [*LB*]

The single was recorded at Berry Street Studios, London in the late summer with Hurrah!'s engineer Brad Grisdale at the controls. (Incidentally, this was the first time that Martin met future collaborator and friend Virginia Astley as, having nowhere to stay, The Daintees were granted the use of Virginia's flat whilst she was away; Virginia's flatmates being friends of Keith Armstrong. They met the next day on Virginia's return.)

Released on 'non-stick' Kitchenware Records, the 'Roll On Summertime' single was housed in a sleeve depicting two smiling young ladies sitting under hairdryers sipping Coke from bottles through straws. The use of its brand name obviously escaped the attention of The Coca Cola Company's lawyers. The sound that leapt from the grooves (including the B-side 'Involved With Love') was an eminently listenable Postcard-inspired jangle that the term 'wimp rock' could have been invented for. References to gender-swapping, desert islands, and feelings of love complete with Byrdsian harmonies and Martin's melodic Fender Mustang guitar-playing firmly set The Daintees alongside the likes of Roddy Frame's Aztec Camera and Edwyn Collins' Orange Juice who were flavour of the month in the music press at the time. Slightly strangely one reviewer favourably compared Martin's voice to Art Garfunkel's – saying he was to Art what David Sylvian was to Bryan Ferry.

However, despite the generally positive reaction to the single, not everyone liked it. 'I met Kevin Rowland in 1982,' said Martin in 2000. 'He was number one in the charts at the time with "Come On Eileen". I had just gone to collect my first single. He asked to hear it. I blushed. I played it him and he said it was shite. He just shook his head and walked away. I felt that God didn't like me for a while.'

In 1983, a year after the single's release, Martin reflected ruefully: 'Red Rhino made a really bad job of distributing the single. It was unobtainable. Apparently London pirate stations were playing it all the time. John Peel played it. Kid Jensen's producer said we're more of a Radio 2 band. I think Radio 2 has a lot more class than Radio 1. The music is by musicians and songwriters. We are hoping to do a session for Terry Wogan!'

The next Daintees line-up change was due.

Not wanting to sack Steve, I decided after a while that I would leave The Daintees but Chris and Adam insisted on playing my songs so eventually Steve Minto got sacked. It was horrible but we were very hard-faced and simply got on with it. Steve was replaced by Jamie once again. It was getting to be ridiculous, worse than kids being in each other's gangs.

We were quite ruthless at times. I mean there was never any money as we were all dole wallahs and there was no security anyway.

When Jamie joined it got much better and he actually put a backing vocal on 'Roll On Summertime' too. [*LB*]

On Saturday mornings Martin, Jamie, Adam and Chris would meet at Martin's house in Gainsborough Avenue for rehearsals. A typical set-list of the time would look something like this: Roll On Summertime / Cecil / Let's Make a Day / Watch Where the Kisses Blow / Turn Me Around / I'll Give You My Heart / Monkey / Tremelo Men / Piece of the Cake / Smile on the Sunnyside / Miles Away / Marie 'n' Jim / Around & Around (by Chuck Berry) / Neon Skies / 55 Friends.

Keith got us a short tour with Aztec Camera in late '82 – three gigs in fact: Edinburgh, Dundee and Glasgow. We still weren't sure how to use PAs properly and I still considered us to be a bedroom band but we did surprisingly well and got a great deal of fun and pleasure out of it. Aztec were very kind to us and offered us another gig the following night in Aberdeen and then some others in London (The Venue) and the Midlands and our hometown Sunderland. They don't know how much they helped us. It was essential as we were just learning to perform on a bigger stage. [*LB*]

The Daintees' transport for the tour consisted of Adam Lynham's Mark 1 Ford Consul Cortina (registration ETN 727C – trivia fans!). Not quite superstardom but a step in the right direction.

'Aberdeen was a really good gig,' smiled Martin after the tour, 'we did an encore there. We could have done one at some of the other dates but the Aztec Camera manager wouldn't let us run over time. In comparison The Venue was really dead, no atmosphere. It's hard to really put yourself into it when you've got no feedback. As soon as Aztec Camera came on, whoosh, straight to the front. We did win them over at the end a bit. At Edinburgh someone sabotaged the PA settings between us soundchecking and playing our set. Two of Aztec Camera were running round trying to sort it out as we played. They had a better sound on all of the dates. That's expected when we have only ten minutes to soundcheck. We didn't take too much notice of the sound quality when we were playing. You become too involved in the playing to notice.'

'We didn't make a profit on the tour,' added Chris Mordey. 'In Scotland Aztec gave us some of their money. It was worth playing for the publicity though. It was a nice working holiday. We didn't expect to make money. Aztec Camera were really nice to us.'

Working with The Boy Wonder had a significant impact on Martin, as he reflected in 2000: 'I met a young Roddy Frame at Edinburgh University in 1982 and he was light years ahead of me. I was blown away by him. He changed my life instantly.'

A review from the tour of the gig at The Venue in London picked out one particular influence: 'With guitars held Haircut-high, this dinner-and-dance combo sang 'we could be miles away' and they definitely are – nearly two decades away with memories of Roger McGuinn's country rock.'

There was very much a Byrds-like quality to several songs, particularly the aforementioned 'Miles Away' and also 'I'll Give You My Heart' – all 'Mr Tambourine Man' guitars and vocal harmonies. But equally the diverse range of styles that would come to fruition on the first album *Boat to Bolivia* in 1986 was already in evidence – 'Neon Skies' comes on like a classic rock anthem;

'Cecil' is a pure pop song; 'Tremelo Men' is punked-up Duane Eddy; 'Piece Of The Cake' sounds like it's from a Rogers & Hart musical. If anything it was the lack of a distinct 'sound' that tended to confuse the listener, although the developing onstage banter and fun and games easily compensated for that. The banter was becoming increasingly important:

> One night we were playing at a Newcastle gay club called Rockshots, and this guy wearing full drag over jeans and Doc Martens climbed onto the stage and sat with his arms around my legs, calling up 'Play Billie Holliday for me'. I started some banter with him and suddenly this huge weight lifted from my shoulders. It was like I'd been frightened to look up. Then I had finally done so and found that it felt all right. [*LB*]

Guitarist, keyboard and harmonica player John Steel was at that time working in cousin Keith Armstrong's HMV shop. He had been learning his trade playing guitar and singing in an Everly Brothers-style duo with school friend Graeme Ash. He had seen The Daintees with Aztec Camera at the last Soul Kitchen gig at Tiffany's in Newcastle in late '82. 'I thought they were brilliant, and in fact preferred them to Aztec Camera. Martin, even at this early stage, was clearly a natural performer and the band had a tremendous energy about them. Adam Lynham looked impossibly young and was still underage, I think, at this point.'

Soon after that gig John started working for the newly formed Kitchenware Records, humping gear and helping out with recording demos. In a Kitchenware press release from that period he is described as '[forming] the link between the management and the musicians. Someone who can view the situation from all angles. An arbitrator and a technician.'

John was asked to play keyboards and harmonica for The Daintees on some demos commissioned by Phonogram. This involved an interesting journey down to London for the session, as John recalls: 'We had got a van from somewhere to take us and the gear down. Martin was driving and in those days he liked to drive fast. He must have averaged 100mph from Newcastle to London. The really scary thing was that the seats in the back of the van were deckchairs. I thought we were all going to die!'

Those Phonogram demos (overseen by A&R man Ashley Goodall) included an early version of 'Piece of the Cake' – almost fully formed as a song and an arrangement (with John Steel on harmonica) and very similar to the version that would later appear on *Boat to Bolivia*. There was also an energetic version of 'Tremelo Men' and the pure pop of 'Let's Make a Day', 'Turn Me Around' and 'Lifetime' – the latter featuring John on piano showing how his multi-instrumentalist skills were beginning to widen the musical scope of Martin's songs.

I then decided to go back and find Anth as I missed his spontaneity and we brought in a drummer called Marty Yule. [*LB*]

Marty has had a versatile music career. He began as the drummer in various punk bands in the North East, including I Breathe First, before going on to occupy the drum-stool with the legendary Toy Dolls for nearly a decade and a half. He now runs the Hot Rats record shop in Sunderland, and spoke in 2008 about how he started with The Daintees: 'I was 17 and had known Anth for a while, and he asked me if I was interested in joining The Daintees. I jumped at the chance. I remember going round to Jamie's place in Washington for the audition and sure enough I was in the band.'

Initially over the moon at joining The Daintees, what didn't impress Marty so much was having to carry his drum kit up and down the stairs of the rehearsal studios in Clayton Street, Newcastle – particularly at four in the morning after a long drive back from a gig. There were lighter moments, though: 'Just before that tour, though, we had a very surreal experience one day coming out of Clayton Street to see an open-top bus coming down the street with Tommy Cooper on the top deck at the front. We looked on it as a sign!'

After some dates with The Bluebells (including a gig at Keele University where Martin pleads mid-song, 'by the way, we haven't got anywhere to kip tonight, so if anyone's got a guest house...!'), this next Daintees line-up were asked to support Aztec Camera on another short tour including a gig at the London Lyceum on 15 March 1983. The bill also included The Farmer's Boys and Screen 3. An *NME* review by Richard North was not exactly gushing with praise, however: 'The Daintees were the first into this pussy cat's den, providing the crowd with semi-acoustic, beat combo dance music that twanged but did not tingle. Their set, comprised half and half of cover versions and soundalike originals – they reminded me of a swinging Butlin's showband. Their version of Chuck's 'Around and Around' was suitably the weakest I've encountered.'

Listening to a recording of that gig proves the *NME* writer wrong in that the Chuck number was the only cover played – but he did have a point with some of the material; thirty minutes of tight, melodic, but mostly unadventurous, three-minute pop songs mainly concerned with losing and/or winning in love with Martin not yet having the confidence to venture banter-wise much further than the basic song intros: 'It's a good song; it's better than the last one – I think!' Aside from the single 'Roll On Summertime', two songs that do stand out however are, yet again, the ballad 'Piece Of The Cake' and the catchy 60s pop-inspired 'Cecil'. Early signs of Martin's songwriting development.

After a few months Jamie decided to write his own songs and left of his own accord. At least he got a guitar out of it as we got £1500 on our first publishing deal [with April Music]. Jamie got an old Gibson 330, Anth an Epiphone semi-acoustic bass. Marty, who was an absolutely brilliant character, got a lovely little jazz kit like Ringo Starr's. With our new gear we did some demos at Park Lane studios, Glasgow. The songs were 'Crocodile Cryer', 'Trouble Town', 'Better Plan' and 'Louis'.

After the demos we toured with new Kitchenware signing Prefab Sprout, who had recruited Aztec Camera's drummer Dave Ruffy for the whole tour. We all became great friends on that tour, jammed together, learned our trade live and The Daintees became a force to be reckoned with live.

In August '83 we played a gig in London at Dingwalls, Camden supporting The Smiths. We were second on the bill and a band called The Telephone Boxes were third. Anyway we finished our sound check and went into the dressing room – The Smiths had gone out for something to eat, and had left Morrissey's daffodils on the table. So Anth shouts up 'come on let's take the daffodils' – and so we took them and threw them into Camden Lock. Mr Morrissey was not happy – he had to send someone out in a taxi to get some more. [*LB*]

Also at this time the three-piece Daintees recorded a gig at The Bunker community centre in Sunderland with the aim of releasing a six-track mini-LP due to be titled *Daintees Go Mad On Mushrooms*. The tapes, however, were allegedly lost.

A centrespread in the *NME* covering all four Kitchenware bands seriously raised the profile of all concerned. Part of the piece offered Martin the opportunity to voice his thoughts: 'The music is more gutsy now. We probably got a bit bored of being soft all the time. I think we've been influenced a bit by rehearsing in the same place as a lot of local punk bands. I've always thought we're more of a live band than a studio one anyway. When we go into the studio, we can't always capture the excitement that we feel live. We're not like Paul Weller who can practically live in a studio, so we lack experience. I can't get used to the fact that you pick a day, 2 October say, and you have to be in the mood to record your song that day. It just doesn't work like that. I don't really care what people say about us. Some will like us and some won't. What's the point of worrying? We'll just keep on playing and whatever happens will happen!'

This was followed up in the same paper's 26/11/83 edition with the aforementioned likes/dislikes feature called 'Portrait Of The Artist As A Consumer'. Both Paddy McAloon and Martin were 'grilled', with the latter quoting The Chefs, Vic Godard and The Undertones among his favourites – his 'hates' being 'violence, selfishness and Frank Zappa'. (Paddy's faves included Sondheim and Stravinsky – proving he was clearly on a higher plane.)

We recruited another member, John Steel. John was a great help at the time because he was more of a polished musician and had an enormous appetite for hard work which always made me feel guilty so I would end up working harder. He was also an extremely versatile musician. [*LB*]

John had been asked to help out yet again at further demos in Maddock Street Studios in London on 27 and 28 November 1983 – at which point it was assumed by all that he had gradually joined the band as a full member. John, like Marty, vividly recalled the pain of the Clayton Street studio: 'We would rehearse at a studio in Clayton Street in Newcastle that was six floors up. It was a real hassle as we had to hump the gear up and down six flights of stairs every time we played a gig. I distinctly remember Martin and Anth tending to go missing on those occasions – but then they were from Sunderland!'

Also from late 1983 The Kane Gang's Dave Brewis recalls a Daintees gig at the Soul Cellar under Grey's casino at the bottom of Grey Street in Newcastle: 'The gig was absolutely mad and chaotic with the band looking like a young early-1960s pop group and doing mainly 'fun' material. There were some good songs, and 'Tremelo Men' the instrumental, and a great atmosphere about the night. The old amps, guitars and suits were made to look good, but it was far from a retro night, I think they were reacting against the po-faced music of the day like only kids can. If Martin had wanted to be a pop star ever, he would have continued this type of image and music. I imagined them all driving round in an old Ford Anglia, all the time, and by all accounts so they did. It was definitely a time that was ripe, in that most bands involved around Newcastle just knew something was about to happen. It was a new age.'

Martin continues:

> In winter '83 the demo we did in Glasgow resulted in us being signed to London Records but keeping our independence with Kitchenware, which took us into 1984 optimistic to say the least. Songs such as 'Look Down, Look Down' and 'Running Water' were coming, we were hardening up live, becoming very confident, maybe too confident. There were no rules on gigs. We'd play till the plugs were pulled out – very spontaneous. I became very good friends with Hurrah!'s new drummer Damien Mahoney who had joined them from a band called The Passage. I think Damien was a great influence on Hurrah and gave them an intensity they lacked before he joined. All three bands were touring a lot then, roadying for each other, helping each other out. It was a very amiable relationship between us all. [*LB*]

The first months of 1984 saw The Daintees playing live as part of a Kitchenware package tour headlined by Prefab Sprout with

Hurrah! first on the bill. The development in The Daintees' live performances, from the early Aztec Camera support gigs, was astonishing. Real charisma, stagecraft and genuine musicianship were well to the fore combined with a significant surge in the quality of Martin's songwriting (e.g. 'Slaughterman' and 'Slow Lovin''). This resulted in some classic gigs during this period, not least the one at Brighton Polytechnic in February (referred to in Keith Armstrong's sleeve notes to the *There Comes A Time* compilation released in 1993 – but Keith's memory must have let him down as they did a few more than 'four songs in an hour-long set'). Armstrong's introduction set the scene: 'The Frankie Goes To Hollywood Award for pure energy and wild sex goes to ... The Daintees!'

Martin is on fine form with the chat and the band have improved significantly with the addition of John Steel's inputs on guitar, harmonica and keyboards. There's also a real breakthrough in the playing as they break songs down prior to building them back up again – prompted by Martin's now infamous 'knock it down, knock it down'. The gig also featured the first ever playing of a future Daintees staple 'Running Water' – albeit with just one verse. The never-to-be-released 'Cecil' is again a standout, but the high point comes with a new song called at this point 'Hypocrite' – a real step-change in quality and proof that this band and its leader had the potential to explore musical and lyrical areas that would have seemed way out of their league twelve months earlier.

A gig at London's ICA earlier in the tour also showed how things were moving in the right direction, according to *Melody Maker*'s Ian Pye: 'Surprise of the night were The Daintees who cheekily stole the show from the much vaunted Prefab Sprout. Singer-guitarist Martin Stephenson was obviously at the head of the queue when they dished out reserves of charm boasting more presence in the twinkle of his eyes than most bands manage in their entire set.'

Around this time a prospective record company rep came to see The Daintees live, in the shape of Michael Levy of Magnet Records – later Lord Levy of alleged 'cash for honours' scandal after he sold Magnet to Warner Brothers in 1988 for £10 million. Marty Yule recalls the meeting: 'He was wearing these badly coloured jeans and orange round-toed cowboy boots. He said, "Boy George works for me, and I tell you he works his arse off". We collapsed in a fit of giggles.' The Daintees didn't sign to Magnet.

On 5 February Martin, Anth, John and Marty convened at the BBC's Studio 5, Maida Vale to record their first radio session for David 'Kid' Jensen's Radio 1 evening show. Produced by Dale Griffin, the resulting broadcast on 20 February demonstrated to the country a well-crafted set of songs played by a band who were rapidly becoming impossible to pigeon-hole. 'Neon Skies' – haunting rock (featuring Newcastle violinist Brian Davidson); 'Cecil' – pop consciousness; 'Slaughterman' – all Ry Cooder guitar and vicious lyrics; 'Look Down, Look Down' – violent country-rock. This was a significant development from 'Roll On Summertime' in both songwriting and playing and pointed to The Daintees becoming much more than the Kitchenware house jesters.

Keen to develop the new songs further, Martin and the band then went into Newcastle's Lynx Studios with the Kane Gang's Dave Brewis in the production chair. Dave remembers: 'My first production sessions were demos for 'Crocodile Cryer' and 'Trouble Town' at Lynx over a couple of days. The whole band were mostly uncontrollable and over-excited, not to mention under-rehearsed, but somehow I got the tracks finished and mixed. They weren't brilliant recordings. The band needed more rehearsal time to sound good in a studio, my memory being that it came back off tape the way they played it, and I couldn't make it sound any better than that. In later years Martin used this state of affairs to his advantage creatively – he never did rehearse ever to my knowledge. He harnessed his own chaos. Not long afterwards Paddy McAloon was persuaded to have a crack at recording the band – a version of 'Crocodile Cryer'. He told me it took days just to get an acceptable rhythm track, as the band were so loose! Paddy's arrangement was the one that stuck.'

The 'Paddy' recording of 'Crocodile Cryer' (now officially called 'I'm A Hypocrite') was released later that year on a cassette available from *NME* entitled 'Raging Spool' (also featuring Aztec Camera's version of Van Halen's 'Jump'). This early version has all the elements in place that would make it such a key part of the band's first album two years later – the swirling organ, melodic bass and plaintive vocals proving that very little else needs adding to a song that works perfectly.

Marty was then sacked from the band at the instigation of London Records head Roger Ames. Ames had played drums in his native Trinidad and apparently had a thing for tight timekeeping for drummers and bassists – he sacked Lawrence Donegan (Lonnie's son) from the Bluebells around the same time for similar reasons. Donegan went on to play in Lloyd Cole's Commotions and Marty signed up for many years in the legendary Toy Dolls. Thus he became the first link between the Daintees and Olga's Toy Dolls, with guitarist Gary Dunn and drummers Paul Smith and Malcolm Dick also eventually playing for both bands. In fact Paul Smith, known for his dry wit, would later sum up the difference between the bands as: 'it's gone from slow shite to fast shite.'

Marty Yule was replaced by Lucas Fox who played drums on 'Trouble Town' and was later sacked. Marty was a great miss but wasn't progressing as rapidly as the rest and simply couldn't keep up. It wasn't an ugly separation, it was just something that was inevitable. His personality was a great miss as everyone loved him but he was holding The Daintees back musically. Marty was very unchildish and professional about it and still did the odd tour in '85 as he was a great live drummer. [LB]

John Steel remembers Marty's involvement fondly: 'It was apparent that Marty was struggling technically in the studio as a drummer. But he was a great live drummer and a dapper dresser to boot. I think some of the character of the band left when Marty went.'

Meanwhile, the single 'Trouble Town' was released.

'Trouble Town' was recorded in summer '84 and The Daintees made their first video and the single went to number 101 in the charts, which we thought was amazing. [LB]

According to Anth Dunn, the single could have fared considerably better in the charts as it was on Simon Bates' playlist but he went on holiday for three weeks and his replacement chose not to play it!

> It was produced by Sade's producer Robin Millar who was a very nice man and very inspiring to work with as we were still petrified of recording studios. [LB]

'Robin was a real perfectionist,' remembers John Steel. 'We must have run through "Trouble Town" with him in rehearsal at least 40 times. Looking back I think it was over-produced.' Martin would later express a similarly unenthusiastic opinion of Millar's work. This wouldn't be the last time that a producer would incur the Stephenson wrath; but perhaps it was just early signs of a discomfort with the music industry processes which would grow significantly over the coming years.

The revolving Daintees drum stool was now filled by Lucas Fox whose claim to fame was playing with Lemmy in an early Motorhead incarnation called Bastard as well as London punks Warsaw Pakt (not to be confused with Manchester's Warsaw – later Joy Division) and then went on to join Sisters Of Mercy off-shoot The Sisterhood. 'Lucas was in the band for about six months and only played a couple of gigs with us,' says John. 'He was a character but somehow didn't really fit in. Although his experience helped a lot with the development of our studio technique.'

Sam Brown (daughter of UK rock 'n' roll singer Joe Brown and sister of Robin Millar's engineer Pete Brown) sang backing vocals on 'Trouble Town', which were faithfully mimed to by Anth and John in the resulting video filmed at High Force waterfall in County Durham. This and a video for the unreleased song 'Poor Angel' (a perhaps too close-to-the-bone song about a young girl dying of cancer) were later included on a Kitchenware compilation entitled *A One Way Ticket To Palookasville* (even later reissued as *Hits From The Kitchen*).

To the more casual Daintees listener, i.e. one who had never attended a gig, flipping the single over brought something of a surprise. 'Better Plan' and the 12" extra track 'Jealous Mind' started to give an indication of the depth of variety in this band's repertoire. The latter song explores the ups and downs of a serious relationship to a gentle, swinging acoustic guitar, while

'Better Plan' comes across as a gender-confused version of the Velvet Underground's 'Waiting For The Man', with the band sounding like the Sex Pistols on Newcastle Brown!

Collectors! – A mega-rare version of the single was pressed with a different sleeve showing 'Crocodile Cryer' as the A-side – although the vinyl still played 'Trouble Town'. This obviously signified the band/Kitchenware's original intentions.

Released on September 28, the 'Trouble Town' single was promoted by a short tour of seven dates titled, with devastating wit, The Magnificent Seven Tour, with Marty Yule back on the drum stool, taking a break from his band The Evil Muthas. Speaking of Marty – no piece about The Daintees can be written without reference to his legendary terrible jokes. So, with apologies for the loss of quality control at this point ...

My Dad inherited a chicken farm. Unfortunately they died because he planted them too close together.
He used to keep racing pigeons. They always beat him.
He's got a pigeon with 666 on its forehead. It's an omen pigeon.

Moving on into 1985 ...

Our initial advance from the record company had run out by early '85 so we had to do a tour with Roy Buchanan to make the money for our wages. The tour was The Daintees' first trip to continental Europe. Roy is a legendary American guitarist who is the guitarists' guitarist and was looking for a young English band to back him on his tour, so we met him in London and had a rehearsal with him; it was really weird.

The idea was that The Daintees would play their set of songs first then play Roy's blues set after that, which worked out about four hours solid playing every night. Marty Yule decided to play with us on this tour and we were all really nervous in case we cocked it up for Roy. [LB]

Roy Buchanan was then, and now, regarded as one of *the* great electric blues players. His pedigree was impeccable, having played in The Hawks, forerunners of The Band, and at one time being favourite to replace Brian Jones in the Rolling Stones.

I remember when we were learning the songs sitting in the rehearsal room, waiting for Roy to turn up, shitting ourselves. Marty was like a ghost, sweating all over, really funny. Roy came in the room, what a nutter, looked like he was a hit man for the Mafia, really cold eyes. Plugged his Telecaster in and said, 'OK boys, let's hear some blues.' Me, Anth and Marty were all watching John because he was the only one who had done his homework and just as we were going into the first chorus Roy stopped. So we stopped, our hearts in our throats. Then Roy spoke: 'OK boys, you've got that song, here's the next one.' The relief on Marty's face was hilarious. He thought he was about to be sacked and Roy in his own way was saying everything was OK. [*LB*]

Marty adds a further chuckle: 'I remember one night on tour with Roy when his manager took Anth aside to have a quiet word with him. Anth wouldn't tell us for ages what it was but eventually he gave way. The guy just asked if he could stop yawning on stage! You see, most of Roy's material was basic 12-bar blues and for a bass player to play that stuff for 20 minutes a song, I suppose it got a bit dull for him. We cracked up!'

Roy Buchanan was a great influence even though he was from a completely different era. We got on like a house on fire and would talk and play songs to each other till the early hours. He had some great stories and he taught me how to play 'Swan Lake' on the guitar. He is one of the most interesting and wacky characters I have ever met.

On the tour we played Finland, Germany, Sweden, France, Holland, Norway and finished with a night at the Hammersmith Odeon where Jeff Beck and Cozy Powell turned up to see Roy. [*LB*]

John Steel was suitably awed by what the dates signified: 'The Roy Buchanan tour was a great experience. We would play our support spot and then back Roy, although Martin would usually not join us for Roy's set. I think he felt a bit uncomfortable. I remember a gig in Paris at the legendary New Morning club. This was a venue that had seen all the jazz and blues greats perform. Art Blakey and The Jazz Messengers had been on the previous week. Scary!

'With it being quite close to the UK, a lot of the Sunderland crowd came over and were hassling us to get them in for free, which was a bit awkward. So Martin decided we should do a runner, and we absconded to a restaurant, which didn't go down too well with them – including Martin's girlfriend Angela.'

A quick search of You Tube will find plenty of clips from the Roy Buchanan and The Daintees Rockpalast gig – an interesting and somewhat different spectacle for Daintees fans.

Three cheers to Roy Buchanan, we all miss him! [*LB*]

After the Roy Buchanan tour Martin and the band were straight back into more gigs, this time smaller venues but now as the headlining band. Their European travels had obviously had quite an affect, as yet again there was an obvious improvement in both songs and performance. New additions to the set list included 'Song About The Member' (a scathing attack on people who need to join a club to justify their existence) and 'Louis' – a light-hearted boogie through the streets of Sunderland that was beginning to become a real live favourite – often interspersed with stories, band introductions and the *Old Grey Whistle Test* theme tune led by John Steel on harmonica. John recalls a novel way of getting the crowd onto the band's side: 'I remember a very strange gig from that time in Edinburgh. The venue was a roller disco by day and the kids who had been skating got free entry into the gig. So we played to about 40 uninterested kids and a few students. It was hard work at first until Martin jumped off the stage and started doing martial arts kicks and shapes, which the kids loved. He got back on stage and said to me 'gotta know how to work 'em' – and from then on the gig was a breeze!'

Hand in hand with this artistic progression, though, was a hint of desperation at their lack of progress re record releases. This was borne out by comments made onstage by Anth and Martin like, 'this was released on the Polydor label' ('Cecil') and 'this was released on EMI in Australia 20 years ago!' ('Caroline'). John Steel was feeling the financial pressure particularly and was offered a gig with Microdisney which he turned down out of loyalty to The Daintees. Added to this an increase in the already substantial quantities of alcohol consumed before going on stage (there's obviously more drinking time when you're headlining) resulted in some extreme behaviour, most of which was incredibly funny (how many bands have you seen bouncing on trimpets? – mini-trampolines), but which occasionally went a little too far. One example of this was a gig at the theological Froebel College, Roehampton in February that year. A combination of alcohol, an article in the music press proclaiming Paddy McAloon to be the 'new Messiah', and the recent memory of a Roy Buchanan song called 'The Messiah Will Come Again', resulted in Martin coming on stage backed only by John Steel's churchlike organ-playing, announcing 'God bless you. The Messiah will come again!' The band then went into 'Song About The Member' – with its first line of 'give him an idol to worship' – and the drunken theological students were suitably unimpressed, and not particularly Christian in their responses, shouting back many a hearty 'Fuck Off!'

Dedicated early Daintees fan Dave Driscoll recalls a gig in early 1985 at the University of London Union: 'I admit it... From the end of 1982 to 1985 I was a Daintees groupie. It all started when my friend sent me a postcard, saying he had just seen this great band supporting The Bluebells. "They're The Crickets! Fuckin' great!" It was The Daintees. From the records, it's virtually impossible to imagine how great Daintees gigs were! This particular gig was serendipitous to say the least. My friend and I had travelled up to London to see The Room, but they weren't playing, and had been replaced with an obvious replacement: The Men They Couldn't Hang. My friend wandered off to get the beers. I was enjoying the cod folk stylings of TMTCH, when I started thinking, *Bollocks, how long do you need to get a couple of beers?* so I wandered back to the bar, noticed a side door open to the left of the bar and poked my head through. The Daintees! "Are you a social secretary?" I was asked. "YES!" "Oh, OK then." (You either have blagging technique or you don't!) I made my way through and found my friend. "Ah there you are," he said. "I think I have missed three songs. I could hear 'Hypocrite' and was looking for a video-screen, thinking *where on earth have they got a video of The Daintees?* Saw the band and thought *walk this way!*" I had expected to be told: "Oh, I looked for you but couldn't find you!" ... I was such a forgiving fellow in those days! I was later to find out the gig was for University social secretaries, with a view to booking the band for a University tour. So on stage were The

Daintees: Martin Stephenson, Anth Dunn, John Steel and (The Mighty) Marty Yule, pissed to shreds and playing with as much fun and abandon as I had seen in ages. The banter and songs were great. The thing I remember more than anything else was when Martin shouts "Drums! Drums!" on "Trouble Town", as Marty was having a crafty fag. Suddenly, jettisoning said crafty fag, Marty started to tub-thump. The jettisoned crafty fag had actually managed to lodge into the folds of his sweatshirt, and started to smoulder. I will go to my grave with the vision of Marty trying to blow his smoking arm whilst drumming!'

In March The Daintees recorded their second radio session, for guest DJ Feargal Sharkey on Gary Crowley's Capital Radio show. The version of 'Trouble Town' was a considerable improvement on the single and was followed by a truly hair-raising 'Look Down, Look Down' (later released on the 'Inferno' EP), including Martin's introduction that rounds off with 'there's nowt wrong with drugs, I think they're fuckin' great! – actually I think they're shit.' Sublime Saturday afternoon entertainment.

After the initial zap to the beginning of '85, the rest of the year was a nightmare; money ran out, Anth got a bar job with all of us heavily in debt. There was only me, Anth and John in The Daintees and we were really down. No dole because of tax and no wages because of debt. So it was back to busking literally for food because after a while it becomes embarrassing going to your parents for help: you can only do it for so long then it becomes humiliating asking for food and money when you are supposed to be independent. I did a lot of busking with Chris Mordey and Adam Lynham during the day and never went out at night. The only consolation was that my songs were coming in waves and I felt I was developing and maturing a lot.

I used to go and watch this drummer called Paul Smith when I was younger. Paul was about 34 with glasses, a really dry character and very talented and fortunately I got him to do the odd gig with The Daintees. This was the boost we needed and Paul pushed our standards way up. It was fun to play again and although there was still a great lack of money, The Daintees were coming out of a terrible spell. Paul had four children and a wife to look after so he couldn't play for nothing but he bent over backwards for us and he is the best drummer I have ever played with.

Also in summer '85 I had an excellent collaboration with song-writer Virginia Astley. She asked me to play classical guitar for some dates she was doing and also play acoustic guitar on her recording of 'I Live in Dreams'. Virginia influenced me a great deal and gave me great confidence in working with strings. It was really easy learning her songs as when I got off the train at Kings Cross we went straight to the tube station to meet Anne Stephenson, her violin player, and started busking. I thought that was great! We played a lovely gig at St James' Church, London and one in Riverside Studios, Hammersmith. Very quaint and English; cellos, violins and flutes. [LB]

The summer and autumn of 1985 was a busy period and Martin, with The Daintees and his new collaborator, set out on a mini-tour of Scotland entitled the Stolen Thunder Review, a Keith Armstrong play on Dylan's 'Rolling Thunder Review'. A highlight of the shows was Martin and Virginia's duet on the Leonard Cohen song 'Suzanne'. Unfortunately not all audiences were receptive to these more delicate, acoustic sounds, as Martin recalls: 'We played a gig in Aberdeen which was a bit of a disaster, 'cos it was full of spiky zombies and people just taking the piss. We ended up getting very upset and just walking off. Like every human being now and again you're really vulnerable. It was one of those moments and I just flipped. I tried really hard to keep going but it was hopeless. The audience were hostile and drunk and it was like banging your head against a brick wall. I like silence, you see; I like people to listen. I like to get a really tight feeling with the audience, I like them to feel really close to what we're doing. That's when the songs work best, you know'.

As well as the St James' Church and Riverside gigs, Martin also supported Virginia at the Electric Screen Cinema, Portobello Road. Virginia (on flute and vocals) and her band consisting of Anne Stephenson (violin), Jocelyn Pook (viola), Audrey Riley (cello) and Nick Pretzel (percussion) provided a very different accompaniment and this period definitely aided the development of new, acoustic-based songs like 'The Old Church Is Still Standing' and 'The Wait'.

During the summer, Martin dossed down in Virginia's Pimlico flat on the camp bed. It was around this time that he wrote 'Rain'.

The 'I Live In Dreams' session was recorded at Elephant Studio in Wapping and emerged on the *Record Mirror* cassette 'Spools Paradise' in September, and in November on the 12" version of Virginia's release 'Darkness Has Reached Its End', under its new title of 'Shadows Will Fall Behind'.

That September news broke that Martin and Virginia were to record a four-song EP for Kitchenware with two songs apiece. This idea was aborted and from the recording sessions in the North East, only 'Synergy' has seen the light of day (on the 'Inferno' EP in 1986 and later on the *High Bells Ring Thin* album). Virginia's trip to the NE was not completely wasted though as she and Martin did some busking in Newcastle – and later in the year she attended Keith Armstrong's New Year's Eve party where she apparently struck the Kitchenware boss after overhearing him making insulting comments about her!

Despite that, this was by no means the end of Virginia's working relationship with Martin –a relationship which provided yet another opportunity for musical development.

> Her best song in my eyes is still 'A Long Time Ago'. It also gave me the chance to do my quieter songs such as 'Rain', 'Coleen' and 'Candle in the Middle' against a more appropriate background. That was a beautiful summer for music; thank you, Virginia. [*LB*]

In October The Daintees had another record out. This time, though, it was a track on a freebie given away with the London glossy fanzine *Jamming*. 'Running Water' could not have been more different from the Virginia Astley collaboration, featuring Damien Mahoney (ex-The Passage) on drums (Marty Yule and Lucas Fox had gone for good and Paul Smith was unavailable) powering Martin, Anth and John along in fine style.

The record deal with London Records had been thrashed out and now at last was the chance for The Daintees to prove that they could translate their on-stage energy and wide-ranging musical style into a coherent whole – so they went to Liverpool to record an album.

Chapter 2

There Comes A Time
(1986 to 1989)

It had been over three years since The Daintees had released debut single 'Roll On Summertime' and two years since they had signed to London Records and released 'Trouble Town'. This time lag and the wealth of songs they had built up and seriously road-tested in the meantime, meant that a severe case of impatience and frustration at the lack of an album release was developing around the band. Original Kitchenware label mates Prefab Sprout and The Kane Gang had already released their debut albums (to much acclaim) and the Sprouts had gone one further, and better, with the release of their classic second album *Steve McQueen*.

That all changed in the cold winter of 1985 as the band arrived at Liverpool's Amazon Studios – scene of the recording of the Teardrop Explodes classic 'Bouncing Babies' single some seven years earlier. Amazon was a relatively low-key studio located next to an MOT testing centre in Kirkby on the outskirts of Liverpool.

Nick Lowe (Elvis Costello, Graham Parker etc), Elvis Costello himself and Clive Langer/Alan Winstanley (Madness, Dexy's Midnight Runners, Lloyd Cole and The Commotions) had been suggested as potential producers for the project, but in the end young up-and-coming Amazon in-house producer/engineer Gil Norton was given the job.

Gil had started at Amazon on a YTS scheme and worked his way up to producing China Crisis' *Difficult Shapes And Passive Rhythms* album as well as co-producing Echo and the Bunnymen's *Ocean Rain*. In short, he was the sharp new kid on the block and the thinking was that he and The Daintees would be a perfect match.

'Gil was only about 23 years old,' said Martin in 1987, 'and very keen on music, totally music orientated, hated money – he had to, to be able to work with us as we had fuck-all.'

John Steel also has positive memories of the choice of producer: 'Gil was great – a real cheeky chappy and much more relaxed than Robin Millar. He created a sound that was simply an extension of The Daintees' natural sound.'

Around this time Gil famously played Martin a demo tape of a new band he was lined up to produce, but Martin didn't think much of the sound and advised him to give them a miss. The band was The Pixies and fortunately Gil didn't take Martin's advice.

Pre-production rehearsals and early takes went very smoothly. Clearly the Roy Buchanan tour and headlining gigs had tightened the band up considerably since the demos with Dave Brewis a couple of years earlier. All the band put their heart and soul into the performances – they were determined to make it something special as the time had clearly come.

Gil Norton creates a wonderfully lush yet low-budget production throughout, perfectly complementing Stephenson's ambitious yet rootsy songs.

The opening track, 'Crocodile Cryer', was described on the matrix notes of the 12" single version as 'A F'N CLASSIC' – never has a mere run-off groove communicated such a truth. The song was written on 3 January 1984, three days after the funeral of Martin's maternal grandmother Jane Bird Bell. The narrative is taken from the perspective of a distant 'friend' attending a funeral purely to discover what value the contents of the will might hold for them. The protagonist is painted as totally parasitic and callous – even to the extent of justifying their actions by quoting a higher force: 'won't God be pleased with me for mourning'. Stephenson's later well-developed knack of disarming the listener by juxtaposing a populist reference with a historical/spiritual one is well to the fore – how many people could write a song that mentions Lourdes *and* Elton John? Musically the track is based on a simple two-chord acoustic guitar strum but builds to a finale after the middle eight and last chorus via some mighty organ (by John Steel) and lead-guitar playing, along with that rare thing – sympathetic-sounding synthesised strings.

Shortly after the album was released, Martin reflected on the writing of this exceptional track: 'What I wanted to do originally was write about the aftermath of a funeral. At first I just wrote down points about the funeral that I experienced, things that had got on my nerves about it. But that just seemed a bit obvious, you know? Then it sort of struck me. What I like doing, say if you write a poem about a tree – rather than say, "this is a tree, it has branches, it has leaves," it's more interesting if you *become* the tree, write the poem as if you *are* the tree, as if you're the tree talking. I think that gives you an interesting angle. So I thought I'd take one of these people, these crocodile cryers, and I'd try to get inside this character, this woman, say, who's very false and just getting into the will to see what she's been left. It's the same principle as the tree thing, you know. You actually become the character, you become the focus for your own contempt and it seemed to me to make it more dramatic. I think it works very well.

'The initial picture I got to write that song, I just remember my Mum was in the sitting room and she was really upset and there were a few of the family around. And the next door neighbour, Mrs Hoskyns, was there. And I can just remember a knock on the door. It hadn't quite hit us until then that it was my Mum's mother that had died, and then there was this knock on the door. I remember going to the door and there was a bloke with a black suit on, you know, and I looked past him and there were three black cars and more of these blokes all dressed in black, standing eerily around the cars. And it just struck me that they'd come for my Mum's mother and we'd never see her again; my Mum would never see *her* Mum again. That was the initial picture I got for that song. And it's there every time I do that song, that picture'.

Next up is 'Coleen' – to quote the sleeve notes, 'a song conveying a brother's sadness toward the termination of his sister's lesbian love affair' – again not your usual pop lyric, and set against a jaunty Thirties swing tune, once more somewhat disarming. The combined effect works purely because of the listener's admiration for the nerve of the man to try and pull it off in the first place – with not a little credit to John Steel's guitar solo. The song, sung in the first person, unsurprisingly caused some embarrassment for Martin's sister: 'Well, you see, it wasn't about my own sister. It was simply a situation, but people picked up on it and made assumptions that weren't true. So yes, she was very embarrassed about it and upset, and so now I'd check things out with my family first before I wrote about them. I was trying to put another angle on love, really, rather than just writing about a boy and a girl.'

'Little Red Bottle' – the alcoholic's lament, dedicated to Roy Buchanan – deals with a subject that would later mean more to the song's composer than he surely ever realised at the time of writing. The song begins with the main character resolutely defending his drinking, hinting that a drunk is inherently more interesting than his sober counterpart. This gradually dissolves into a slow section that sounds like our hero is drowning – and the lyrics begin to bear this out. Eventually the song leaps into life with a kick as the alcoholic gets more and more angry with his uncontrolled state – in live performances Stephenson would literally bawl the last verse and chorus to emphasise the plight of this trapped being whose only consolation is that 'blues to some are gold'.

An early sign of the finger-picking ragtime guitar that would begin to feature so prominently in Martin's playing in the late 90s, 'A Tribute to the Late Reverend Gary Davis' at the time seemed like a throwaway track. The music scene of 1986 did not include many references to Blind Blake or Big Bill Broonzy – the 'NME scene' of which The Daintees were somehow a part was dominated by The Jesus and Mary Chain's feedback and The Smiths' flora. Martin, as discussed earlier, had been introduced to country blues by his cousin Jamie Harwood – hence the dedication on the album sleeve. His playing is efficient compared to his later proficiency, but ably accompanied by John Steel on double bass and assistant engineer Marc Crellin on tambourine.

'Running Water' (co-written by Martin and Anth Dunn), from the *Jamming* freebie single, is a souped-up piece of country rock. Production credits go to High Times Inc. – a pseudonym for Martin and Kitchenware boss Keith Armstrong. The music is well complemented by an almost Western-style lyric concerning a character who attempts to rob a garage with a plastic gun, but the assistant dies of a heart attack during the incident and the unfortunate failed robber is put in prison for manslaughter. Martin sets the scene: 'Wink was the character in the song. One day in 1980 he came to my Mum's house and we sat and talked. He wanted me to go thieving students' bicycles on Westgate Road [in Newcastle]. He said he had these big wire cutters to snap the locks, then it would just be a case of piling the cycles into the back of the van. I declined and the incident within the song happened about a year later. A friend of mine called Roy Errington gave Wink a replica gun and he and another accomplice raided an all-night garage. The old man at the till saw what he thought was a real gun and literally died of a heart attack on the spot. The boys bolted and Wink cracked with the guilt a good while later and admitted everything. So they got time.'

In the days of vinyl, 'Candle in the Middle' closed side 1 in some style. 'An alternative Country and Western poem', it is a paean to the lonely and desolate and displays a tenderness that is completely unexpected on a debut album, where the drive to impress from the start usually disallows such maturity. Add some wonderful pedal steel guitar from session man Dave Rowlands and the result is another classic, although one that has never featured regularly in live performances. John Steel remembers: 'Dave Rowlands' pedal steel playing on that track was classic. I've used it as a benchmark in my playing ever since.'

'Piece of the Cake' opens side 2 with a roaring John Steel harmonica riff leading into a song of sticky sentimentality that would have sat comfortably on an Orange Juice record. The 'cake' and 'film' references are as corny as hell, yet The Daintees get away with it by virtue of a delicious melody (Anth Dunn's bass line is almost as melodic as the vocal tune) and an equally glossy production. Another song a million miles away from the tone of most of their contemporaries but all the stronger for that.

More fiery country rock comes next in the shape of 'Look Down, Look Down' – a song about bullying with the narrator exhorting the victim to 'speak loud and CLEAR!' The song's natural aggression became a useful tool in live performances – witness the Capital Radio session version on the 'Inferno' EP for an example of this sensitive band of alleged 'wimp-rockers' kicking some serious ass!

Next is a song dating from spring 1983. 'Slow Lovin'' is as smooth a piece of schmooze as Bacharach and David never wrote. It conjures up summer nights, moon in June and all the other clichés you can come up with. The character feels he should be leaving his comfortable home town life and striking out for fame and fortune in the big city – but his heart is with his girl and his conclusion is that he would be 'leaving for leaving's sake'. Another, more down-to-earth angle on it, is that it is just about the guy holding back his orgasm. Either way it is a song about passion. Indeed the passion of the musicians to get things right spilled over during the recording of this song and John Steel almost walked out following a row with Martin over the 12-string guitar part – but Gil Norton calmed things down.

'Caroline', like 'Little Red Bottle', had deeper echoes in its composer's life. The song deals with the trauma of miscarriage but in a healing, positive way. Stephenson is telling his cousin (the 'Caroline' of the title) that her loss is simply a way of making space for the child that eventually *is* born. (Later, in 1987, Martin's partner Angela miscarried and their sadness was later expressed in the beautiful 'Spirit Child' on the *Yogi In My House* album). Such a delicate subject matter is actually dealt with in a harrowing but necessarily open way in 'Caroline' as Martin talks about his mother's two miscarriages which made space for him and his sister.

Martin revealed in 1986: 'When I got to a certain age, my Mum said, *I once had a miscarriage*. And at first I thought, *Oh no, a miscarriage*, but then I worked it out, I thought, it was a really good thing, 'cos I wouldn't be here if she hadn't had it. I had a hard time when I wrote "Caroline": I had to get my Mum on her own and explain it. She's alright now, as long as she knows I'm not taking the piss.'

This is a song that is never easy to listen to – I have often skipped the track in the past when listening to the album – but Martin must be admired for his honesty and sheer ambition in tackling the subject. As David Quantick pointed out in the *NME*: '...but you play "Caroline", with Stephenson's soft, warm, convincing voice, and listen to him sing those horribly blunt words, and it somehow works because it's him. It ought to be a terrible song, a complete embarrassment to the ear, but it isn't. And this is one of the ways you spot a great songwriter: they rush in where angels fear to tread.'

The album (in its original format) closes with the classic 'Rain'. Written, recorded and mixed in 40 minutes ('using a little classical guitar I bought at J.G. Windows music shop in Newcastle around 1982') this song, simply about experiencing a summer thunderstorm, employs no clever lyrical devices, nor does it break through any musical barriers. It just exists – an acoustic guitar, a voice and a gentleness rarely found in modern music. Its author describes it as his 'most favourite song' and he must have played it live at just about every gig since its conception – complete with its harmonics ending in the style of U2's The Edge! 'I remember "Rain",' said Martin in 2003. 'The early hours of the morning with Gil Norton and the lights of the SSL desk as we recorded it in one take. That felt like we were hitting onto something.'

So the album was 'in the can'. The initial plan was to title it *Crocodile Cryer* after the opening track but a chance comment by Keith Armstong produced the phrase *Boat to Bolivia* – and it stuck.

The album was re-cut in 1987 with the addition, 'by popular demand', of the missing title track which had been released as a single the previous year. A venture into the reggae genre produced by Paul Hardiman at Jam Studios in London, it manages somehow not to sound conspicuous, simply because of the sheer diversity in style of what had gone before. Martin was inspired to write the song after seeing the image on the front of the album sleeve. He would later tell the hilarious story of a Daintees gig in Birmingham attended by two very disappointed Rastafarians who had obviously heard 'Boat to Bolivia' (the song) and, not unreasonably, expected to hear some UB40 soundalikes. He stopped the gig and publicly apologised. The Rastas laughed and watched the rest of the show.

The recording of this track, however, did prove to be a significant pointer to the future uncomfortable relationship between Martin Stephenson and the music industry. Pressured by the management to produce a hit single, some high-profile 'names' were drafted in – Paul Hardiman (The The), Dennis Bovell on bass (Orange Juice, The Slits, Matumbi) and Wix on keyboards (Paul McCartney). Apart from being ignored when stating that 'we've got our own bass player – Anth', Martin and The Daintees (now including Gary 'Strange' Dunn on guitar) spent most of the session in the pool room, thus feeling completely disconnected from the song. The later song 'There Comes a Time' was a direct response to this and was introduced at live gigs thus: 'I really love my songs and when producers get their hands on them it's just like watching someone fondle your girlfriend in front of you.'

As Martin recalled in October 1986: 'There was a clash. It sounded great on paper, but in the studio, it was awful. It was Gary's first session and he was going to the toilet every half hour, crying because he really wanted to get it right. And I was just really upset. I just couldn't talk to anybody. I was going in the pool room all the time and I wrote 'There Comes a Time' sitting on the pool table in a really foul mood.'

Unsurprisingly 'Boat to Bolivia' didn't feature in live performances for many years – the bad memories clouding a nice, but not exactly crucial, song. This gathering of industry greats would result in the single reaching number 70 in the charts in November 1986. (Useless information: it is possible to catch a boat to Bolivia – across Lake Titicaca from Peru. So now you know!)

On its release in May 1986, the album *Boat to Bolivia* must have come as something of a shock for fans of the early Daintees singles. The sheer breadth of musical styles on show was a massive leap forward from the Postcard-inspired jangle of 'Roll On Summertime' and the new-wave pop of 'Trouble Town'. The use of acoustic guitars, pedal steel, harmonica and double bass showed how the connection with pre-punk music was beginning to be made. In an interview at the time Stephenson acknowledged the similarities in his songs to those of Leonard Cohen, Tom Waits and Paul Simon whilst denying any direct influence.

Lyrically, this collection of 11 (later 12) songs showed a degree of insight and understanding of the human condition that gave a hefty hint to all who listened that this was potentially something very special. This feeling of timelessness combined with the desire to involve the listener as much as possible is further emphasised by the back cover's dedications and song explanations which, unusually for the 'cool and mysterious' pop world, go into some detail as to the 'year in the life of...' origins of the compositions. The back cover also features photos of Martin and Anth looking impossibly young.

The front cover shot (by Australian photographer Bleddyn Butcher) shows Martin and his then partner Angela sitting almost forlornly in Newcastle Central Station – an appropriate setting for the start of this musical journey and perhaps an apt expression of anticipation for the emotional rollercoaster ahead.

Press reaction to the album was very positive:

'Aching with giddy emotion…this is an album to savour and cuddle tightly to your breast' – Mike Gardner, *Record Mirror*, 24/5/86.

'Here The Daintees dream in an often brilliant world of their own, laced with country, drenched in tuneful accessibility; crafting idiosyncratic pop from human beings mining hope and honesty in the day to day. A wonderful record which you should seriously consider buying' – John McCready, *NME*, 10/5/86.

'The best debut since Dexy's' – *The Observer*.

'The album stretches out like a cat to bring you a travelogue of American ethnic idioms as witnessed on the banks of the River Tyne' – Martin Aston, *Melody Maker*, 3/5/86.

'I came expecting to enjoy this album; I went away with it close to my heart' – Dave Henderson, *Sounds*, 10/5/86.

Kitchenware's status as Newcastle's answer to Postcard ensured a certain level of 'hipness' would be afforded to all of their early releases and The Daintees' image, with hats and cravats heavily featured, was certainly in tune with what the style gurus demanded. In fact they even reached the dizzy heights of number 22 in *The Face* magazine's albums of the year for 1986 – the year of Prince's *Parade* and The Smiths' *The Queen Is Dead*. Combine this with a number 24 showing in the indie hipsters' bible the *NME*'s end-of-year list (ahead of Talking Heads' *True Stories* and The The's *Infected*, no less) and the 'cool' factor for a debut album couldn't have been more positive.

A somewhat incongruous Kitchenware ad for the album was placed in the music press to announce the release thus: 'Bored shitless with crap records? Then get a *Boat to Bolivia*.'

Sales chart-wise things weren't so great – the album peaked at number 85 during a three-week run. However, the necessary impact on the industry and the public had been made and Martin Stephenson and The Daintees profile was sufficiently high to provide London Records with the impetus required to push the band on further down their designated career path. But things were not quite that straightforward.

> The album was scheduled to go out in spring so we had to do something between January and April to eat, so we did a gruelling support tour with John Martyn. Just before that John Steel and Anth did some roadying on a European tour for Alex Chilton.
>
> For the John Martyn tour we couldn't use Paul Smith as he was playing in Australia with Smokie so we drafted in our old chum Mr Dave Ruffy, ex-Ruts and Aztec. I don't know if you've ever met Mr Ruffy but I can tell you he can't half cheer you up, a truly excellent character. Anyway, we did 28 long dates in England with John Martyn and got some hard-earned experience playing big halls as a support band. That was the last UK support tour The Daintees did. [LB]

A review in the *Sunderland Echo* of the band's support slot at Newcastle City Hall talked about '…the simple pleasures delivered by The Daintees. Playing a short, sweet set and impeccably fronted by the lovable Martin Stephenson, the Sunderland band won us all over with tight songs, great melodies, and the sheer fun they put into the performance.'

Much later, Martin reflecting on the John Martyn tour: 'It was a 28-date tour, and I didn't even know who he was until we started. At first I was frightened of the man because he's a strange bloke, and he can be an aggressive man. But I got to know him and he's got some good ideas with tunings for the guitar and that sort of thing, and he definitely influenced me. You can't help but take in things if you work with someone like that.'

After the John Martyn tour the band appeared on Channel 4's revolutionary new pop programme *The Tube*. In a 30-minute Newcastle special Martin, Anth, John, Paul and Claire Dunn were filmed playing in Macey's wine bar. But all was not well within the ranks:

> Unfortunately the tour was so gruelling that at the end of it John

Steel jacked it in. He started tour managing. I don't blame him. It just makes me sad that he left as things began to pick up. [*LB*]

John Steel's main reason for leaving prior to the album release was lack of cash, but his departure was also brought about by the unusually arrogant way in which Martin communicated to him a significant change in the order of things. The band were no longer to be called The Daintees. From now on they would be Martin Stephenson and the Daintees. Whatever the tensions, John's part in the adventure would be fondly remembered by Martin, who noted in 2003: 'John Steel playing the solo in "Coleen" and "Little Red Bottle". That's the best musical memory for me. John was the greatest. It broke my heart when he left the band.'

In his 1987 piece, *Looking Back*, Martin spoke of the speedy search for a replacement guitarist:

He left four days before our promotional tour of our debut album *Boat to Bolivia*. I drafted in Gary Dunn, Anth's brother. Gary is an excellent guitarist and a very gentle person and I've known him through Anthony since 1980. He's been through all sorts of crap and nobody deserved to take John's place more. Gary boosted the buzz back into The Daintees and there was a really special rapport between the new line-up.

Gary Dunn: Guitar (Gazza Strange)

Anth Dunn: Bass (Tone Dunn)

Paul Smith: Drums (Class) i.e. the most sarcastic, dry little git that ever lived!

Martin Stephenson (Marty Glitter)

'He's like a kid on a summer holiday,' said Anth Dunn in May 1986, on brother Gary joining the band. "A tour – wow!" He's really chuffed. Our Mam and Dad are dead proud. They were a bit wary and thought it wasn't a proper job. My Dad was a bit averse at first but as soon as he saw us on TV it was "that's my boys!"'

Interviewed in October 1986, Martin put the debut album into context from his point of view:

We used to do gigs in London and get reviews, and they just seemed to miss the point I was trying to get across. Luckily, the LP is doing that, getting across that I've always wanted to be taken seriously as a songwriter.

Before the LP they'd hear 'Running Water' and just think 'country song'. They'd hear 'Coleen' and just think 'jazz'. So we'd get reviews like 'Dave Edmunds mixed up with...', all that rubbish. They'd just have the impression that I was a bit of a joker. But I mean I'm quite serious about what I do. Most of the things I've written, I'm not really embarrassed about. I've got a few things in the closet that I wouldn't talk about though. Most of the things I've put out are just honest really. As long as they don't upset anyone else. But just because I write songs that maybe have a little more meaning than chart pop songs, doesn't mean I'm any more precious than they are. There's a directness to the songs that's perhaps not what people expect. There's also a lot of different subjects. Most male songwriters steer clear of writing about anything but love, cos that's the easiest way to get an emotional reaction. I try to look at other things. Sometimes it confuses people. I used to be really influenced by the records I bought, and I thought this was a really bad mistake, and you should get your influences away from you as much as possible. So I stopped buying records; the last record I bought was 'Transmission' by Joy Division.

If I do another record, I'd like it to sound a lot rougher than the first album. I'm going to leave a lot more out, create more gaps. A record, you know, can be like a picture. You can present someone with a rough sketch and they'll fill in the details, they'll almost finish the picture for you.

*

The release of the album propelled Martin and The Daintees into an intense period of gigging, interviews, radio and TV appearances in support of the album and the follow-up single releases. The May/June '86 gigs saw them headlining a major UK tour for the first time and further developing their unique stagecraft, including a gig at London's Dingwalls that saw Martin take to the stage covered in plasters having fallen across a gravel path earlier in the day. At that same gig Virginia Astley accompanied Martin on two numbers as the determination to mix things up on stage (an approach at times as frustrating as it is laudable) began to take root. The band would deviate further from the album versions of songs as Martin would slip into stories such as 'Greyhounds' and 'Basher The Slasher' – the banter provided light relief against the backdrop of some of the set's more close-to-the-bone lyrical content.

In-store appearances at HMV in Manchester, Sheffield, Leeds and Edinburgh took Martin and Anth back to their busking roots and were a welcome diversion from the daily grind of touring.

The end of May saw the release of the 'Inferno' EP – with 'Running Water' as the lead track supported by the Feargal Sharkey session version of 'Look Down, Look Down' and the delightful 'Synergy' duet with Virginia Astley recorded at The Cluny Whiskey Warehouse in Newcastle back in 1985. Despite the quality of the tracks on show it was a slightly odd release as it was not on London Records – that is, it was a proper independent release on Kitchenware, distributed by The Cartel independent network of record shops. Unfortunately, due to the passage of time no-one can recall the reasons why this happened – as such it remains a one-off and somewhat rare release.

On 4 June The Daintees recorded a radio session at Yellow 2 Studio in Stockport for Radio 1's Andy Kershaw programme, featuring 'Roll On Summertime', 'Crocodile Cryer', 'Louis' and 'Rain'. Produced by Stuart Pickering, the session was broadcast on 26 June and demonstrated further the variation and tight playing that Martin, Gary, Anth and Paul Smith were rapidly developing.

This was followed by a live appearance on 24 June on BBC2's legendary rock show *The Old Grey Whistle Test*. Trailed by a write-up and picture in that week's *Radio Times*, Martin and the band started with a raucous and passionate 'Look Down, Look Down' followed by 'Tribute To The Late Rev Gary Davis' (with Martin taking some serious liberties with the tempo) and finishing with a stunning performance of 'Crocodile Cryer' (with Mike Timmany on keyboards), preceded by Martin having a battle with the guitar strap on his acoustic to which he responded in typical style 'god bless you'. Anth Dunn recalls: 'For the *Whistle Test* recording our driver and roadie was Martin McAloon [of Prefab Sprout], and we had a marvellous time. We had a drink and nice chat with the presenters Mark Ellen and Andy Kershaw.'

On 24 June London Records released the first 'official' single from *Boat to Bolivia*: 'Crocodile Cryer'. The picture sleeve bore a family snapshot of Martin's grandmother (Jane Bird Bell) with his mother (Frances) as a young child sitting in a field, and on the other side a sketch of Jane Bird Bell done by Martin's girlfriend Angela. This fondness and respect of family and history would feature often throughout Stephenson's musical career and begin to set him apart from the pop world and closer to the traditional values of folk, blues and country music. The A-side was an edit of the album version. The B-side featured an acoustic version of 'Louis' on the 7", but purchasers of the 12" version were treated to a live version of the same song – an extended 'X-Mix' recorded at the Jumping and Hot Club, Bridge Hotel, Newcastle the previous month. This captured for the first time on record the live Daintees at their very best. It is in short hilarious, featuring more banter than it does song and should be listened to regularly by every right-thinking person.

> After one tour we went straight into another and took on one more recruit in the shape of Mickey Watson. What a weirdo, such a square, such a brilliant lad and musician. He plays sax and keyboards. I hope this line-up stays together forever as it's absolutely great fun playing with. [*LB*]

Expanding the band with the aforementioned Mickey Watson saw The Daintees' live form improve even further. UK tours throughout August and again in October were the order of the day and the size of the venues and the ecstatic reactions from the audiences attested to the fact that this band was getting a serious live reputation, with reviews on a par with those for the album. Press and radio focus was intense, with nearly every gig being preceded by an interview for either national or local papers and radio stations. In the *Sunderland Echo* in August, Martin was asked to name his five favourite things:

> Louis – a Sunderland café full of colourful people.
>
> Touring – we can't do without it.
>
> Releasing an album – then we can perform to people who are there because they like us – not just because they're there and want to get drunk.

Parties at my place – we see old friends, have fun and a big fight at the end!

Snooker – not only relaxing, but I usually win!

'Slow Lovin'' was released on 7" single in late August, quickly followed in October by the recently recorded non-title track 'Boat to Bolivia'. The 12" of the latter featured two new songs: 'Slaughterman' and 'Wholly Humble Heart', produced by Dave Brewis. In 2002, Dave gave an insight into their working relationship at this time:

> I was asked to record and arrange demos with Martin and the band quite a lot; to work up new songs in a budget studio (Cluny). Apart from the chaos we got on great, which was a primary thing for Martin, as after his first album working with Gil Norton, he didn't enjoy being told what to do, and we found we could always discuss his ideas and work out things so he liked them. I found Martin very creative in bursts. He would have this initial creativity writing a particular song, then again in performing either live or in the studio, but the whole other studio mechanism was avoided and disliked at all costs by him. By this I mean all mechanical processes of recording, arranging etc. which became my job. The boring bits. Martin also knew when to leave a song alone. He was good at that. I eventually stopped doing arranging work for him, after some of my better work was copied note-for-note with identical performances by other producers being paid lots more than I, in professional studios. I was, in my opinion, doing all the work for them in a £100-per-day rat hole. So I stopped saying yes. The only times I got to record Martin in a good place with a good engineer and a decent budget we enjoyed it, and the tracks got released, which was good, or copied again until the life was gone from them, which was not. It's a common producer's gripe.
>
> My favourite, as one of the 'Boat to Bolivia' 12" B-sides, was 'Wholly Humble Heart', the same version of which appeared on a Greenpeace album for some reason credited as 'produced by Paul Samwell-Smith'. That time they didn't even copy it, it was my recording! Sloppy A&R book-keeping. Samwell Smith did a similar version later as was the pattern.
>
> I enjoyed recording my version. After Neil Conti (freelancing away

from the Sprouts) had whipped up an astonishing brushed drum rhythm, Martin just went for it, and played a bit of acoustic guitar on his cracked Ovation as he sang the vocal. It was blindingly inventive, and Harold Burgen, the engineer, and I sent the lot of them to the pub for a few hours while we got an Akai mono sampler out and dubbed his guitar phrases around and got the atmosphere going with delays etc. I got permission from Anth to play the bass, so I did, tuned down at least a fourth for the subsonic dub effect, and when Martin came back, he actually loved it. I think he may have redone his vocal even better after hearing where the track was headed. We had them back in the pub again till closing time while we mixed – we may even have had a Guinness too – and I still remember the final mix sounding perfect. From start to finish it worked and showed Martin's talents at their fullest. Also it was out of the genre everyone thought he was stuck in. The next thing I remember is someone at the record company not liking the 'gayboy' line, and then it was re-recorded as an album track with everyone in the band playing the dubbed parts and my version was gone.

The track 'Slaughterman' was recorded at the same time, and was more standard fare for The Daintees. I noticed all the gigging they had done in a couple of years had really made them into a good band, especially the Dunn brothers. Martin's talent of seeming to sing directly to the listener had also evolved. His best vocal takes were always the first ones after being in the pub. To get the atmosphere perfect one time, Martin insisted on all the studio lights being turned off. Then he could totally relax and get into the spirit of the music. We had to turn the lights back on as he couldn't see his lyrics!

1986 finished off with some pre-Christmas gigs in Manchester and Newcastle and culminated in high-profile shows at London's Mean Fiddler on 15 and Newcastle Tiffany's on 17 December. A busy but very successful year was over and thoughts were turning to the second album.

The following year saw Martin and The Daintees spending comparatively less time on stage and much more time in the studio than in 1986. Several demo sessions were convened with Dave Brewis at the helm as new songs that had started to see the light of day in '86 began to be developed. 'There Comes A Time', 'Nancy', 'The Old Church Is Still Standing' and 'I Pray' were among the first new songs to be tried out as well as a never-to-be-released track called 'Start The Boil' which saw The Daintees picking up an African high-life feel for the first and, to date, last time.

In January another TV appearance beckoned with Martin performing 'Coleen' solo on the first ever edition of Channel 4's *The Last Resort*, hosted by Jonathan Ross. A slightly forced bit of banter between Ross and the clearly uncomfortable Martin Stephenson followed. Martin: 'No jokes or I'll flatten you'; Ross: 'My dog has no nose … I'm still standing!'

Martin would later reflect on the show: 'It was the first programme and I didn't know what the hell was going on. It was like a bloody carnival when you went in. There was a bloke with one leg and a juggler and Donald Sutherland sitting in a corner moping and Jonathan Ross was a bit stroppy, probably because it was the first programme and he was trying to make a name for himself, trying to get on. And I just felt like I was being really patronised.

'We turned up for the sound-check which must have taken all of five minutes, and they shoved us around like cattle; I just felt like they were taking the piss out of us. There was a girl from *Brookside* on and I felt really sorry for her because Ross was taking the piss out of her and I just felt it wasn't right in a way. Still he got his karma later when he had Peter Cook on – he really sorted him out. And at least Jonathan Ross was big about it: he could take as well as give. So in the end it was all right....'

Also in January 1987 the re-publicised 'Trouble Town' single from 1984 broke into the UK singles chart, peaking at number 58. To this day it remains Martin and the band's highest placed single.

Most of 1987 was split between being in the studio 'working on the second album', as the music press kept reporting, and playing ad-hoc gigs prior to a full tour in June of that year. Joyous gigs in Leeds, Manchester, Newcastle and at the London Town & Country Club showed that the live band just kept getting better. Several gigs were recorded – whether a live album was ever considered is not clear but what high-quality recordings have emerged from that era showed Martin Stephenson and The Daintees at the absolute peak of their powers. They mixed the songs from the first album with fully formed versions of new songs that gave a strong indication that the second album would be at least as good as its predecessor. A typical set list from the June tour showed there was no fear in terms of giving the new songs an airing: Get Get Gone / Little Red Bottle / Trouble Town / Crocodile Cryer / Slow Lovin' / Coleen / I Can See / The Wait / Goodbye John / Me and Matthew / Neon Skies / Boat to Bolivia / There Comes a Time / Running Water / Look Down, Look Down / I Pray / Piece of the Cake / Nancy / Candle in the Middle / Caroline / Rain.

Another TV appearance, this time on Thames TV's *Meltdown* late-night music show, saw the band playing 'Crocodile Cryer', a very intense 'Look Down, Look Down', 'Wholly Humble Heart' and 'There Comes A Time'.

Meanwhile in the studio, the work continued with Dave Brewis, who recalled in 2002:

> In 1987 I went to Bath to record with the line-up featuring the Dunns plus Paul Smith on drums and Mickey Watson on keyboards. Martin invited Steven Foster Pilkington to play violin, also a bagpipe player from the town centre who sadly didn't turn up. It was like the Bash Street Kids on holiday. The first day was spent recording the whole lot jamming, although the brief was to do two specific songs: 'There Comes A Time' and another which was changed in favour of 'Nancy', as Martin had just written it. I had permission from Keith Armstrong to do this change-around but London Records weren't happy, as it took the decision away from them. So when I finished recording, they wouldn't let me mix it, and they re-recorded 'Nancy' with Paul Samwell-Smith, and it sounded identical to my version (seen *Groundhog Day?*); eventually they released mine on the album, after later allowing me to mix it properly. The two recordings were so alike I wouldn't have known which was mine if my name hadn't been on it. I liked that song a lot regardless.
>
> 'There Comes A Time' has a great vocal from Martin, all in one take, and is only hampered by my over-the-top kitchen sink arrangement, which I wouldn't do now. They should have recorded that one with a different producer!
>
> For that week in Bath, London Records sent everyone involved £15 each per day living expenses, so on the second day Martin, Anth

and Gary were skint as they'd all bought new pairs of shoes with the week's money, and been to the pub with the change. So they lived on boiled vegetables from the market and home-made soup until they went home. The rest of us ate out. The actual recording time was well used, as everyone was used to working together, and enjoyed it. They were genuinely one of the UK's most entertaining live acts at this point. Slick, even. I heard that they were the highest-paid band on the college circuit without a hit record. Sounds like faint praise, but think about it!

In the autumn of '87 the decision was made to make the new album at Ridge Farm Studios in Surrey with Paul Samwell-Smith as producer. Samwell-Smith had made his name as bass guitarist with classic British blues boom group The Yardbirds in the 60s, playing alongside the likes of Beck, Clapton and Page. He began producing whilst still in The Yardbirds and began to enjoy this role more than that of the humble bass player playing behind these legendary guitarists, so took up the role permanently. His claim to fame was producing all of Cat Stevens' 70s breakthrough albums including *Tea for the Tillerman* and *Teaser and the Firecat* as well as albums for Carly Simon and Jethro Tull. Clearly he brought with him an element of depth, experience and no little spirituality which it can be assumed seemed to tally with the new songs that Martin was working on.

Prior to going down to Ridge Farm, Martin took time out in September to play some gigs with an Australian blues dobro player by the name of Gypsy Dave Smith. Dave was taught the guitar by his elder sister Patty, who was involved in the folk revival scene of the early 60s. He was a contemporary of the Australian guitar legend Tommy Emmanuel; they had met in their early 20s and Emmanuel had influenced Dave considerably. He had left Australia in the early 80s after travelling 20,000 miles in one year in Oz. He realised that he could have gone several times round the world, so he set off and ended up in Holland via Asia and Italy, eventually making it across to Newcastle in 1986. Dave, and his dedicated but carefree attitude to music, would become very important to Martin over the next few years, often providing Martin with an escape hatch from the prison of the music industry that would very soon start to entrap him.

The working title for the second album was *In the Greenhouse, My Grandfather and Me* – a line taken from a new song Martin had written called 'Me and Matthew'. The rest of 1987 was spent at Ridge Farm, where the sessions took a lot longer to complete than for the debut album. Whilst the time may have dragged it did give the opportunity for some interesting meetings, as Martin exemplified in 2003: 'I remember chatting with the studio's night watchman. He said he had a guitar under his bed. I asked him for a jam. We did and when he sang I recognised his voice. It resounded in me, like a church bell does in an altar boy: 'Call out the instigators / 'cos there's something in the air / we got to get together sooner or later / 'cos the revolution's here and you know it's right.' Speedy Keen! So I met a master.'

On the subject of using Paul Samwell-Smith as a producer, Martin had the following to say: 'I didn't realise he had been Cat Stevens' producer till I met him, and in fact I bent his lug all night about The Yardbirds. But I'm really glad we used Paul because he is such a great mediator and he's such an important producer for these times, because he's so much against the mentality of producers these days who are dominating the music and have a bigger ego than the musicians! He's the opposite to that; he feels it's his job to get the band on tape and enhance the sound, and that's it.'

After the album sessions were completed, and prior to its release, Martin set out on a mini-tour of arts centres and other smaller venues in January 1988, accompanied by Mickey Watson and Gypsy Dave Smith. This desire to mix things up and at the same time get away from the typical gigs expected of him would follow Martin throughout his musical career. It seemed totally normal to Martin to keep his music fresh, original and, most importantly, natural and unforced regardless of what anyone else expected of him: 'I just wanted to pay the quieter songs back for the hammering that they take when we play standard rock gigs.'

Released on 4 April 1988 The Daintees' second album, *Gladsome, Humour and Blue*, was a considerable progression from its predecessor. Martin Stephenson's songwriting development was yet again as stark as that seen between the early singles and *Boat to Bolivia*. Musically, The Daintees were moving into areas that had only previously been hinted at in their own career, and which were a million miles away from the increasingly dance-based noises produced by their contemporaries. Folk, blues, the use of a string section, acoustic piano and dobro gave the album a timeless, organic feel that was honourable in its ambition and genuinely startling in its achievement.

Gladsome... in its original vinyl format came in a gatefold sleeve of monochrome and sepia tones which complemented the music perfectly. A poem, 'I Wouldn't Change a Thing', was on the front cover and succeeded in setting the tone of deep, sometimes dark, almost confessional lyrics that followed. The Ridge Farm sessions provided the majority of the tracks, and there were three songs from the Dave Brewis sessions in London and Bath.

Stephenson's earlier unfortunate experiences with producers were not repeated here as Samwell-Smith creates an entirely sympathetic atmosphere out of a potentially complex and unwieldy group of musicians. The addition of Virginia Astley on flute and her accompanying string section provided an almost olde English sound, compared to the gutsier, bluesier playing of Gypsy Dave on other tracks. Not to mention the songs. It is rare for any album to cover such a wide range of subject matter, never mind so early in its creators' career, and for the result to be so cohesive and rounded.

The opening track, 'There Comes a Time', is Stephenson's rant against producers and the industry in general – taking the artists' work and turning it into 'product'. On another level it seems to be about independence and taking control in general – 'There comes a time, when this life should be mine'. The gentle opening develops into a rousing mid-section with Mickey Watson's accordion and Paul Smith's marching drums prominent in the mix, leading Martin and The Daintees into battle against the forces of corruption and greed: 'We must walk forth, to meet the fatal night' – before exiting triumphant after victory. A genuinely stirring piece of music which could effectively be Martin Stephenson's anthem, so well does it set the agenda on which he has based his musical journey ever since.

'Slaughterman' was written at least five years before *Gladsome...* was released. Indeed, along with 'Crocodile Cryer', it could be seen as a watershed in Stephenson's songwriting as he moved forward from the simpler pop songs of the 1982 to 1985 era. Described on the single sleeve as being about a young footballer whose father, the Slaughterman, tries to stifle his ambitions, it again emphasises individuality and the need for controlling one's own destiny. Not for the first time on the album is the seriousness of the subject broken for a moment with a disarming line – 'No would-be-Ian St Johns are gonna bring me down.'

Martin explained the lyrics in 1988: 'It's like rebellion against a forceful parent who doesn't agree with what you want to do. I took the example of a young footballer from round here called Tommy Mason. He was a really talented player, he signed for Sunderland, but he never really did much. I thought of his rebellion and mixed it with a bit of mine. I was getting a lot of hassle from my Dad at the time, just through sitting in front of the fire, playing the guitar, not getting a job. I could just imagine him getting the same hassle, and I could just, like, relate to him. That's what it's about.'

Musically the track is almost too-typical Daintees with the popping bass, tight-as-you-like drums and jangly guitar – a sound that could easily have been bottled and sold for album after album if its creators had allowed it.

'The Wait' is a different kettle of folk altogether. An acoustic guitar backed with simple but effective violin and cello (courtesy of Anne Stephenson and Caroline Lavelle) support the singer's plaintive story of a relationship gone awry due to the uneven distribution of emotional power. The 'victim' is at the mercy of his/her partner to such an extent that 'whether I glow or dim' is dependent on 'your every whim'. Sure it's depressing but these things have to be faced up to – and set in the context of such a beautiful, stirring melody it can even start to sound positive. 'The Wait' has become a firm live favourite over the years regardless of whichever musical form Martin has favoured at the time – its intensity never diluted for a moment.

In 1999 on the *Martin Stephenson* (Floating World) album, 'The Wait' was revisited with the addition of a rap taken from a Strange Relations song called 'Subterranean Rhythm'. In fact 'The Wait' performed live is a good example of Martin's increasing desire to weave lyrics from many songs, not just his own, into old favourites to develop something completely new.

A restrained version of the 'standard' Daintees sound opens 'I

Can See' with the lead vocal almost whispered and enhanced by more female presence (via Sheryl and Sheila Parker's backing vocals). The melody is gorgeous and the song could easily have come to a conclusion after the second chorus. However, the lyrical theme of throwing off the shackles of depression by finding belief in some higher being ('the moonlight man') is continued into a delightful, almost Gospel-based outro: 'Free the shattered mind, throw the keys to heaven.'

Track four, 'The Old Church Is Still Standing', sounds like it could have been written centuries ago. Gentle acoustic guitar precedes a lyric with an ostensibly religious theme, but which develops more into a timeless picture of a community set around a church; a church that doesn't judge its congregation and is looked on by all as a monument of wisdom. Martin describes the moment of the song's conception: 'Some songs give you really strong pictures just before you put them together and with that I had an image of an old church surrounded by factories and houses that are falling down, and still managing to keep a smile on its face.'

In this writer's opinion the next track, 'Even The Night', is one of the finest songs Martin Stephenson has ever written. It is a desperately sad tale about a man who has lost his wife and children, set to a melody that almost defies description – but I'll try. Strings, flute and piano support the main vocal line of 'Even the night has turned its back on me' – which builds to a peak at the end of the song that surely must break the heart of even the hardest cynic. Lyrically, the song paints such an evocative picture of 'the crying man', with lines like 'with a soaken coat from a passing car' and 'your back is arched and eyes look far'. It's as close to poetry as any 'pop' song can get.

The song reflects the situation Martin went through some years later following his split with Angela. This is not the first time he has 'sung his own fate' as he puts it – suggesting that some outside, greater force is at work in his writing. He remarked in 1988: 'I really believe that when songs like that evolve, they have their own minds, and they actually use songwriters as much as we use them … a good song will never be forgotten. I wrote 'Even The Night' on the train coming back from London to Newcastle. The train was full of young soldiers; it was winter and everyone was in jovial spirits. I wrote it on the back of a Christmas card for my Dad.'

Like 'Slaughterman, the next song – 'Wholly Humble Heart' – had also featured on an earlier release although this was a different take, albeit building on Dave Brewis's basic arrangement. Back there it was a very minimal drum and vocal track that was a long, long way from the 'recorded in L.A.' single version that was released in late 1988 (featuring vocalist Andrea Mackie for the first time on a Daintees record). The album version is possibly the best, capturing the middle ground between the three versions (a fourth, the 'Irish' version appeared in 1997 on *Beyond the Leap, Beyond the Law* – but that's another story). Rhythmic and almost, dare I say it, dancey, the song is an upbeat protest song – or so it seemed. The sleeve notes to the single expressed Martin's thoughts and anger at Clause 28, the legislation brought in by the Conservative government ruling that local councils 'shall not intentionally promote homosexuality or publish material with the intention of promoting homosexuality'. However the song itself was about more than that, as Martin explains: 'It was just written for anyone who can't get love. It's quite a subtle song. I wrote it very quickly and it was only later that I realised it was about my mate Malcolm (Hutchinson). He's a very lonely bloke, but he's a real comedian and everyone loves to be around him and all that, but he's one of the loneliest people I've met. It's just about affection. Everyone needs affection. It's sort of against promiscuity really.'

If a tendency towards the folk music scene had always been hinted at in The Daintees repertoire, the next song, 'Me and Matthew', with its buzzing bees and singing birds, would have fitted comfortably onto a Julie Felix album. Almost too twee, the song is about Martin's maternal grandfather Matthew Carlton and the time he and Martin spent together in the 'summer of '73'. Martin recalls Matthew's gentle nature: 'He was a wonderful character: he talked to children like adults and, in fact, some children would talk to him as if he were a child. The song deals with the smells and tastes of childhood and the adult/child barrier.'

It is certainly a natural step from the family-orientated stories of 'Crocodile Cryer' and 'Caroline' and does in fact boast some wonderfully resonant lyrics – 'Unfold your magic sweet clasped leather palm, for there lies your baccy, old man'. Timeless. Timeless and twee – yeah, that sums it up! 'Me and Matthew' is perhaps more significant for the first appearance on a Martin Stephenson recording, after the first verse, of Gypsy Dave Smith on dobro ('go on Dave!') – his inspired playing would feature often, both live and in the studio, in the future.

'Nancy' continues the family theme but this time things are not so cosy. Nancy is the rebellious teenage daughter incurring the wrath of her heartbroken father. 'I would say that "Nancy" is a very tragic song,' Martin observed in 1988. 'I think it's based on my Dad's relationship with my sister and how at 17 and 18 she had a really sharp tongue with my father, who was argumentative at the time. After they had a row she'd say something to my Dad that was really hurtful and walk out. Then I would see him, really hurt and being the father figure, the pillar of strength, he couldn't exactly break down and cry.'

Lyrically, the song uses a language of days gone by as if to emphasise further the generation gap in question – 'my wayfaring one' and 'blinkered and huffed and cold as the mire' are lyrics that few writers of Stephenson's generation would use – with the exception of Steven Patrick Morrissey, perhaps. Musically, The Daintees are on top form, led by Gary Dunn's wonderfully melodic guitar-playing. The end product is a classic – end of story.

Next up, 'Goodbye John', sees Martin using a different style of lyric-writing – as he explains: 'In 1985/86 I started using a dictaphone. Also I would use alcohol to remove self-consciousness – fucking with my head, bypassing my programming – and basically started playing and having fun with it. "Goodbye John" was the first result of this. I went on a binge in The Sandpiper pub in Fatfield, Washington. Came home in the early hours, had the dictaphone next to the bed and when I woke up in a dream-like state I just started rapping into the machine. "July it was a fruitless month" pause "chibed, molested" pause "and at the end of it a birthday" pause. When I got to the end of the tape I would transcribe it onto foolscap paper; collage it together; snip out big chunks of it and record it as a loop onto tape – a one-off almost.'

The end result is quite magical – this Burroughs-style stream-of-consciousness lyric set to a simple three-chord strum that is taken somewhere else entirely with the addition of Gypsy Dave

Smith's D-tuned dobro. Along with Mickey Watson on tambourine the song was recorded 'live in the studio' at only the third attempt. It would become a regular live favourite – particularly during the Daintees reunion tour of 2000 when Gary Dunn's lead-guitar-playing took it even further into the stratosphere.

The album finishes off with the jazz chords of 'I Pray' – again a third take done 'live in the studio' and made even more remarkable by the stunning duetting between co-composer Gary Dunn on guitar and Mickey Watson on saxophone. Proof of how tight this band were, the song features on a bootleg CD recorded some two years earlier at Manchester Polytechnic, and you could be forgiven for thinking you were listening to the recorded version – which is outrageous for such a complex and, at the time, recently composed song. Gary Dunn had based the music around a guitar tutorial piece. Quite what Martin based the lyrics around is not so obvious – very much in the style of 'Goodbye John', skipping from one seemingly unrelated line to another, but with some pointed self-analysis going on in there: 'Bring on the mongrel, the fool with the hat', 'Him with his ego, and me with these hooks, should get together some time and Rock this Town' – maybe a Brian Setzer reference?

For two months following the album's release a poetry book, *Something To Carry With You*, was available free to fans who responded to the sticker on the front sleeve. *Something...* gave yet more insight into the Stephenson psyche – desperately touching pieces such as 'Spirit Child' (about a miscarriage), and 'Jim Sixsmith' (about Martin's mentor) showed how prepared the author was to lay his innermost thoughts and secrets bare for the reader/listener to see. Sometimes uncomfortable but always challenging and interesting, the book came complete with photos from the Stephenson family album – yet another connection with the past.

On its release the album gained even more plaudits than its predecessor.

'... sees Durham's wandering preacher in pew-packing form' – Keith Cameron, *NME*, 9/4/88.

'One of the finest and grossly underrated singer-songwriters this country has given birth to has stood in the shadows for too long ... it almost wraps its arms around you, to give you a hug from which you hope you will never be free' – Ron Rom, *Sounds*, 9/4/88.

'Songs that caress and undoubtedly strike a chord somewhere in everyone' – Andy Strickland, *Record Mirror*, 27/8/88.

'... a reminder that pop music is not just an ephemeral device to sell jeans and banking services but the latest chapter in an aural tradition, a chronicle of social history' – Alan Jackson, *NME*, 9/4/88.

'Stephenson builds bridges between love and hate, between cradle and grave, between folk and pop, between the past and the present' – Len Brown, *NME*, 9/4/88.

Overall, this classic album served as a reference point for what a band could achieve in the late 80s – taking on board the direct communication of punk and blues, the poetry of folk and the close working-class family ethos of country. A milestone in modern music.

In an interview in May '88 Martin gave an insight into his songwriting process: 'Too many musicians think they are the Messiah, here to spread the word. They believe they are responsible for what they do, but they're wrong to feel that, because it's not really them. It comes from behind them; they're just being used. A songwriter is just a medium. I know it sounds a bit hippyish and a bit precious but, when a song comes to me, it's such a quick, sharp thing that, even as I'm writing it, I feel it doesn't belong to me. That's how *I* feel ...'

He was similarly forthright in his opinions on the music business: 'These days everyone in the business seems to want everything for themselves. They're all intimidated by each other and constantly competing, whereas I've been taught by friends like our dobro player, Gypsy Dave Smith, about how people used to share songs with each other. They'd write a song and give it to someone and, like a joke, the song would change subtly over the years. I've recently been giving away some of my songs, simple, little things. Because songs don't belong to anybody, that's the way I see it.'

Martin and The Daintees launched themselves into the expected round of gigs and interviews in support of *Gladsome, Humour and Blue.* The live band was again expanded by the introduction of backing vocalist Andrea Mackie. Andrea, originally from Aberdeen, had been singing in working men's clubs in the North East when she was spotted by Martin and asked to join the band. Her soulful vocals were initially featured on a new live arrangement of 'Slow Lovin'', taking it even closer to its soul origins. Andrea would also provide more scope for developing the band's sound in future recordings.

The live band now comprised Martin, Gary, Anth, Paul Smith, Mickey Watson and Andrea, plus Caroline Barnes and Caroline Lavelle on strings. A full headlining UK tour took up all of April (supported by Lovetrain and the relatively unknown Melissa Etheridge), before the band's debut headlining European tour in May, taking in Scandinavia, Germany, Italy, France and Belgium in an exhausting schedule.

'The *Gladsome* tour saw us at our absolute best,' remembered Anth Dunn in 2000. 'The Manchester International 2 gig was the best gig of my career. The audience really made it. The highlight was "Little Red Bottle" – it started with a cello and viola piece that Mickey Watson wrote and then the full band comes in. We rehearsed so hard for that tour; we were very tight. The audience reaction was incredible.'

On 21 April a cut-down Daintees consisting of Martin, Gary and Anth recorded another session for Radio 1's Andy Kershaw programme. Produced by Dale Griffin, 'Goodbye John' and 'Me and Matthew' were played very similarly to the album arrangements (but minus Gypsy Dave's dobro). Two unreleased songs – 'Far Away Meadows' and 'Migrants' – followed, the former sung a cappella like a traditional folk song, while 'Migrants' hinted at something new altogether, almost Robert Wyatt-esque with Gary's jazz chords giving it a harmonic structure similar to 'I Pray' from the album. It was Martin's vocal that was different, as he attempted to sing across a range far wider than anything he had done before. Yet again, you never knew exactly what you were getting with any Daintees performance.

The level of visibility in the UK during 1988, both live and in the media, should not be underestimated. Rarely a week went by without a mention in the music press and on stage the band were attracting a serious following as they began to play 2,000+ capacity venues such as the Town & Country Club in London and Universities and City Halls the length and breadth of the country. *Gladsome, Humour and Blue* had peaked in the album chart at number 39. Add to that a spot in the *NME* albums of the year (again) alongside REM's *Green* and U2's *Rattle and Hum*, and some serious progress, if measured in regular rock star terms, was being made.

At the end of May, London Records arranged for Martin to re-record 'Wholly Humble Heart' in Cherokee Studios, Los Angeles under the direction of producer Russ Kunkel, with the aim of releasing it as a single. No Daintees were involved in this session (though Andrea Mackie added backing vocals in the UK later); instead Kunkel had put together a session band made up of the great and the good of the hot US players of the time including guitarist Hugh McCracken, whose track record included Steely Dan, Billy Joel and John Lennon's comeback album *Double Fantasy*. A somewhat uncomfortable Martin did the session but wasn't completely happy with the arrangement, as he recalled in a 2000 interview: 'My psychological trip then was to please people, but I was surrounded by a lot of energies that had different needs. Suddenly I was in a position where I had become my best mates' employer in a way. The Daintees were just a band of mates and I ended up as the boss – that caused me stress. I just wanted to be the same as everybody else; I didn't want that responsibility. People with different needs – management, Gary and Anth, Angela – caused a lot of head problems. I didn't have the kind of character that could say "no" to people. My space was invaded all the time and I didn't know how to protect myself. I don't blame anybody for it: it was just a lesson on my journey.'

When the resulting single was released on 25 July, however, it wasn't a hit, despite being promoted via a video showing the band playing, intercut with shots of Martin, Angela and the band goofing around in a somewhat typical 80s/MTV sort of way. It seemed that London Records were struggling to know just how to position Martin and the band from a commercial point of view. Were they an indie albums band or was there the potential to cross over to the singles market? And if so, what was required in terms of making that change? In retrospect it seemed that nobody really knew and no-one particularly asked Martin if he wanted it anyway. This issue would raise its head several more times over the next couple of years. The new version of 'Wholly Humble Heart' (the LAX mix) was good but took the track as far away as possible from Dave Brewis and Martin's original concept and, in a way, encapsulates the whole direction issue.

On a positive note the B-sides of the new single were excellent: a non-album-track, 'Come Back To Me', with its wise-above-its years lyrics such as 'All those morbid words make sense now/All the love songs I once hated/Are all I ever listen to', set to a calypso beat; and two tracks recorded live at Manchester International 2 by Piccadilly Radio back in April – 'I Can See' and 'Slow Lovin'' – showing Andrea Mackie's contribution to the live band was developing. The highlight, though, was an outtake from the *Gladsome* sessions – 'Get Get Gone': a seemingly throwaway 'meaning of North East life' tale with Martin supported by Gypsy Dave on dobro and his own foot-stomping. It was a million miles away from the 'professionalism' of the Russ Kunkel sessions. Then, and all these years later, it is so clear which is the more natural sound. It is also the only song ever written to feature the lyrics 'snivelly wivelly old tramp'.

Back in the UK Martin played a solo spot at the Cambridge Folk Festival in July. The Daintees then played two nights at London's Sadler's Wells Theatre on 4 and 5 August. Martin was on top form at these gigs, mixing up the set as much as possible, throwing in the odd poem, playing some of the moodier album tracks very straight but with much passion, before the night ended with high comedy. As the encores stretch long past the hall's curfew time, impatient roadies start to unplug the amplifiers, forcing the band to sing a cappella and sending Martin off to the drum kit where he whacks the snare with childlike defiance. Eventually a roadie carries Martin off stage before he scuttles back on to have one last bash on the drums as the crew dismantle the kit around him. A proper Daintees gig!

In August Martin was the subject in the *NME*'s 'Material World' feature, where musicians list their favourite records, films etc. Musically Martin mixed in some old classics (Velvet Underground – 'I'll Be Your Mirror'; Van Morrison – 'Brown Eyed

Girl') with songs by some of his contemporaries (Virginia Astley – 'Hiding the Ha Ha'; Gypsy Dave Smith – 'Remember') as well as 'anything by The Chefs and Girls At Our Best.' Films included *It's a Wonderful Life*, *Kes* and 'any Charlie Chaplin'. And under the subject of 'Drinks': 'I've just had five cans of bitter with friend and guitarist Gary Dunn on the train to London. There's something really wealthy about having a pint in your hand, especially if you're skinny and training for a beer gut. I like a pint of Theakston's with Gypsy Dave Smith; it's much better than talking or thinking.'

Prior to embarking on another UK tour, the band went back into the studio, this time with Warne Livesey as producer, to re-record 'There Comes a Time'. Released in October, the new version was not dissimilar to the Dave Brewis album version; if anything it was slightly more kitchen-sink-like. Either way, it flopped. However it did give us the opportunity to hear two further live tracks from the Manchester International 2 gig. Joyous versions of 'Little Red Bottle' (Anth's favourite) and 'Coleen' (with an overly enthusiastic audience sing-along) showed just how good this band were becoming. They were tight, but as loose as they needed to be in the circumstances, showing just how artist/audience barriers were broken down at Daintees gigs with Martin desperately trying to wrestle the vocal chores back from the stalls ('this is a football match!') – an accurate reflection of the 'big cheesy grin' syndrome that would always accompany any Martin Stephenson gig.

A predominantly northern UK tour took place, migrating down south for the winter to culminate in two gigs at the Hammersmith Odeon in early December.

1988 had been a pivotal year for Martin Stephenson and The Daintees. They had clearly 'arrived' in terms of following up the debut album with a more than worthy successor. They had made a name for themselves on the UK 2,000+ seater gig circuit with a live act that was as unpredictable as it was riveting to watch. And yet some serious doubts were emerging in the mind of the band's leader. On stage at Newcastle City Hall in April, Martin Stephenson made this comment: 'That's the trouble with music today. Because it's all about money, there's no mistakes, no spontaneity. But I'm not going to get crushed.'

*

1989 started out with Martin again getting away from the pressures of the full-band format by playing a 30-date tour of arts centres and small theatres with Gypsy Dave Smith. This alternative approach allowed Martin and Dave to vary away from the standard Daintees repertoire, and gave Martin the opportunity to bring in new blues-, folk- and country-based songs of his own as well as looking back to the rich history of those genres. Just before embarking on these dates, Martin offered up some interesting thoughts on touring: 'Really if you've got any sense you can only take a band out three times a year at the most, though twice is best, because if you do too much people get sick of it. Plus it's not very clever financially: you can lose quite a bit of money. On the last tour, Anth, Gary and me were getting £60 a week and we had a cello player who was getting £300 a week, so you really have to be careful with the financial side of touring. So doing this solo tour is just another way of carrying on working, playing in a different way, in different environments and situations. Rather than playing universities all the time, it gives me the chance to play in little theatres, different places. You have to work harder though. All the people in the band are better musicians than me really, so they sort of pull you along a lot in a way because they're so much better. When you're on your own you do have to work quite a bit harder, but it's good for you.'

These low-key dates were followed by something much more high profile altogether. In March/April Martin took the opportunity of touring in the Americas for the first time via a solo support slot on a Hothouse Flowers tour taking in the USA and Canada. The Hothouse Flowers had caught a Daintees gig in Dublin and were suitably impressed. The three-month-long tour took in New York, Boston, Baltimore, Philadelphia, Montreal and Toronto and placed Martin in a not too familiar position of opening act, playing solo to an audience almost totally unfamiliar with his material and his Geordie accent. At least it was different and provided another opportunity for Martin to adapt his stagecraft to meet a particular situation. 'What I love about my career is when I have a chance to play with other musicians and talk with them. When I was on tour with the Hothouse Flowers we would do a gig, travel all night and play music all the time. And that's why I love music.'

The long journeys on the tour bus between gigs also provided some time and inspiration in the songwriting department, with a number of songs that would feature on future Daintees albums (including 'Long Hard Road') being written during this period.

Martin and The Daintees were signed to Capitol Records in the USA, and a double album, under the title *Gladsome, Humour and Blue*, was released just ahead of the tour. Rather awkwardly, it incorporated *Boat to Bolivia* – previously unavailable in the USA (although it had seen a Canadian release).

Following the Hothouse Flowers tour the focus was on a third album. Martin revealed in April that year: 'I've got all the songs ready. Mind you by the time I get in the studio, probably another one's come along and they've all changed places. I've got a pool of about thirty songs to choose from, which is worse sometimes than having a pool of twelve, 'coz everyone's arguing about which songs to use. Hopefully we can start recording soon.'

The Daintees played a semi-acoustic set at the annual Cambridge Folk Festival in July with *NME* reviewer Stuart Baillie picking up on one of Martin's endearing traits: 'For comic relief Martin headbutts the microphone regularly, but refrains when one particular attack, with all the dexterity of a young Jackie Charlton, threatens to maim the front row.' New songs 'Morning Time' and 'We Are Storm' were previewed – further proof that material was in the bag for the third album.

As no new material was available for release in 1989, the record company decided to re-publicise the 1982 single 'Roll On Summertime' in much the same way as it had done with 'Trouble Town' two years earlier. A slightly strange decision, as the material on the single bore very little relation to where Martin and The Daintees were at in 1989. It didn't trouble the chart compilers.

London Records were keen to push Martin on in a bid to outdo the 40,000 sales of *Gladsome, Humour and Blue* and reap the financial rewards that all the rapturous reviews and ecstatic audiences seemingly indicated were due. So a plan was hatched to record the third album in the USA with Pete Anderson in the producer's chair. What wasn't immediately apparent to everyone was that the record company wanted Martin to go over there on his own, without The Daintees.

Chapter 3

The Cylinder of Hell
(1990 to 1993)

Date: July 1989; Location: Capitol Records Studios, 1750 North Vine Street, Hollywood. Martin Stephenson is struggling to lay down the vocal part for a new song entitled 'Migrants'. An engineer called Charlie, becoming impatient at this young English guy with a weird accent, decides to have a word: 'Say fella, you know that microphone you're using?' 'Aye?' says Martin. 'Well Frank Sinatra used that to record "I've Got You Under My Skin" in 1956.' 'Oh, really!?' says Martin, stepping back to look at this legendary mic. 'Yup, but it's doing fuck all for you right now son!'

Allegedly designed by the aforementioned Old Blue Eyes to resemble a record player spindle with a stack of 45s ready to play, the Capitol Records Tower had been the home to many a bastion of the music business since its construction in 1954. Nat King Cole, The Beach Boys, Billie Holiday, Frank all recorded there – and of course all The Beatles' US releases bore the Capitol label. With the blinking light at the top of the tower spelling out 'Hollywood' in Morse code, it was here that Martin Stephenson with his Daintees (almost) arrived to record the third album, *Salutation Road*, in the summer of 1989.

'The Cylinder of Hell' – Martin Stephenson

'On the corner of Hollywood and Vine sits The Cylinder of Hell. A phallus with a panoramic view of LA. In the basement is Capitol recording studios where Gene, Frank ... you name it, cut all that incredible stuff. Beneath the basement is an old multi-storey car park. That's how the studio gets its reverb and echo. They feed mikes through the floor.

'I saw souls on the walls of The Cylinder of Hell. Gold records plastered in the reception area where the security guard looks you up and down. I saw Helen Reddy's soul on the wall of The Cylinder of

Hell. I saw John's, Paul's, George's, Ringo's too. I felt a celestial view-ing of the epicentre of one of the great boils in the modern-day Roman Empire.

'I meet Spike from The Quireboys at the door of The Cylinder of Hell. I get shocked when he opens his mouth and is a Geordie. I say, "You look like Paul Stanley out of Kiss but you've a Wallsend accent." He laughs and says, "Yeah, my favourite pub is the Broken Doll and my tipple is a pint of Salem D."

'Then Spike and I get introduced to Hale Milgram. Hale is at that time Top Dog in Capitol Records, i.e. Satan for the week. That's how quick you can lose your job in The Cylinder of Hell. So, as the lyric goes in that wonderful Eddie Cochran song: "We climbed up two flights, three flights, four / five, six, seven flights, eight flights more / Get to the top, we're too tired to rock!"

'Yep: "The Death of Rock 'n' Roll".

'An old dense carpet that me and my few brothers are humbly rolling up.'

The record company pressure to push Martin Stephenson for-ward as a major artist in his own right, unsurprisingly began to have a detrimental affect on The Daintees as a band. The initial plan was to send Martin over to the States on his own on the same basis as the 'Wholly Humble Heart' single sessions with Russ Kunkel the previous year. Martin, however, was not happy with this and insisted that Anth Dunn went with him. This upset Gary Dunn and so a compromise was reached between Martin, the Dunns and London Records that Anth would go over to play on the backing tracks and Gary would fly out later to add guitar overdubs.

The critical acclaim that the first two albums had received, coupled with the sound fanbase developed through the live shows, had persuaded London Records that it was time to 'go for broke' with Martin Stephenson. As well as putting him in Capitol Studios, legendary horn section The Tower Of Power were hired, along with session musicians Skip Edwards (keyboards), Jeff Donavan (drums), Larry Knight (guitar) and Don Reed (vio-lin) – most of whom temporarily formed the basis of Michelle Shocked's touring band. Producer Pete Anderson was given the job of moulding this somewhat uncomfortable amalgam of musicians into a chart act. The choice of Anderson as producer was down to Martin's publisher, Ian Surrey, who was particularly impressed by his work with the aforementioned Ms Shocked and had begun to bend Martin's ear with her *Anchorage* album in early 1989.

Sessions were split between Pete Anderson's Mad Dog Studios in Venice, CA and the Capitol Tower. The backing-tracks sessions were completed very quickly, in less than a week (at the same time Anderson was recording Michelle's *Captain Swing* album – Martin recalls walking out of the studio and into the TV room to wake Michelle up to tell her it was time for her to do some singing now!). Despite the uncomfortable atmosphere that had developed between the band and the record company, the respect for Pete Anderson and his main engineer Dusty Wakeman was total, as Anth Dunn confirms: 'Pete and Dusty were excellent; they had such an extensive musical knowledge and knew how to use the studio very quickly, and got the best out of us and the session guys around us.'

The production team were completely unaware that Martin and The Daintees were a band. They thought that Martin was a solo singer-songwriter who had specifically requested session musicians to back him. In fact when they later caught The Daintees live and saw how strong a band they were, they realised that the sessions could perhaps have been done differently.

Pete Anderson recalls the culture shock that affected Martin on his arrival in LA: 'Venice is not the worst part of LA, but it's not the best. There were a few little gangs, a lot of Mexican gangs. There was a liquor store down the street about a block away and Martin always wanted someone to escort him there. He'd say, "Pete, I'm afraid I'll get killed, someone will knife me." I took him to my favourite Mexican restaurant and he was like, "They're going to kill us" – I'm saying, "no, they're not!"'

Dusty Wakeman adds: 'The Venice Mad Dog was in kind of a rough neighbourhood. I remember one night, Martin and Anth said goodnight and left the control room. About half an hour later I walked down the hall, only to find them peering out of the curtain on the exit door. They were afraid to go outside, so after that, we would walk them to their car.'

Following the Capitol sessions, London Records were aware

that this was not the album they were expecting and requested that some more single-based material be written. Hence 'Endurance' and 'Long Hard Road' were later recorded at Rockfield Studios in South Wales. Despite this Martin still didn't reckon the album would spawn any hits: 'I suppose "Long Hard Road" has a bit of a dance feeling to it. Anyway, I went out on tour for a month, which I think finally persuaded them to put it out.'

When it did appear in May 1990, *Salutation Road* was, nonetheless, keenly snapped up by the hardcore of fans who had followed the Daintees since *Boat to Bolivia* and before. Housed in a sleeve which, on the front, accurately depicted Stephenson as the troubadour guitarist sitting on his case and, on the reverse, rather cornily set him against the backdrop of a colliery playing a tuba, *Salutation Road* was still another collection of Stephensongs waiting to be heard.

The opening track, and first single, was 'Left Us To Burn' – a strikingly atypical song both lyrically and musically in its con-demnation of the effect of Tory politics on the North East, coupled with a jazzy, almost Sade-like groove. It wasn't the first time that Stephenson had aligned a song to a political cause: 'Wholly Humble Heart' had strong links to the anti-Clause 28 movement, but that was primarily through a heartfelt sleeve note rather than any specific lyrical content. 'Left Us To Burn' was different; it was very direct, as Martin confirms: 'It was written about changes in the environment where I was living around Sunderland. Everyone could sense what was going to happen to the shipbuilding and so on. So, I was just talking about the thing that was there that was wiped out, and the sadness of that because it's people's livelihoods, you know. I don't like to use music for political motives too often because it becomes tiresome if it's in every song, but that was something that affected me. If I met Margaret Thatcher I couldn't feel any violence to her. All I could do is laugh at her.'

Despite its undoubted commercial appeal, with swinging bassline (courtesy of Mr A Dunn) and smooth-as-silk sax, 'Left Us To Burn' failed to trouble the Top 75 chart compilers but did set the album off on an original and challenging note. The single sleeve again featured artwork by Angela Cape, whose simple but effective illustrations – almost like chalk on a blackboard –

captured the lyrical content of the song (and that of the follow-up single 'Endurance') perfectly.

Next up, 'Endurance' – specifically recorded with the aim of being a hit single, it contained another traumatic lyric, albeit of a more personal form, about the testing nature of love. Martin's notes on the album promo sheet set the scene: 'It's all about two people having a big fight and storming out of the house in opposite directions. As they each reach the end of the street, they both realise they've forgotten their keys, head back to the house and have another fight! He climbs in through a window while she cools her anger and she thinks, "If this road is for endurance and endurance means a son, if endurance means a marriage then this pain is purely fun".'

A few months later, he added: 'It's about my own philosophy: when I'm going through a bad time in a relationship and I feel like running away from it, I think of it like the weather. You might have had bad weather for a week, but it always breaks.'

This need to fight hard to keep a relationship going when times are tough stood very much at odds with the typical rock 'n' roll messages of casual sex fuelled by alcohol and drugs and – potentially, in some eyes – set Martin up as some sort of New Puritan religious fanatic. In a telling interview with the *Melody Maker* in 1990 he set out the basic concepts that inform his songwriting: 'A lot of people are tempted by rock 'n' roll because it's sex-orientated and you can be cool. But I gave up being cool when I was 11 – I realised I just wasn't! People join rock 'n' roll bands because they want money, drugs and sex but that's not what motivated me to make music. I was motivated into writing songs by the death of my grandparents, things like that. I'm not interested in telling people that they can shag everybody they want. There's too many people doing that and it's sad. I don't want to play a part in that, because I believe in love. I believe in a one-to-one relationship with a woman, and I don't believe in everyone seeing what you are doing. Songs like "Steamy Windows" just make me cringe. A 50-year-old woman and that's her contribution to say that she's getting shagged in the back of a car! I just think it's a bit thick. There's more you can do, you know, especially after what she's probably been through.'

'In The Heal of the Night' is a mandolin- and drum-powered

folk song of an altogether more 'spiritual' nature. 'Imagine God and his mates sitting around a fire, and they are singing all the great songs that we will never hear – the song unsung. In fact, all the ones that Dylan and Co. would love to get their hands on! I based the idea on those guys who used to wander through villages – before the days of the media – and just shout the news.'

The stark contrast of these glorious unsung, pure songs is set next to the reality of the rock industry that Capitol Records so epitomises where '... the folk hero is full of badges and peripheral – gold discs'.

But could Martin be considered a spiritual songwriter? He addressed the issue in 1990: 'I don't like the word "spiritual"; it confuses people. They think you are a higher force or something. Everybody has got the same feelings, but people don't talk about them. You know I have limited intelligence, I have vulnerabilities and instead of trying to hide them, which a lot of rock 'n' rollers do, I open up. This is me, I have 3 CSEs, this is what I think. Image is for people who lack honesty and personality; people put shades on because the eyes are the key to the soul. I like to see myself as a Geordie who has written a few good songs here and there. I've just been in a position to express my inner feelings about myself and my family. I never work too hard on how I'm going to be viewed; it's for other people to do that.'

Led by a gorgeous Georgie Fame-like organ riff, 'Big North Lights' is a welcome low-key diversion from the heavy subject matter of the previous tracks. 'A sailor owns a small boat which is available for hire for a trip up the river where he will show you his personal big north lights. They may or may not be too impressive to you but they are his world!' (Another reading is that it is simply stating the obvious superiority of the North of England over the South, over the USA etc. But that just wouldn't fit with Martin's 'humble lights' line so perhaps it is just a personal observation from this writer!)

Inspired by spending three months on a trans-US sleeper coach with the Hothouse Flowers, 'Long Hard Road' is something of a disappointment. A fairly standard trumpet-led rock beat accompanies an even more routine lyric of the 'band-on-tour-bus, driving-across-US-from-town-to-town' type that has been done to death by every band and its brother over the years.

The addition of some 1960s-style 'psychedelic' phasing in the middle eight kind of puts the final nail in the coffin of a below-par song. Martin hinted at this drop in the quality of the writing at the time: 'Someone told me you get five or six years to write your first album and then you have to do the rest in six months.'

Despite this pressure to keep the songs coming and other tensions around London Records' attempts to split the band up, there is no doubt that Martin does deliver several classics on *Salutation Road*, and 'Spoke In The Wheel' is definitely one. In essence it is one of those songs of Martin's that actually suffers from any deeper analysis; suffice it to say just put it on at a hefty volume and wonder at the way a different language seems to be created around a stunningly simple chord sequence (enhanced majestically by Pete Anderson's lead guitar). 'I think I was trying to describe something that was indescribable – the Universal energy ...' A fine example of the song taking over the writer, if ever there was one.

'Heart Of The City' is another relatively routine, if pleasant, ramble through typical rhythm and blues territory, albeit with a helluva swing to it. Andrea Mackie shares the lead vocal and her voice sits beautifully next to Lee Thornburg's muted trumpet. The overriding impression, though, is more pub-rock than cutting edge – it just don't sound like Martin and The Daintees (funny, that!)

Neither does 'Too Much in Love' – '... a song dealing with the age gap in relationships. Try to imagine a 50-year-old man falling in love with a 20-year-old and his confused feelings of love and guilt, and his attempts to deal with his emotions.' Another relatively lightweight song that surely would never have passed the in-built quality control mechanisms to get on either of the previous albums, it's a further indication of the pressure-points building up within Martin's head as he was rushed into this album.

'We Are Storm' puts the album back on track with another true classic. The delicate guitar-picking combined with Martin's examination of a passionate relationship is genuinely stunning and ranks among the best songs he's written at any stage of his career. Like 'Spoke in the Wheel', a unique form of English is used to convey the feelings of tension, heartache and emotion that inhabit the four short verses. 'It's about the grip lower consciousness has on humanity, as that is how people are easily farmed. Keep a human distracted by needs and he is easily kept in lower conscious. Hence easily manipulated on a grand scale. Just like with all these tags we have like computers and mobiles. We are actually paying and carrying and promoting our own bondage. And it's personalised. En masse we are enslaving ourselves as a group. Spiritual awareness dimmed.'

'We Are Storm' has been a regular feature in live sets over the years, culminating in the stunning ten-minutes-plus version of The Daintees' 2000 tour which included references to the 'Cylinder of Hell' rap, 'The Oral Tradition', 'Knock on Wood', The Seeds' 'Pushing Too Hard' and a piece about the Galleries shopping centre in Washington (anyone spot any other references, answers on a postcard ...) despite Gary Dunn's protestations to 'play it straight'!

'Migrants' produces a significant change of pace with its hark back to the jazzy 'I Pray' from *Gladsome*.... Accompanied by strings, keyboards and brushed drums, Martin breathily exhorts us to 'let mindlessness emotion be', before a baritone sax takes us off to somewhere even more ethereal. Again the use of words that live way outside the usual scope of pop/rock songwriters are to the fore ('clangour'); unsurprisingly it is when these traditional values, words and instrumentation are used that *Salutation Road* as an album is at its best. Lyrically the song tells the tale of a couple running off together during the 2nd World War ... further emphasising the timelessness of the song. Martin was never happy with the vocal performance on 'Migrants'; a far better version had been recorded for the Andy Kershaw session back in April 1988 with Martin's voice in great shape accompanied by his acoustic guitar and Gary Dunn's electric.

'Morning Time' is another standout as it is removed from the production values that were tending to stifle the true spirit of the songs. An acoustic guitar is picked and hit to accompany the story of a sixteen-year-old Martin taking the number 194 bus into Newcastle from Washington for the first time. 'I'm gonna catch me the big north lights.' In another way it is a story for anyone setting out on a new journey – I can picture Cyril and Nadya Povyshev playing it as they set off from Russia on their way to the Highlands of Scotland for the E-group Gathering in August 2000.

The album finishes in upbeat style with the wonderful title track (named after Martin's local at the time, the Salutation Inn in Tynemouth), dedicated to Lindisfarne's Alan Hull. 'It's a song about coming home and that wonderful feeling when you see the first landmark of home,' says Martin. 'And there's nowhere better to come home to than the North East.' Pete Anderson captures the best of the combined musicians on this track: the brass and backing vocals lift the simple chords to a celebratory climax as our hero marches his band home, away from the hell of Hollywood, to the safe sanctuary of the North East of England.

Following the Capitol sessions there was a gap of several months while London decided just what to do with the recordings. A significant budget had been spent so far (around £120,000) and it wasn't immediately apparent how the money was going to be recouped. Hence the sessions in Wales were convened in December, which also gave Mickey Watson and Andrea Mackie an opportunity to contribute to the album.

Dusty Wakeman recalls: 'A few months after the Venice sessions I was on tour in the UK with Pete Anderson, Jeff Donovan, Skip Edwards and Lee Thornburg as part of Michelle Shocked's band. We got to see Martin perform in Dublin. He was great, of course. We also hooked up in Newcastle and visited the pub owned by Anth's girlfriend Sarah's parents. He was living with her above the pub – a bass player's dream!

'After the tour, before returning to the US, we all met in Rockfield Studios in Wales to record two more songs for the album. After the tracks were done Jeff and Skip left. Pete and I stayed for a few more days of work. The last night before we were supposed to leave at 5:30am, we worked till about 11:00pm. As we were wanting to have a pint after we finished, we were worried the pub would close before we got there. I stayed at the studio to work with Mickey, while the rest went to the pub. They came back with half a dozen various liquor bottles filled with the local ale (the only way to get it "to go", apparently). Pete, being wiser, went to bed while I stayed up celebrating with the guys. When I left at about 3am to go pack and get ready to leave, they were developing a full head of steam. While I was packing they kept moving this large plant closer to my door and knocking on it. When I looked out, I would see this demon shrub getting closer and closer, until finally it was right outside. You probably had to be there, but it was hilarious at the time. When I finally went back to the party, they were trying to sing old standards and not fall out of their chairs. On the table were half a dozen empty scotch, vodka, rum etc bottles, looking like we had consumed even more than the vast amount we did consume.'

Given that he hadn't been required on the *Salutation Road* sessions, drummer Paul Smith had left the band (albeit, as it turned out, temporarily) and was replaced by Durham-based drummer Malcolm Dick, another Toy Dolls alumnus.

A 35-date UK tour, playing in total to some 25,000 people, went ahead in February and March despite the lack of a released album to promote. Martin, Gary, Anth, Mickey, Andrea and Malcolm Dick were supported, and occasionally augmented, by Gypsy Dave Smith, the Hotlicks Cookies (with Martin's old Daintees mate Graham 'Shippy' Anderson and Ray 'Round Eyes' Burns) and Five Guys Named Mo.

What with the further expanded nature of the band and the extensive and varied repertoire available to them, the live Daintees were now an even more exciting proposition. New songs were mixed in with old; Andrea took a delightful lead vocal on 'Migrants'; Mickey Watson played the bassline to 'Salutation Road' on a tuba. Gigs would culminate in a rousing version of 'Down by the Riverside' with Martin memorably leading the band walkabout through the auditoriums.

'Left Us to Burn' was released as a single on 16 April 1990, accompanied by 'Big North Lights' and non-album track 'Eyot' (a lovely country rock story). The 12" and CD versions included a live version of the ballad 'Kathy', a heart-rending story of a man who falls in love with a blind girl – a song that reduced Gypsy Dave Smith to tears at a gig some years later (Dave had heard it every night on the tour but one night it got to him). *Record Mirror* accorded the record 'Single of the Week' status, picking up on the anti-Thatcher message – 'Just try and make this man pay his poll tax.'

The album *Salutation Road* was finally released the following month and the music press response was, once again, very positive on the whole.

'It's the sort of heart-warming collection that will leave listeners sighing in contentment' – *Music Week*.

'Given time these Stephensongs will warm you down to the bone marrow' – Mat Snow, *Q*, June 1990.

'*Salutation Road* is the homecoming embrace you'd always hoped awaited you' – Tim Peacock, *Sounds*, 2/6/90.

Despite this, and although *Q* magazine rated it as one of their top fifty albums of 1990, there were some dissenting voices.

'Nothing that makes one scream for more of the same' – David Quantick, *NME*, 5/5/90.

'There are tracks that simply sound hollow or forced ... but a couple of gems shine through the gloss' – Dave Jennings, *Melody Maker*, 12/5/90.

Chart-wise the album only reached number 35, despite a widespread interview and ad campaign along with three separate spates of touring in the UK alone. In June 'Endurance' was released as the second single backed with two tracks salvaged from the 1987 Dave Brewis sessions – 'Men Can Be Flung' and 'Release the First'. Another failure sales-wise, its main claim to fame as a single is that of generating the worst and shortest review of Martin's career – *Melody Maker*, 2/6/90: 'Endurance ... you'll need it!'

In 1992 Martin summed up his feelings about *Salutation Road*: 'Those songs are still my kids, like, but on that album they're dressed up in more expensive clothes and I don't really think they suited them.' And later, in 2001: 'I suppose the duffers for me were "Long Hard Road" and "Too Much in Love" – shite songs. I think my vocals on "Migrants" are dreadful and it's not a good version. If the songs like "Left Us to Burn" and "In the Heal of the Night" were recorded ambiently they would actually show their class more. The same with "Salutation Road". "Morning Time" is cool, I think. Song-wise I would give it 8/10. Production technique 9/10. But for the production being true to the art and the artist being true to his art – 2/10. Which is my fault for being weak. The session guys on the album did a good job and so did Pete and Dusty. The Dunn boys held their own easy but it was deffo a commercial attempt. I don't regret it, though, because it was actually a good experience and taught us how never to record like that again.'

Time has perhaps dulled some of the criticism that was initially levelled at the album by the hardcore fans. In fact some folk, predominantly brass players, rate it as their favourite Daintees album. Engineer Dusty Wakeman is one big fan of it: 'I LOVE *Salutation Road*. It's one of the very few albums I've worked on that I listen to for pleasure. I have a home in the Mojave desert, and *Salutation Road* lives there; the highest compliment I can pay a record. He's out there with Sinatra, Bob Marley, Miles, Coltrane, Eno etc. Sometimes you bond with the artists more on one project than another, and I got to be really good friends with Martin, Anthony and Gary, which added to the experience.'

Pete Anderson speaks along similar lines: 'I don't think I realised how good it was until I saw Martin and the Daintees come back to the States and play some of the songs with the arrangements live, supporting the Violent Femmes. I was really impressed with his musicianship and what we had achieved in retrospect. I generally have a difficult time listening to records that I've done but I enjoyed all the work I did with Martin. He was great to work with because he was definitely an artist and a poet.'

The joyousness at the live gigs during 1990 could not hide the fact that all was not well with the band and with Martin himself, particularly as the financial pressures mounted: 'I was depressed. I felt responsible for everything. I felt autistic. So trapped that I couldn't cope with life. Intense anxiety all the time. I was very unhappy and lost. I had run out of child and the grown-up world was eating me up.'

Pete Anderson understood the predicament fully, recalling in 2001: 'I can imagine Martin being uncomfortable with the music industry back then, because what we've seen happen subsequent to making this record in the last ten years is that the music industry has collapsed and is continuing to collapse for reasons that would make anyone that has a basic talent, which Martin has in abundance, uncomfortable. Because he is artistic, he is poetic, and he was born to make music and the record industry has long since abandoned the idea that if you had any talent, you would be neatly able to fit in with what they do. That is, they try and market you as something that they think you should be. They are not really music people, they're just bean counters, people with opinions but no education or basis for their opinions, that somehow got that job.'

The Daintees, in fact, almost split up at this point. Gary Dunn had decided that his future lay elsewhere and auditioned (successfully) for the lead guitar role in James as the Mancunians looked to expand their line-up in the wake of the success of 'Sit Down'. Gary eventually turned the offer down.

Interviewed in 1991, Martin synthesised the commercial dilemma very neatly: 'It was external business pressures from people who don't like music. You can be the best songwriter in the world, but if you don't have the money to make your own records you've got to go to the men with the money and when you borrow money they feel it's their right to tell you how to write songs when they don't really know how.'

*

After the fallout of the *Salutation Road* album and in between a hefty tour schedule with The Daintees (including the Reading Festival in August), Martin took some time out in October 1990 to spend five days in Lynx Studios, Newcastle (run by AC/DC singer Brian Johnson's wife Carol) recording an album that didn't surface for nearly three years. The *High Bells Ring Thin* sessions could not have been further away from the Cylinder of Hell episode, and give as true a picture of where Martin's music was at, as any recording could do. Ably assisted by the multi-talented Mickey Watson, (with Mond Cowie, ex-Angelic Upstarts guitarist, engineering) Martin produced an album that was ultimately truer to his songwriting and production values than any of The Daintees' albums. Typically, London Records refused to release it as it didn't contain a potential hit single. A story at the time that the tapes had been lost in a fire was obviously later proven to be apocryphal. Its delayed release in 1993 came about purely as a mutual exercise in fulfilling contractual obligations.

When the album finally did see the light of day the CD sleeve featured a dedication to Emma Gray Watson, a young girl who worked as the secretary at Lynx Studios and was killed in a car crash after the album was recorded.

Away from the pressure cooker atmosphere of The Daintees, Martin pulled in musicians whom he had worked with on and off over the years in either a live or street busking setting. Gypsy Dave Smith's dobro makes a welcome return to a Stephenson album; The Hotlicks Cookies add their unique brand of country blues and Paul Smith and Andrea Mackie make telling contributions. Old friend Graham Anderson (of the Hotlicks) even got his Dad's Vintage Jazz Men to play on the sessions, adding a wonderfully diverse touch to the proceedings.

Opening track 'You Really Had a Heart' sets the scene: a delicate love song, with Martin's voice accompanied only by acoustic guitar and some deft percussion from Paul Smith. The feel is closer to the busking and live work with Virginia Astley back in 1985.

'Looking For Some Peace of Mind' is one of the few songs on the album that could conceivably have been on either of the first two albums. Mickey Watson (bass and keyboards) and Malcolm Dick of the Daintees 1990 live band (drums) back Martin's plea for an end to all the emotional and financial hassle that had gradually built up over the last two years – the overriding atmosphere is confessional. Andrea Mackie's soulful voice reinforces this on a beautiful middle eight.

Recorded first take (as much of the album was) 'Song About The Member' uses a traditional folk song structure to convey a story of a weak-minded individual who clings to organisations, religious or otherwise, to justify his own existence – 'he's a member of anything that moves'. A perfectly reasoned first couple of verses are concluded by a somewhat over-the-top recommendation that this character should be hanged.

The traditions of American folk music are celebrated further on 'Should My Friends Be Gone', which featured in The Daintees' live set later that year. Martin stamps his foot and Ray Burns takes off on harmonica, set to a lyric extolling the virtues of friends and family.

Next up: classic cornball Stephenson on 'Don't Be Afraid of the Night' – 'we've got Mickey Watson and Gypsy Dave Smith on

Ovalteeny harmonies and Ray Burns on chromatic harmonica'. Simply 'a great song for putting the bairns to bed' and about as far away from Murder the Disturbed as you can get!

Originally featured as part of the poem 'To Charles Baudelaire' in the *Something To Carry With You* poetry book, 'Far Away Meadows' continues the folk theme in the most traditional-sounding song on the album. Carol Gascoigne's violin follows Martin's vocal on this ode to the beauty of his home country.

Fitting perfectly with the atmosphere of the album, Martin's duet with Virginia Astley, 'Synergy' (initially hidden away on the back of the 'Inferno' EP in 1986), was recorded five years previously at Cluny Studios with Dave Brewis. It shows a maturity of songwriting and subtlety that significantly predates even 'Rain' from the first album. The development from the early Daintees songs of '82 to '84 is stunning and as such can be seen as a real milestone in Martin's musical journey. Virginia's voice and flute match perfectly with Martin's voice and guitar, and it is something of a shame that no other recordings of their work together appear to exist.

'Wake Me in the Morning' is riotous and wonderful at the same time: a raucous run through a slow blues led by Gypsy Dave's dobro, supported (in a slightly wobbly fashion) by Paul Smith's marching drums and Mickey Watson's tuba. Martin finds it difficult to keep it together amidst the hilarity, and as such it's not immediately obvious what the lyric is about. Until the final verse that is, when the similarity to Ian Dury's 'Wake Up and Make Love With Me' becomes apparent – 'wake me in the morning, and watch your boy rise!'

'I Live in the East' tells the sad tale of a boy who is abused by his father, while his mother works away as a 'singer in the Air Force Band'. Ukulele, harmonica and double bass (hail the Hotlicks Cookies!) provide a lovely traditional sound. Another song that was played live on The Daintees' tour, as well as being aired on BBC local radio in the North East for the Children in Need appeal.

Recorded at Salt Mine Studios with Frankie Gibbon, this version of 'Him, Her and the Moon' is therefore the original as it was recorded over three years before the version that would appear on the fourth Daintees album *The Boy's Heart*. Mickey Watson is the

Frances and Alfie Stephenson on their wedding day

Martin aged 12

Jim Sixsmith, Martin's mentor in his teenage years

ETN 727C

The figure in the house over the road in the background is Mr Tommy Conway, he always stands at the door but never appeared when you wave at him, I don't think he likes us my dad was born in the house with the arrow and P's was Jessie, my car is the horrible Ford escort behind Adam's collector's item it cost £50 and the wheels were jacked up not the truck and I didn't know how the gold flame chews or made out the wrong immersion I suppose

The Daintees and friends, London Records 1982

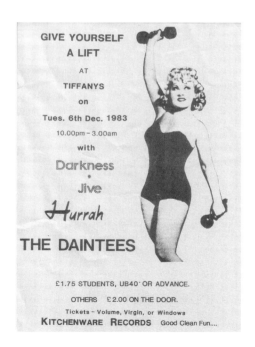

Kitchenware gig poster 1983

Anth Dunn & Martin, Trouble Town vocals, Powerplant Studios 1982

Enjoying the sun, London 1984

Daintees live, 1986

Sheffield Poly' 1987

...Lynx Studios, Newcastle. High Bells Ring Thin Sessions, 1990.
With Shippy (above) and Round Eyes Ray (below)

Daintees, Dublin Olympia 1990

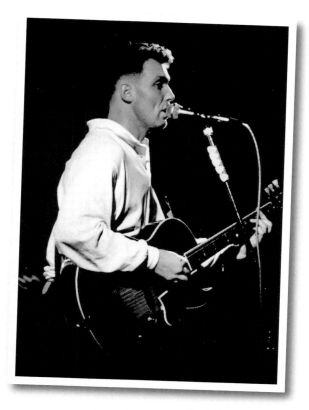

Edinburgh Queens Hall 1991

...with Shippy and Joe, Jumpin'& Hot Club, Newcastle 1992

...with Paul Handyside, Jumpin'& Hot Club, Newcastle 1993

star player on this track, providing the delicate brushed drums, piano and haunting clarinet part. If anything this version is truer to the feel of the song than the later Lenny Kaye-produced take which rather overdid the echo on Martin's vocal. Whatever, it's magical, beautiful, ethereal and lots of other things that this writer's vocabulary is unable to express – just listen.

'Every Night' is just classic Martin and Gypsy, and shows just why their many tours together later in the mid-90s were so special. It is wonderful listening to two musicians who have an almost psychic understanding between them. Additionally the song is a fine example of Martin writing a country blues song in the classic style of Mississippi John Hurt and Blind Boy Fuller – widening his scope even further. Sharp-as-a-pin imagery comes flying out at the listener as the raconteur bemoans his bad luck and hard life – 'On this rock of savage and abandon', 'As we watch our every brother dangle'.

The mood is lifted by the late night jazz swing of 'Music and Life', a perfect vehicle for Andrea Mackie's voice that is the last time she would feature on a Martin Stephenson album for many years. Rick Taylor's trombone completes the picture.

Closing track 'Let's Call the Whole Thing Off' is an offbeat classic. Martin duets with Cathal Coughlan on a slightly perverse take of the George and Ira Gershwin standard. The Vintage Jazz Men provide a suitably swinging backing, the whole thing sounding perfectly respectable until the second verse, when references to acid and bananas come in from somewhere and finally Cathal resorts to calling Martin a 'bastard'! Best not to get too deep with this one, methinks.

Among other things the album is a testament to the versatile talent of Mickey Watson, with whom Martin later split as Mickey couldn't handle his 'spontaneous' approach to live work. A real shame as the two of them obviously had a real rapport, which was demonstrated further at several low-key gigs in the North East at the time. One gig at Newcastle's Bridge Hotel pub, a Jumpin' and Hot Club night, showed Martin at his most relaxed in years, playing guitar while Mickey swapped between piano, saxophone, bass and percussion. The duo played a delightful gig running through a bunch of Martin's songs, mixed in with considerable banter, aided and abetted by Shippy and Round Eyes.

Outtakes that never made the final album include 'Old Black Jerome', about a soldier returning from the war to find that his sweetheart has run off with 'Black Jerome': 'Here's a gun, go out and find them, and blow them both to kingdom come.' Featuring the Vintage Jazz Men once again, with Martin on pre-war-radio-style vocals, the song was recorded live in a South Tyneside pub.

Additionally 'Hop Down in E Minor', a ragtime guitar piece, and 'Wild Sex And Drugs Party', a rap about, well, a wild party, have managed to survive the ravages of time (and alleged fire) and can be tracked down on a rarities compilation.

About half of the album was gradually released in 1992 in the various formats of the 'Big Sky New Light' single, but after a rumoured 'freebie' release with *The Boy's Heart* came to nothing, it was actually 12 April 1993 before *High Bells Ring Thin* was finally available in its entirety. Due to the low-key release (limited advertising and promotion by Kitchenware whose links, and presumably budget, with London Records had been severed) it has since become one of Martin's most sought after albums – and something of an obscure classic to boot.

Despite the 'thin on the ground' promotion the music press still got hold of it and, as usual, were generally positive despite acknowledging it was something of a belated 'clearing the decks' exercise by Kitchenware.

'... leaves us hoping we're witnessing the end of a chapter rather than a swansong' – Peter Paphides, *Melody Maker*, 15/5/93.

'... fans will find plenty to cherish' – Gary Leboff, *Vox*, 6/93.

'A rich and peculiar talent ... pleasant rather than earth-shattering' – Stuart Maconie, *Q*, 6/93.

To these ears *High Bells Ring Thin* is, up to that point, the album truest to Martin's rationale for writing songs in the first place, as he explained in an interview in 1992: 'The only way I can express my knowledge of the world is to explore the self, the family and the community. Each of us has a specific experience of the world, and that's all you can offer as a songwriter – the world as seen through your eyes.'

Following back-to-back US tours supporting Violent Femmes and Melissa Etheridge (returning the favour from two years earlier), The Daintees rounded off a hectic and emotional 1990, playing a handful of UK dates including a gig at The Town & Country Club in London that was broadcast on TV in its entirety as part of Thames Television's *The Concert* series. The show gives a good account of a typical Daintees gig of the time, with all the supporting cast getting involved as the gig reaches its climax. Martin, though, appears uncharacteristically subdued and Anth Dunn confirmed there was a fair amount of tension around the band at this time – particularly with Martin. The difference in Martin's demeanour between the Town & Country Club and the Bridge Hotel gigs with Mickey Watson, could not have been more stark.

*

1991 was a strange, almost dour year for UK rock and pop music. During the 80s, the post-punk phenomenon of independent labels had somehow managed to develop into a very limited genre known as 'indie'. In the late 80s, after the highpoint of the C-86 sub-genre, indie had started to take a battering in terms of popularity and 'coolness' from the hip hop-based dance music emanating from Chicago and New York and being played in clubs and at gatherings (both official and unofficial) all across the land. The hippest and smartest bands of this era were able to morph together Byrdsian guitar-based indie, with the ecstatic, sweaty grooves of 'rave' – and in some cases produced some genuinely original and classic music, e.g. Happy Mondays and Stone Roses, flagbearers of the Madchester scene.

However by '91 there was a clear lull in the careers of the aforementioned Mancunians as they battled with the challenges of repeating the success of the albums that had brought them to prominence. Dance music was still hugely popular but in terms of potential great leaps forward only the emergence of the earliest indicators of Bristol's trip-hop scene, led by Massive Attack and Portishead, could be classed as anything truly innovative.

For the first time in many years the main focus in terms of new, interesting, guitar-based music was in the USA: specifically a city in the north west, Pacific state of Washington called

Seattle. From here Nirvana released their keynote album *Nevermind* – and a host of Seattle-based bands followed them, including Soundgarden, Alice In Chains and Pearl Jam. Influenced by an abrasive combination of punk and metal, and lyrically driven by front man Kurt Cobain's inner demons, Nirvana would have a huge influence on US music over the next ten years or more. Even established bands such as REM would later be inspired and elevated by grunge, and a whole host of US 'college-rock' bands (Sugar, Pavement et al) used it as their starting point.

Meanwhile here in the UK, aside from the delightfully anarchic KLF, we had to put up with Bryan Adams' '(Everything I Do) I Do It For You' power ballad being number one for the best part of four months. Grim, indeed.

1991 was also a dour year musically for Martin Stephenson and The Daintees. This was due to a combination of burnout from the intense activity of the last five years since *Boat to Bolivia*; Martin's inability to control the tension between his artistic output and the ravenous needs of the music industry; and finally a new issue that was starting to have an impact – his drinking: 'I was a chronic alcoholic by then,' he admits, 'and a lazy bastard.'

Meanwhile, in January, Kitchenware saw fit to release the 'Let's Call the Whole Thing Off' track with Cathal Coughlan from the *High Bells Ring Thin* sessions as a limited-edition single. It was available at gigs and from Kitchenware via mail order.

While songs were being written and worked up for a planned fourth album, Kitchenware busied themselves with some typical record company scam devices. Firstly, George Michael had released a song as a single from the *Listen Without Prejudice* album called 'Waiting For That Day', which bore a striking resemblance to Martin's 'Crocodile Cryer'. Martin recalled in 2001: 'Keith Armstrong was adamant that we could have this guy – real serious about having his ass. If you listen there is, oh, at least seven seconds of it that sounds the same. I found it creepy trying to make money out of someone whose track sounds like yours just because they are successful. I thought it was a bit dark so I kept out of it.'

Secondly a news item (emerging from Newcastle) went around the industry that Martin had been asked to write a song for Joan

Baez. 'Yeah, another Keith Armstrong scam. I never thought that anybody would want to sing my songs. I would have avoided that concept – anxiety, insecurity!' It seems neither Mr Michael nor Ms Baez were particularly troubled by either story. Nevertheless it did manage to make a few interesting column inches in the music press that were a bit different from the usual 'working on a new album' mini news articles.

Ahead of that new album some fresh material was being worked up. Malcolm Dick had left and Paul Smith was back on the drum stool; Andrea Mackie returned to her jazz project with her husband as the new material was rockier and not considered suitable for Andrea's singing style.

At lunchtime on 23 April 1991 the basic Daintees four-piece band (augmented by Frankie Gibbon on Hammond organ) played an 'open rehearsal' at the Newcastle Live Theatre, previewing a number of new songs that immediately showed a 'back to basics' approach in terms of both songwriting and arranging. New songs included 'The Boy's Heart', 'Big Sky New Light' and 'We Can Roll', as well as some that would remain unreleased – 'Turning the Wheel', 'Do It Again' and 'Groove Bin'. The overall sound indicated a shift towards indie guitar pop – well away from the transatlantic sound of *Salutation Road*.

Following this, some demo sessions were arranged with Pete Wingfield in the producer's chair at his Chipping Norton studio – the output of which Anth later described as sounding 'middle-aged'. A rumoured reunion with Gil Norton never happened and the band again linked up with Dave Brewis to work up some demos.

Gigs in 1991 were thin on the ground: there was an appearance at the Heineken Big Top festival in Bristol in August, followed by two nights at Edinburgh's Queen's Hall as part of the Fringe Festival. Mike Chavez reviewed one of the Edinburgh gigs in the Kitchenware newsletter *Rollmo'*:

> 'The final show of a short series of dates saw Martin and Co. at the Queen's Hall. Despite massive competition from the Edinburgh festival, the venue was full and the 900-strong crowd decidedly convivial. They weren't to be disappointed either as a real scorcher was in store tonight.

'Opening with a new song "Big Sky New Life" [sic], the show jogged along through old faves and a further couple of newies, "The Boy's Heart" and "We Can Roll". A little local flavour was added, too, with the appearance of young Edinburgh fiddler Fraser McNaughton, who joined Martin for a fine rendition of "The Wait". Fraser had interviewed him for the local press on the telephone a week earlier and was somehow roped into playing!

'The encores came along all too soon and were far and away the highlight of the evening, ranging from the sheer aggression of "Look Down, Look Down" to the silence-inducing "Kathy" – a song about a man and his blind wife, invoking a real knife-cuttable atmosphere. "Come Back To Me", a comedy calypso about being chucked by your girlfriend, was thrown in for good measure and the show was done.

'Hearing the new songs it is apparent that there has been a shift away from the acoustic folky numbers to a weightier, indie sound. The addition of Frankie Gibbon on Hammond has added some extra depth to produce, hopefully, more widely-appealing music. This would appear to be a solid move, as the band sure could do with a hit record when the new LP is released. The group is approaching a vital stage in its development and it is important to consolidate the support they have and also to attract new fans.'

Martin also did a solo gig at London's Mean Fiddler and three nights at Glasgow's legendary King Tuts Wah Wah Hut in October.

Another reason for this relative lack of activity was that Martin's wife Angela was pregnant with their first child. Daughter Phoebe was born in November.

By the end of the year it was apparent that something radical and inspirational needed to happen to kick the band out of their torpor. That inspiration would come, much like the main influence on the music scene that year, from a US source. But from the east coast rather than the north west.

*

Martin and The Daintees (with Frankie Gibbon on organ) convened at Trinity Heights Studios, Denton Burn, Newcastle in January 1992 with legendary Patti Smith Group guitarist, and curator of the psychedelic garage scene, Lenny Kaye in the producer's chair. This was, first and foremost, a chance for Martin to meet a personal hero: 'I'd kept Lenny's plectrum after seeing him play with Patti at Newcastle City Hall in 1978. He came back to Newcastle and did the album for next to nothing. He's a real hard worker although the first thing he wanted to know was where Westgate Road was 'cos that's where he knew all the bike shops were.'

The overall feel of the album *The Boy's Heart* is of 'back to a four-piece band basics', with very little extra instrumentation aside from Frankie's Hammond organ and some guest vocal performances from Pauline Murray (ex-Penetration and Invisible Girls) and Cathal Coughlan (Fatima Mansions). This approach led to the Dunn brothers collaborating with Martin on writing the music to three of the songs: 'Big Sky, New Light', 'Sunday Halo' and the title track.

It was a conscious decision by the band to record in the North East and the record undoubtedly benefits from that, as was confirmed at the time by Lenny Kaye: 'I think, in terms of this record, it's really important for Martin to make a record surrounded by the people he loves. I mean, we've utilised local musicians and that sense of spirit, especially as an outsider coming here, the spirit of what Newcastle really is, is in the blood of this record'.

Martin expanded further on this theme: 'Anth and me started out playing rockabilly and we had all these dreams about playing in America and you have to get it out of your system. But every time we've come to making an album, it's been someone else's decision, saying "try this or that producer, record here" etc. It just got to a point where I thought, "hold on, who do I want to work with?" My first gut feeling was Lenny. The record company said I could work with whoever I wanted, but they didn't have much money – so we're on a pretty low budget, but we're making the record we want to make.'

Opening song 'Big Sky New Light' sets the scene with a Gary Dunn guitar riff that shows up The Edge for the amorphous, weak wimp that he is. The song takes a not so subtle swipe at the record industry-related constraints of the previous two years in its urge to 'break free from down time', and as such sets a wonderfully positive tone for the rest of the album. As the only single released from the album, the song, thanks to some high-profile championing by Simon Bates no less, actually made a modest dent in the singles chart on its release in June '92 – The Daintees' first 'hit' since 'Trouble Town' in 1987.

Back in 1990 Martin had mentioned in an interview: 'I'm writing songs for a play about a First World War poet who died at 23 in the Battle of the Somme.' Whilst the play never came to fruition, the song and the concept of The Boy's Heart certainly did.

William Noel Hodgson was a lieutenant in the 9th battalion of the Devonshire regiment of the British Army. He was also a poet and writer publishing under the name Edward Melbourne. He is generally regarded as the 'forgotten war poet', especially compared to peers such as Owen, Sassoon and Graves. Born in Thornbury, Gloucestershire, he was educated at Durham School before gaining a First in Classics at Christ Church, Oxford. Like so many other young men he cut short his studies to enlist in Lord Kitchener's New Model Army. From that moment he was destined not for a life of learning, but for death, alongside thousands of others on the Somme. After being awarded the Military Cross in October 1915 he was killed in action on 1 July 1916, the first day of the Battle of The Somme, at Mansell Copse.

Hodgson's links with Durham were further established by a poem he wrote in 1914 entitled 'Durham Cathedral'. A North East writer called Jack Medomsley wrote a biography of Hodgson called *The Gentle Poet*, which was published in 1989. It was reading this book that inspired Martin Stephenson to base a song around one of the war poet's lesser known works.

To a Boy

Oh, arrow-straight and slender
With grey eyes unafraid,
You see the roses' splendour
Nor reck that they shall fade.

Youth in its flush and flower
Has a soul of whitest flame,
Eternity in an hour,
All life and death in a game.

> May youth forever weave you
> His magic round your ways,
> And time the robber leave you
> The boy's heart all your days.

Hodgson wrote 'To a Boy' in 1914 before he went over to France, hence the optimism within, as if the dangers that lay ahead were either unknown or underestimated. It is not surprising at all that the theme of the poem, holding onto the naivety and magic of youth as one gets older, should have appealed so much to Martin's instincts at the time he first read it. It would be incredibly crass to draw a direct comparison between the poet's optimism and the barbarism of the war and Martin Stephenson's battle against the music industry. But in principle these two writers are coming from the same viewpoint – that youthful talent must always battle against the evil in the world, no matter what the personal battleground in question.

The ensuing title track is a collage of images flashing between the First World War and 1960s America, as Martin explains: 'I saw the poet in a re-birth after dying on the battlefield. He is reborn as Lenny Kaye! The second part is about a story that Lenny told me. When he was 14 he and his mates drove from Pennsylvania to San Francisco, enjoying their first joint, enjoying the freedom of this really long journey for a bunch of young guys. So the poet is reborn as one of those young boys in the car. The message is about all the young lads who had to go to war – reborn as young hippies.'

The main core of the song would often weave its way into later songs, both live and in the studio, particularly a song Martin wrote in 2001 after the death of his Mum, Frances, entitled 'Home'.

Lightening the atmosphere somewhat, the Van Morrison-inspired 'We Can Roll' is the sort of song you tape (don't people still tape?!) and send to your best mate when he's just fallen head over heels in love with his new girlfriend. To this listener it's a celebration of falling in love, phoning in sick to work and just living life. Which isn't too far from what it was actually about, as Martin confirms: 'The song "We Can Roll" is about middle age, a couple re-discovering each other once the children have flown.' It doesn't need any more analysis: just listen and let that big, beaming smile take over your face.

'The Ballad of the English Rose' (written back in 1989 on the Hothouse Flowers tour bus) depicts a view of England as a violent, colonising nation 'sinking to a level of despair'. Its subject matter is not open to debate, but coming from Martin Stephenson, it just sounds a touch forced. We expect a more subtle approach to songwriting subject matter than this; in fact it is his only political song since 'Left Us to Burn' and, whereas that shocked with its direct approach, 'English Rose' sounds more than a little contrived. It is also very difficult not to be reminded of Tenpole Tudor's 'Swords of a Thousand Men' during the instrumental breaks. Martin bravely acknowledged this fact during live renditions in later years.

'Neon Skies' had been written way back in 1977, when Martin was just 16. One of his first ever compositions along with 'Cherryade and Rock 'n' Roll' (which wouldn't appear on a release until 2008's *Western Eagle*), it had even been recorded at Spectro Arts Centre, Carliol Square, Newcastle in the summer of 1978, with Martin, Chris Mordey, Steve Minto, John Farrer, and Tommy Watson. Any concerns about returning to a 'lost' song from the writer's teenage years were allayed as 'Neon Skies' is, quite simply, a classic. Performed live for the 1984 Radio 1 Kid Jensen session, Martin could have sold this song ten times over to Neil Young, Bruce Springsteen, or any other 'serious' songwriter you care to mention. As a vehicle for getting The Daintees of 1992 back on track it is perfect and probably should have been considered for a single. Written in two parts (how progressive!) the first, slower, section is a moody ballad seemingly about losing love to a heartless soul: 'I'm only one chapter in your book of love' – and finding solace in the psychedelic tripping brought on by too many magic mushrooms. The second section is a riff-driven reprise that doubles the tempo and doubles the heartbeat accordingly, bringing the song to a fitting climax.

The pièce de resistance of the album is undoubtedly 'Hollywood Fields'. Martin outlines the background: 'The song "Hollywood Fields" is about a boy witnessing the persecution/modern-day crucifixion of his Mother. From his school he can see the factory where she works and at playtime goes to the fence to try and catch a glimpse of her. He sees the white overalls pouring out to have their packed lunches hundreds of yards away. He thinks he spots his Mother and she symbolically moves to the middle of the field that separates the school and factory. She dances and she dreams. Her son is at the fence and he understands perfectly what is happening. The children flock and mock, as do his Mother's workmates. It concludes: "peasants are the workers, and peasants are these children, and all who laugh at dreams." These last few lines indicate that the child in the song doesn't perceive himself as one of the Children. He is his Mother's son.' It is a compelling tale which, although rarely featuring at live gigs over the years, has never lost its power.

Side Two (OK, this is the last Martin Stephenson album to be released on vinyl!) opens with 'Sentimental Journey'. Like 'Neon Skies' it develops from an initial low-key quiet section into a double-speed finale. The lyrics seem to hark back to a time of 'real emotions' and question where that time has gone. Unlike earlier songs that subtly suggested a return to earlier values, 'Sentimental Journey' is more definite and specific as it hits home in its closing section – with Gary Dunn proving that he is the guitar hero we knew he could be.

OK – we knew Martin Stephenson could never be one-dimensional, and 'Sunday Halo' proves that most convincingly. After an intro bass riff of worryingly modernist tendencies by Anth Dunn, followed by a Bowie-esque rap (so it mentions loads of European cities!) delivered by Cathal Coughlan, Martin waxes lyrical about the family radio as his mother vacuums up his marbles.

I have mentioned in this book already (and will do many times more) the ability of Martin's music to take you unawares. A typical example is the classic '8.30 Mowbray Morning', a song of such gentleness relating the attempts of our hero (at the tender age of 20) to make love to his intended amongst the distractions of a busy park. He finally wins me over (don't know about her!) with the killer line 'you're two years older than me and you give me the horn'. Sounds cold and callous to the outsider, but then you've never heard the song if you think that.

'(Least We've a) Map in the World' is a flawed attempt at writing a Simple Minds-inspired, flag-waving anthem. Unfortunately it doesn't do a great deal more, for this listener, other than remind me why I dislike such songs, despite its undoubtedly well-meaning protestations to save the earth.

'Him, Her and the Moon' appears on this album in a different guise from that on *High Bells Ring Thin*. But the effect is the same: a beautifully poetic ballad that can lift you higher than the moon, once in the right frame of mind.

The album finishes with the punk classic 'Cab Attack'. An apocryphal tale of a taxi driver being beaten up by his fare, the song could have been taken seriously were it not for the references to Mond Cowie of the Angelic Upstarts in the outro. Rarely played live these days, although often requested, it aptly demonstrates one of the extremes of Stephenson's songwriting as well as being outrageously great fun.

Listening back to the album with a critical ear for the first time in several years, it is apparent that despite some flaws Martin and The Daintees really were back on track again after the blip that was *Salutation Road*. It's certainly Gary Dunn's best album – his guitar-playing really coming to life has he finds his own style and sound. The 'gang' mentality of the four-piece band, while never previously appropriate, seemed to bring out the best in all concerned, with no little credit going to Lenny Kaye, who reflected: 'The album brought out the real feel of the band; the fact that they have been together for a while and understand each other's rhythms. That is why this is a band record because before it's the strings thing, then the orchestra thing and jazz and all that stuff, then all of a sudden we're back to being a four-piece that rocks as well as being able to encourage its more intimate self. This album brings out an aggressive side to Martin's music that hasn't been heard before.'

Dressed in a strange collage-effect front cover, focusing on an unnerving clown's face, *The Boy's Heart* was released on 13 July. Dedicated to Martin's daughter Phoebe, the album had minimal impact chartwise but once again reviews were, in the main, positive:

'The title track conjures up images of Burl Ives jamming with The House of Love … bizarre head-spinning stuff' – Paul Davies, *Q* magazine, 7/92.

'... songs that end with the ponderous inevitability of a walrus on a moped' – David Bennun, *Melody Maker*, 11/7/92.

'His best LP to date ... forget fashion, what's good is good' – Nick Duerden, *Select*, 8/92.

'This is a quality LP from a man in his prime ... take heed all ye unbelievers!' – Gary Crossing, *The Big Issue*, 8/92.

'The songs ... have the virtue of not sounding like anyone else' – David Quantick, *NME*, 4/7/92.

'*The Boy's Heart* is the boy back on course' – Craig McLean, *Vox*, 8/92.

'They've not made their definitive album yet, but they're definitely getting there' – Mike Chavez, *Paint It Red*, 8/92.

Ahead of the new album's release Martin and The Daintees (Gary, Anth and Paul Smith plus Graham Henderson on keyboards) played a handful of gigs in May and June including appearances at both the Glasgow and London Fleadh festivals and a sell-out gig at Manchester University playing to over a thousand ecstatic, sweaty students. This, plus a single of the week award for 'Big Sky, New Light' in the *Melody Maker*, proved that, despite accusations of them being immensely unfashionable in some parts of the music press, The Daintees still had an audience out there, keen to see them and keen to get hold of the new album.

A showcase gig on 13 July to launch the album at London's Town & Country Club (supported by new Kitchenware act Hug) saw the back-to-basics approach of the album reflected in the live performance and showed Martin keen to focus on the new material. He noted in 1992: 'I told the lads we were going to do things differently this time – not to worry about having hit singles and stuff. And I told 'em that times might be harder, but it's what we had to do. I'm not a songwriter really. I'm a finger-picker. I could just about make a living from that. But as a songwriter, I rely on alcohol too much. I'm the sort of bloke who, when it's a lovely sunny day, puts his coat on and goes down the pub. I'm getting a bit more health-conscious now I've got a little girl, but I still like to drink to fuck up that computer in your head. To stop me worrying about being cool and silence all those voices in your head.'

However, the pressure from London Records was still intense and, whereas the first three albums had all sold in excess of 30,000 copies, ultimately *The Boy's Heart* struggled to reach the 15,000 mark – a telling statistic that mirrored the fact that all was not well in the Daintees/London Records camp.

In September Martin, accompanied by Graham Henderson, supported Del Amitri (just peaking with their hit 'Nothing Ever Happens') on a short European tour: 'I connected with Graham closely as he had just left Fairground Attraction and was finding his own way, so we became really good mates and travelled together. We supported Del Amitri around Europe and we were into this "travelling with a light step" thing. He had his accordion and I had my guitar. Del Amitri would have the big bus and all the gear, soundchecking for five hours. We would just get on the train and turn up, do a two-minute soundcheck and then go and do a gig in a café across town in Hamburg or wherever. He's a great musician, Graham, a very well-read man, great piano player and very nice to be with. I got a lot of soul food from him.'

Following the Del Amitri tour, Martin played a handful of gigs solo in Austria and Italy supporting Bob Geldof, no less. I have to confess that I struggle to get my brain around the hugely different personalities of Messrs Geldof and Stephenson being on the same tour. Interestingly though, Geldof's 'musical' persona is actually quite different from that of his more well-known one, as I can attest to having being dragged to one of his solo gigs in the 00s by my wife, a fan. Several of his between-song quips curiously reminded me of some of Martin's banter, e.g. 'this one sold 71 copies in Poland', 'you're applauding now but none of you bastards bought the album, did you?!' etc. Martin recalls the experience: 'Geldof blew me away. He was a character, a typical "lad". I saw so much good and so much bad in one person.'

Also that month, Kitchenware announced what was in effect a farewell tour, the official line being: 'The gigs give fans their last chance to see Stephenson perform with his band The Daintees. Martin has decided on a new approach for future recordings, including some collaborative writing which he hasn't done previously. Although this marks the end of an era for Stephenson it marks a fresh approach for the New Year after a fulfilling decade of The Daintees.'

In reality both parties had pretty much had enough. In cold hard terms the albums weren't selling enough units to satisfy the accountants and Martin was not prepared in any way to compromise his art to improve matters. If anything he was looking to take an even less 'commercial' path musically.

Circumstances also meant the end of Martin and the band's relationship with tour manager Mick 'The Mick' Owen. 'Mick was a good friend of mine,' recalled Martin early in 2009. 'Not only did he look after the Daintees like his own kids, but he also worked with me on all my solo tours too, including the three-month Hothouse Flowers tour in the USA in 1989 and headlining Glastonbury Festival that year.

'Mick was very close to Bob Geldof and started with the Boomtown Rats in 1977 as a T-shirt guy but soon slipped up the ranks. It was Mick who put me on Bob's tour in 1992. Mick always looked out for me and I for him. He was very fond of the Daintees and really understood all the characters in the band. If ever asked his occupation he would answer either "International Jewel Thief" or "Roof Felter from Alberquerque". We lost Mick about five years ago to cancer and there is not a day goes by that I don't miss him; he was a very funny and loving man and was my friend and brother.'

The final tour, taking in some 30 dates throughout October and into November saw The Daintees supported by new Irish band The Devlins, who would later become a million-selling act on the back of their *Waiting* album and *Batman Forever* soundtrack tie-in 'Crossing The River' (and ironically would later work with Martin on his *Beyond the Leap, Beyond the Law* album in 1996).

The gigs were predominantly celebratory affairs, tinged with an element of anger at the music business in Martin's delivery. Martin introduced some new songs including the solo 'Think Only of the Child', dedicated to 'the mechanic and his wife out of *Coronation Street*'.

A review of their show at Sunderland Polytechnic by Victor Jara in *Paint It Red* summed up what this great band meant to many: 'Here we have a band forced into splitting up when their career was at a peak and not when on the slopes of mediocrity ... if the band's members can individually recreate the magic and charm of The Daintees then they are at least assured of credibility and affection, if not actually riches.'

And so on 2 November 1992 at the Glasgow Pavilion, The Daintees played what was deemed to be their last gig. The end of an era.

Chapter 4

The Troubadour
(1994 to 1998)

'There been times that I thought I couldn't last for long
But now I think I'm able to carry on
It's been a long, a long time coming
But I know a change is gonna come'

When Rene Hall created the mournful, horn-led arrangement for 'A Change is Gonna Come', little did he know that Sam Cooke's 1964 hit would soon become an anthem for the American Civil Rights movement.

Dylan himself had offered up a heart-breaking 'Blowin' in the Wind' a year earlier, communicating his anger through a series of rhetorical questions, but Cooke saw a light at the end of the tunnel and gifted us his hope only a few months before his life was to end tragically at the Hacienda Hotel in Los Angeles.

30 years later, in 1994, the Civil Rights movement in South Africa was celebrating the country's first multi-racial vote and the election to the presidency of Nelson Mandela. Among the celebrations could be heard the unmistakeable notes of Sam Cooke's song of hope. The change had indeed come.

But in the UK, somehow insulated from major change, the political landscape was as it had been for the previous 15 years. A Conservative government (with a large C) and a conservative context (with a small one). We were getting excited about the recently completed Channel Tunnel and the impending paroxysm of joy that would be the National Lottery. Musically, the UK was experiencing desperate times. A sequence of underwhelming number ones from Mariah Carey, Wet Wet Wet and Chaka Demus and Pliers sent youngsters careering back to the indie scene where Oasis were ready to emerge, smoking, swearing and preparing for mayhem. Along with Blur, Pulp and a whole bunch of considerably average bands, the very retro-looking genre to be known as Brit-Pop was about as radical as the local music scene could manage. If change was long overdue in the UK, it would come in response to a plague of mundanity music-wise.

For Martin Stephenson the times were also a-changin'. In the process of winding down his relationship with Kitchenware/London Records, he had reached a significant milestone on his personal journey. Alcohol would still be the drug of choice and there would yet be new record deals to rope him to the corporate mast, but 1994 would be the catalyst for a period of self-examination that would lead him to divest himself of the traditional trappings of the music business and focus on the music. It would prove to be a key point on his particular voyage.

Martin's contract with London Records was actually a six-album deal and he and The Daintees had only made four. Hence the tapes for *High Bells Ring Thin* were magically recovered from the 'fire', and the inevitable compilation album was suggested.

There Comes A Time, the final Daintees album, was released on 15 March 1993. Subtitled *The Best of...*, it was put together by Kitchenware boss Keith Armstrong in December 1992 and provided a solid summary of the previous six years of recording. The cover featured a nice Bleddyn Butcher shot of Martin's hat with the 'July it was a fruitless month' inscription, and the sleeve notes by Armstrong nostalgically drew to a close the career of one of the most interesting and inimitable British bands of modern times.

For those of a sad-collector persuasion, the version of 'You Really Had a Heart' is unique as it is from the Pete Wingfield-produced demo sessions of 1991.

The music press were unsurprisingly unanimous in their praise:

'Time, once more, to discover a long-lost songsmith, proud owner of a distinct deftness of touch' – *Q*, 6/93.

'This band should've been massive ... very highly recommended' – Victor Jara, *Paint It Red*, 4/93.

'A tip of the hat to the man in the hat' – Patrick Humphries, *Vox*, 6/93.

'Stephenson has been overlooked for far too long and latecomers would be advised to get hold of this collection as an ideal starting point' – Terry Staunton, *NME*, 3/4/93.

Martin later expressed his feelings on the compilation: 'I personally thought it was a bit too early to do it. I felt like I hadn't really achieved anything. It's the kind of thing Bob Dylan brings out after 20 albums! I didn't have any input into it 'cos I wasn't bothered. The only use I've found for it is making tapes for drummers when they've been learning the set'.

Looking back, *There Comes a Time* would be a significant moment, following in the footsteps of the now fondly remembered *High Bells Ring Thin*. Bringing together a fan's-ear collection of the best that had gone before, its future reappearance in the discount racks of the likes of Fopp, Andy's Records and MVC (mourn their passing, all) would lead to a serious re-examination of Martin Stephenson and his music, while also finding a new base of admirers among those new to his music. Around the country 30-somethings would pick the disc up and mutter something like, 'whatever happened to him? He was great!' Inevitably purchased, the strains of 'Little Red Bottle' would be, for many people, the first time they'd heard Martin on anything other than a cassette tape or long player.

For many other artists, the arrival on the scene of a greatest hits package denotes either a falling star in the firmament or, alternatively, an attempt to cash in on present fame. For Martin, it signified a proud review of his canon and a line in the sand. For his many fans, it provided an opportunity to re-visit times past – and for a large percentage of that group, it was the beaming smile that they recalled most compellingly. And that smile would grow wider in 1994 with the arrival of Martin's second daughter, Esme.

There Comes a Time ends with the lullaby, 'Don't Be Afraid of the Night'. The pace and tone of the song now seem oddly prophetic. Something was in the air. The change was gonna come – and while 1994 saw no official releases, and very little recorded activity anywhere, 1995's twin offerings of *Yogi In My House* and *Sweet Misdemeanour* would see the troubadour embark on a number of paths, often straying in different directions, tangential and curiously simultaneous.

Many journeys would be started at this time, some of which,

as Neil Young reflected in the sleeve notes to 1977's *Decade*, would take unexpected paths. Young's only commercial hit single 'Heart of Gold' put him, in his words, 'in the middle of the road. Travelling there soon became a bore, so I headed for the ditch. A rougher ride, but I saw some interesting people there.' One sensed that Martin Stephenson would be taking a road less travelled in 1994.

In May 1993 Martin had headed out on his first solo tour since The Daintees split. Taking in folk clubs and arts centres, he was now free of the commercial pressures that had previously encumbered him and very shortly thereafter free from Kitchenware. His 11-year relationship with Keith Armstrong, Phil Mitchell et al was over.

*

Back in 1994 the best clue as to Martin's musical inclinations would be his live appearances. They didn't stop. He plays the Borderline in London on 11 February 1994 and a detailed examination of the evening reveals our master of ceremonies on top form. A recording of the gig opens, significantly, with the sounds of laughter as Martin eases in to the show with some typical banter. The audience is asked to guess what he will open with – a fiver is offered – and like the sound of a starting motorbike, 'Look Down, Look Down' picks up the pace and rattles along.

There are previews of songs that will appear on 1995's *Yogi In My House*, including 'Taker On The Globe', 'Think Only of the Child', 'Spirit Child', 'Gone the Gypsy Davey' and 'Solomon', the latter of which paints a dark-period Johnny Cash with a dramatic accordion accompaniment. To the delight of the crowd the band strikes up a rousing 'Crocodile Cryer' and although Martin inadvertently christens a new version of 'Coleen' by starting at verse two, the Stephenson audience is forever tolerant and the cheeky North East banter redeems the situation again.

Between-song 'raps' are not yet the length and depth of those a current audience would experience, but we learn of the birth of Anthony Dunn's little boy Lenny, the story of how Slim Gaillard was abandoned by his father and became a regular Charlie Parker bandsman, learning eight languages in the eight years of travels he accomplished after losing his particular way. The Slim

Gaillard story could have been wrought to bring an audience to tears, but mindful of his role as sometime musical court jester and teacher, Martin counsels: 'It's positive, man.' This wouldn't be the last example of Martin's better nature and unwillingness to hurt people.

Perennial favourite 'Running Water' and *Salutation Road*'s ominous yet warm 'We Are Storm' bring the set to a close, laughter mingling with applause.

Martin was on fine form, as anyone present will attest. Photographs of that era show the eternally smiling minstrel still in possession of the odd cigarette. One engaging snap taken around then shows him, pork pie-hatted, guitar in hand, cigarette dropping from his mouth, wearing a goatee and a Hawaiian shirt, while another presents us with a Joaquín Phoenix as Johnny Cash look-a-like, illuminating the dark stage with a lit match, clean shaven and angelic, in that disarming Stephenson way.

With the benefit of hindsight, the gig sounds strangely 'throwaway' as if the message were more important than the music, but that is to deny one of the fundamental precepts of Martin's approach. Right up to *The Boy's Heart*, there was a depth to the production values, aurally if not totally appropriate to the sound. It appeared, to this writer at least, that some of the nascent power of Martin's message had been sacrificed for the excitement of being in a studio – soul compromised by production perhaps.

To the onlooker, however, one of the symbols of Martin's evolution to travelling minstrel has been the gradual deconstruction of the recording process. From the swirls and echoes of *Boat to Bolivia* to a running commentary (telling his band what chords to play as the song is being performed) the message was becoming the music and the future would stretch even a fixated minimalist's interpretation of the term 'stripped down'.

What was evident, however, was the reach and depth of the voice. Having always possessed a warm, sweet, soulful burr, Martin was becoming more aware of the power of his voice. Not power in the conventional sense (there was never any real prospect of him replacing Freddie Mercury) but the 'power of the small', to quote something he said to us in 2006.

Any attempt to explore the nuances of tone and delivery take one immediately out of the context of current contemporary music – and that is where part of the astonishingly wide appeal comes from. Not from the off-kilter tenor of Ian McCulloch or the bleaker still Ian Curtis, but from a rainbow of past masters more likely to fill the bill of *Family Favourites*, that old Radio 2 stalwart or to be played in a Midwest honky tonk. Not comfortable bedfellows, these two contrasting backdrops, but somehow spanning the reach and soul of Stephenson's sound.

Looking back to that gig in February 1994 may conjure up a fairly run-of-the mill 'Coleen', but listen closer and a warmth not unfamiliar to the likes of Matt Monroe, Andy Williams or Bobby Darin sneaks out through the jazz chords. Take a listen to Darin's posthumous *All the Aces*, released in 2005, and hear his pared down version of 'Moon River', if you're inclined to challenge the argument.

This gig in particular offers the interesting opportunity to compare the timbre of the between-song banter with the relaying of the song itself. The lilting County Durham tones add the charm, but then the opening bars chime out and it seems we're dropping an octave, if not quite into Tom Waits territory, then somewhere west of Edwyn Collins, somewhere on the corner of Elvis and Hank.

That one constant – the voice – would find new clothes to wear in the years ahead. Years that began with the 1995 signing to Demon Records, a three-record deal begun with the dual releases of *Yogi In My House* and *Sweet Misdemeanour* in that same year. These were sequential, not simultaneous releases, pre-dating the current epoch, when three or four Martin releases in a year would not surprise anyone. Like fanatical twitchers gathered to witness the arrival of a rare migrant finch, Martin's fans have to be on permanent sentry duty in case a Stephenson recording sneaks past them while no-one's watching. *Hell's Half Acre*, recorded in 2004, is a case in point. Like a professional party crasher, blending into the crowd, it sneaked out almost unnoticed in 2007.

If anything, this was a hint at the emotional constipation that would be eased by the change of scene and change of road. Some of the venues would be the same, but somehow the context was beginning to change.

Chronologically, *Yogi In My House* came first, but musically, the following album, *Sweet Misdemeanour* was the starting point, lurking somewhere in the fifties, between the *Pulp Fiction* sound-track and *Lost Highway.*

Elsewhere there are fascinating glimpses into Martin's state of mind at the time. A new record deal, a new found freedom and a host of new and interesting partnerships beckoned. Joe Guillan, whose Gretsch guitar would light up recordings from 1995 to the present day, would be one who would light a particular undiscovered fuse in the Stephenson subconscious.

I met Joe in late 2007 and over a coffee he told me how he'd become a fellow traveller. Martin and he had first met in the mid 80s – a Tyne Tees Television pop music programme had featured The Daintees and Joe too. They'd liked what they'd seen of each other, but wouldn't actually collaborate until a decade later.

Joe cut a striking figure when we met. One might have expected a rockabilly type, arriving on an old motorbike, leather-clad and ever so slightly dangerous. Far from it. Joe cycled into Newcastle that day, fitter than a butcher's dog – and after we met I saw him again, weaving in and out of the stalls on the Quayside market. Just when I thought I'd seen the last of him, he reappeared. He'd found an original vinyl copy of *Boat to Bolivia.* Was I interested? Do bears perform their ablutions in the forest?

Joe's personal legacy was part Hispanic – as evidenced by his surname. His grandfather, who'd come from North West Spain, found himself on a Spanish Navy ship in Tyne Dock when the Civil War broke out back home in 1936. Joe described his grandfather as gently apolitical, so while we will never know what his true motivations were, his next act was to take out his revolver, throw it in the River Tyne and declare himself home. Another predictable journey had taken an unexpected turn and Joe now has an uncle Pedro and an auntie Dolores.

Speaking as someone with a son called Juan Luis and a daughter called Elena (a legacy of a land well loved and a deep, enduring Iberian connection – named Ana, incidentally), this co-author found much to enjoy in Joe's own history.

Joe's love for skiffle, rockabilly and country swing would jar with the indie folk pop that Martin was putting out in the mid-eighties, but as the different paths converged and diverged over the following years, Joe would become an anchor around which Martin could weave his own brand of musical magic.

For me, Joe Guillan is the driving force behind *Sweet Misdemeanour*. If the album were a wine, the tasting notes would focus on Joe. From riotous rockabilly stomps through to reflective ballads and affectionate instrumentals, *Sweet Misdemeanour* provides more fuel for the *less is better* camp, welcoming in an era of staggeringly diverse output that few contemporaries could match and even fewer record companies could stomach.

Recorded during July 1995 at Frankie Gibbon's studio in Durham, the album sees a welcome return to the laid-back, relaxed style of *High Bells Ring Thin*. Old friends Graham 'Shipcote' Anderson and Anthony Dunn share bass duties as Martin teams up with the respected rockabilly guitarist Guillan – in effect, the debut of the band that were to become The Toe Rags a few years later.

More than anything it gives Martin the opportunity to return to his busking roots as he alternates between the rockabilly style of 'All I Do Is Dream', 'Can't Find the Doorknob' and 'Ball of Fire' and the ragtime & blues acoustic guitar of 'Smokey Mokes', 'South Wind' and 'Candy Man'.

The record is a delight, unveiling a clearly exuberant duo, set on covering all of the points from Chuck Berry (and backwards from there). 'Maverick Waltz' appears to usher in 'Oh, Lonesome Me', but does so without lyrics and in that old country waltz style that's propelling Ryan Adams down his particular road these days – see 'The End' on 2005's *Jacksonville City Nights* for a clear marker.

'Can't Find the Doorknob' crashes in, pricking up everyone's ears from Steve Earle's *Guitar Town* to *King of America*-era Costello, with his rockabilly duets, the song sure fires along up to the title track.

In 'Sweet Misdemeanour', Martin shouts out the verse like an angry bouncer on a Sunderland night club door, before the chorus ushers in Messrs Darin and Berry, performing a mid-tempo 'Splish Splash', clearly enjoying the freedom of the moment, a shared appreciation of musical apprenticeships forged in the west.

One of the earliest Daintees songs, 'Tremelo Men', bursts into the room next, Frank Gibbon's production taking you right onto the set of *Pulp Fiction* with Dick Dale and the Del-tones watching from the canteen: 'didn't *we* write Miserlou?'

The song makes its debut on an official release as Joe Guillan's Gretsch tears the place apart, backed by a beaming Anth and a young drummer by the name of Greg Drysdale who would support Martin in various guises in the studio and live over the next couple of years (including a nice vocal on this album's touching 'Keep This Time').

In the context of the shift from corporate employee to troubadour-of-the-people, this was Martin's truest album to date and the precursor for the relentless period of recording that would follow on from the late-90s and into the next century.

'South Wind' pitches up somewhere near 'Danny Boy', with its wistful melody bringing us closer to the British Isles, something Celtic in its refrain, something Hibernian in its longing.

'Talking to the Child' musically recalls 'Rawhide' while telling a far more serious but intriguing tale, as Martin pointed out in 2009: 'It tackles a unique issue of a man being blamed for attempted abduction by a seven-year-old child. It was written in 1981 and performed in 1982 now and again. It is a true story in a sense as my sister made out that someone had tried to abduct us on our way home from school and told me to go along with the lie. My mother got the police to the house, my sister and I were interviewed and she finally cracked and told the truth. I was so young I hardly spoke – I was seven, she was ten. I made the consequence up of a man being wrongly accused. It is probably a cousin of "Running Water".'

'Ball Of Fire' chugs along like a deranged 'Rock Island Line', with the musical footnotes reading like a *Who's Who* of edgy 50s popular music.

It's appropriate that the album's coda, the instrumental 'Smokey Mokes', brings the invigoration to a pensive close, giving you time to rub your eyes, open the curtains and realise that you are in 1995, the year of Oasis and Blur, rather than 1955.

While publicly Martin would feature *Yogi In My House* strongly, rarely taking anything from *Sweet Misdemeanour*, in his solo gigs, the impending arrival of The Toe Rags would provide sufficient sorties to give these rockabilly routines a wide airing.

Or at least, that is the view of the Martin-watcher. Outside of the curtains, the view was naturally less awed, with the Demon deal certainly failing to have a positive influence on the critics' response. Looking back, it seemed that reviewers were prepared to allow Martin some slack to express himself more organically.

The honesty of the recording hit home. A reviewer in *The Crack* declared: 'In the current atmosphere where an artist's value is measured in Mercury and money, Stephenson's idealism is a breath of fresh air.'

David Roberts, awarding the album 3 stars in *Q* magazine, summed up its musical adventurousness thus: '*Sweet Misdemeanour*'s acoustic rockabilly, ragtime and country rock selection has a lo-fi charm which verges on the twee and precocious once or twice but ultimately wins through by virtue of its charm and sheer bare-faced amiable self-indulgence.'

There is much to go along with here. Most of us would nod in agreement that for want of musical expression and concentration of the message Martin would, from time to time, place himself squarely in the firing line. What's not to challenge, however, is the reviewer's assertion of 'amiable self-indulgence'. There's gentleness to the recording, in spite of the raucous solos, that strikes a chord of recognition in many fans. His voice may not be high in the mix, but there's a familiar old soul in there.

Paint it Red magazine was more upbeat in its appraisal, calling the album 'quiff-bobbing, string-twanging, thigh-slapping stuff' (though neither co-author has yet to detect any German Bierkeller themes in there) but making the interesting observation that the record is 'more suited to a juke box than a CD player.'

Magazine interviews at the time offered an insight into the path travelled to *Sweet Misdemeanour*. In a particularly insightful interview given to *The Crack* magazine in October 1995, Martin reveals that the album was inspired by recent travels in the Basque Country and Ireland, where he'd been searching for roots.

As a consequence of this new pared-down sound, there was an opportunity to free up former Daintees to raise families – or 'to set them free', as Martin put it. 'I spent two years dismantling the business and had to break a lot of contracts.'

Sweet Misdemeanour, like its 1995 companion *Yogi in my House*, only cost £2,000 to make – and even then Martin shared out the money made among the musicians on the albums. 'It's often the company men who end up getting the money and musicians sometimes get treated like crap. The industry is like a cake. The commercial side is only concerned about the icing and they forget about the heart – where the musician is.' Martin's words reveal just how recent his more soulless experiences of the music business had been.

'Like riding too fast on a motorbike' was the analogy that ended the interview. Ironic, as several of the punk skiffle contributions on *Sweet Misdemeanour* sound just like that. Thankfully, our hero was spared a 'Leader of the Pack' denouement.

Demon never did provide the marketing punch necessary to keep Martin's profile as high as it had been five years earlier, but a number of radio stations picked up on the listener-friendly quality of many of the tracks, knowing that they could count on Martin and his colleagues to provide some great on-air craic. Phill Jupitus was one who arranged for a session from Martin on his show just before Christmas 1995, when listeners were treated to versions of 'Sweet Misdemeanour' and 'Talking to the Child'.

Unlike other 'in session' moments where the artist's words are less common than hassle-free days at Heathrow Airport, Martin and colleagues could always be relied upon to give good conversation.

His first solo album since the break up of The Daintees (ignoring the delayed release of *High Bells Ring Thin*), *Yogi In My House* was also the first result of the Demon Records deal. Recorded in Frankie Gibbon's house studio at 14 Nesham Place, Houghton-Le-Spring during late 1994, *Yogi* was very much a collaboration between Martin, Frankie and Graham Henderson who co-produced with Martin and also co-wrote three of the songs – 'Solomon', 'New Wave' and 'Dance the Last Goodbye'.

The working relationships that developed between Martin and his two cohorts were, at the time, vital in enabling him to find his feet again as a writer and musician following the split with both his long-term band and management team: 'Frankie? He was an older guy who always had a lot of time for the kids and I've always had a really strong connection with him. I felt safe with Frankie, particularly after I left Kitchenware when I felt a bit lost. I actually did a lot of travelling through Europe and Ireland to find my own path, but I'd always end up going back to Frank cos I knew he understood us. Sort of a musical Jim Sixsmith – a mentor, the older brother I never had.'

Meeting Frankie on one grey November morning in County Durham, I discovered an engaging smile, an encyclopaedic musical mind and a commentator all too ready to share stories from his own musical journey.

Frankie's musical legacy goes back to the late fifties: a deep affection for all forms of musical expression whose zenith, for Frankie, would always be the quiet rapture of choral music.

I recall his enthusiasm for Joseph Stainer's canon, to such an extent that further personal travels have led me to uncover progressive choral artists like Christian Forshaw.

Frankie now lives in a small gatehouse on the Lambton estate near Chester-le-Street in County Durham, in the land of the Prince Bishops, miners and a largely Catholic and Methodist community whose youngsters sought escape through the early Beat days. He achieved notoriety back in the early 60s when, having sneaked out of the house to play with a band in nearby Whitley Bay, he received a serious electric shock when the equipment misfired. His adventures would have remained undetected by his father, had the local paper not led with 'Local Beat Boy Electrocuted'. He may have had to explain himself that morning, but the release of electricity forged a love for music that has taken him from performance to arrangement and production. Learning from contemporaries like Stevie Winwood and Eric Clapton, Frankie learned how to sculpt a song, got to appreciate every nuance of the creative process and engendered in himself and his companions a recognition of the power of music. If Frankie was to be the 'older brother' Martin Stephenson never had, he could hardly have chosen a more apt sibling.

Frankie's recollections of his various collaborations with Martin are not based on a mechanically strict recording studio regime. There was no way that Frankie could, George Martin-like, produce recording schedules and engineering notes to evidence the inspirational moments. 'Hardly,' recalls Frankie, with a smile. 'Martin would be sat with a blank piece of paper. I'd disappear to the toilet, come back five minutes later and he'd have a song written out.'

The recording studio Frankie owns is a few hundred yards

away in what used to be Lambton Lion Park. As a kid, I would spend many summer days trying to figure out how lions from the Serengeti would handle a typical Burnmoor midsummer frost. They certainly used to look angry. Frankie explains: 'The studio used to be the café in the middle of the safari park.' How it came to be abandoned is never satisfactorily explained, although one could easily conjecture that on one particularly biting July afternoon, the lions decided they'd had enough and opted for a reviving hot chocolate down at the café.

As we listened to some recent recordings, Frankie tried to make sense of the years with Martin. 'A real free spirit' was a phrase that re-appeared several times in our conversation. Martin was more interested in the moment – the magic of the music – than any conventional music-production measure of success.

The sleeve to *Yogi In My House* features dedications to French footballer Eric Cantona and spiritual healer Barbara Anne Brennan (whose concepts of colour awareness influenced the later song 'Orange Is The Colour Of Joy'), as well as the title poem 'There's a Yogi In My House', expressing its author's feelings of humility and wonder towards three-year-old daughter Phoebe.

Behind the CD in the jewel case there is a picture of Frankie's dog – part of the deal for using his studio. Very affectionate, are Frankie's dogs, and deserving of the recognition. I recall being regularly 'embraced' by one of them the day I visited.

For the album, a solid band was put together around Martin and Graham with Frankie on bass, Paul Handyside (ex-Hurrah!) on guitar and Dave Ohm on drums.

Yogi In My House begins with 'Solomon', a live staple at the time, which impresses me as much as it depressed the reviewer in *NME* that month. 'A plain boring folk song' was his unfortunate assessment, but on repeated listens a familiar message emerges, urging the subject of the song to travel 'far from the disbelievers'. Backed by ominous Dylan *Desire*-era strings, like a theme tune to a tragic western, Martin is clearly back on form. There is structure, it is not twee and the message is clear and unconfused.

'Solomon' also reflects the influence of Martin and Graham's travels around Europe with its innately Latin feel led by the spoken-word intro from Paul Handyside. Graham initiated the song by writing the main guitar riff when he and Martin were staying in a flat in Germany. Martin put the lyrics to it immediately. It seems virtually autobiographical at times with references to 'the disbelievers' and its observations of 'I see you as a dreamer'.

The line 'why do you travel with the hollow kind?' sounds like an indictment of the latter years on London Records and the shallowness of their attempts to mould Martin into something he wasn't prepared to be: 'I saw it as being about a dream – a dream for people's freedom. But yes, it was one of those songs that come more from the sub-conscious than the conscious.' The final production adds more than a slight reminiscence of the theme to the 60s TV programme *The Flashing Blade*.

'In Fire' is next. 'Fucking hell, we sound like REM!' shouted Martin on a live version a couple of years later and he's not far wrong. Paul Handyside's combined lead and rhythm guitar is straight out of the Peter Buck School of Electric Guitar, whilst the lyrics impart a passion for love no matter how deep the pain. Emotions were obviously running high.

Four songs in and 'Think Only of the Child' brings us back to *Boat to Bolivia*-era Martin, where the North East accent is stressed for effect, as he warns against being processed 'like data'. The inspiration behind 'Think Only of the Child' came from the christening of Martin's daughter Phoebe: 'I decided I ought to organise the christening, you know, do the correct family thing. So I went along to this church in Whitley Bay and saw the old priest there. Man, did he give me a hard time. He basically said that we were using the Catholic Church for our own purposes in order to have a nice christening, and that we as a family should go along each Sunday.

'Well I thought that was a bit rich, because when I was born I was like a fresh plot of land and all of a sudden all these people, including the Church, moved in to stake a claim on me. Like Saatchi & Saatchi putting a poster up in East Germany within twenty minutes of the Wall coming down. What right did they have to do that?

'The same goes for my daughter. Anyway a little while later I was away working in London and I phoned home and asked my wife Angela how things were going. She explained how the priest had been convicted of making indecent videos with young boys – it'd just been on *Look North*. So anyway I'm going to get onto them with a lawyer and make history and sue the Catholic Church. Now that story is not knocking faith and belief, just those who manipulate it.'

'New Wave' is another Stephenson/Henderson collaboration that musically sticks to relatively orthodox rock band territory (its intro is reminiscent of an Oasis song, an interesting nod to the times), whilst lyrically attempting to defy analysis. It is either a positive look to the future or a claustrophobic look back at the past, depending on your mood. The frequent addition at gigs of a chorus of Jonathan Richman and The Modern Lovers' 'Ice Cream Man' further muddies the waters. Best just to let Paul Handyside's guitar wash over you and not worry too much.

'Spirit Child' takes something of the English folk legacy of Nick Drake, a mournful violin and sad piano accompanying a warm ballad, with curiously Cocteau Twins-like female backing. Martin takes the opportunity to introduce one of those spoken-word sections, later extended into long raps, but which, at the time, led to some heavy criticism. 'There are painful head-scratching moments when you stare wide-eyed at the stereo wondering what on earth is he doing?' the *NME* review continued – not every critic was prepared for the new direction. 'Spirit Child' is also one of the saddest songs ever written, tackling as it does the harrowing subject of losing an unborn child.

'Taker on the Globe' is generally regarded as the best track on the album and one of Martin's finest songs. Set to a chord sequence that steals from Dylan and Marley (well, if you're going to steal you might as well pinch from those two), the song is a heartfelt plea for dreams and emotions to win over cold-hearted business and economics. The argument is beyond debate, but it is expressed so beautifully that stating the obvious becomes a pleasure in this instance. Paul Handyside's guitar is again to the fore in a majestic fashion.

While 'Bridge of Nae Hope' was another ukulele slap across the backside for many indie darling journos, it signalled another future path – a path through some indigenous UK grass roots music. Had some of the critics known that a future album would be recorded in a lighthouse backed by two Scotsmen, a father and a son, the record might have escaped being reviewed altogether.

This song, with Davey Crichton on fiddle, and 'Fair Company' both use traditional folk settings to extol the virtues of positivity and good friendship respectively and lighten the picture that this very descriptive album draws.

It would be unfair to describe *Yogi In My House* as receiving a critical panning, rather more a quizzical reaction. But Martin had established himself as an artist of some integrity and his renowned live performances helped dissuade the faithful from abandoning him altogether.

Q's Danny Eccleston found little to impress in the album, arguing that 'Stephenson's story-telling suss seems to have nipped off for a fag, leaving portentous musing – the world is bad but kids are ace, apparently'. Clearly, many music critics felt that the muse had departed, seeing mawkishness instead of an artist at a crossroads. 'Rather less Yogi than Boo Boo' seemed an easy swipe at the time, but it would not be the last.

Indeed, 'Fair Company' was one of the songs that emerged unscathed. Described as a 'blissed out rock opera' it sounds more dated now, but still envelops Martin's compelling melody carefully with relaxed drums and shimmering guitar.

But just as listeners are preparing to re-visit their Doors collection, along comes Martin's tribute to his favourite co-pilot, 'Gone the Gypsy Davey', which sent the critics scattering for cover – the *NME* apparently unimpressed at this 'cat scratch fiddle barn dance'. The lyrics of the song would be reprised at many later gigs as another extended rap in awe at Gypsy Davey – the man, his muse and some incredible stories.

The ever-present Gypsy Dave Smith and his dobro were a feature of the period. On radio appearances throughout 1995 and 1996 the warmth between the two is infectious and the improvisational nature of many (if not all) of their collaborations seems to reflect Martin's state of mind – both then and now.

'Always Us' in its original version here only hints at the evocative live performances that were to accompany it during The Daintees' reunion tour of 2000. That said, it is a stunningly vibrant recording: influenced by Ken Keyes and the California hippies of the 1960s, it somehow manages to avoid the terrible clichés inherent in that movement and becomes a genuine call for peace amongst the rat race of the 90s. Pauline Murray's (ex-Penetration and Invisible Girls) ethereal vocals lead into almost funky electric guitar before the rhythm section kicks in perfectly to support Martin's alternately spoken and sung vocal: 'Free yourself from security sensations and power addictions that make you forcefully control situations in your life, and thus destroy your serenity and keep you from loving yourself and others. Love, love, love.'

Above all, it's a great song to dance to. Having said that, to our knowledge, no one has yet approached Martin to offer a Mark Ronson re-mix. What fun he could have had with the 'Penny Lane' trumpet.

'Always Us' somehow recreates the sight of the Nimble girl rising above the forest in a hot-air balloon, the ethereal intro gives way to Martin's mournful tones and a late-sixties film soundtrack is colourfully evoked.

The celebratory feel of this song is transformed completely by the closing track 'Dance the Last Goodbye'. Originating from another piece of music by Graham Henderson and sung beautifully by Pauline Murray, it paints the picture of the last night of a relationship, where both are trying to part on good terms instead of with the usual emotional traumas. The effect is saddening all the same as the voice, guitar and violin echo into the distance and fade away.

'Dance The Last Goodbye' sees Martin on fine form. The tune is original, the message 'deep in our hearts there is the will to speak' and Murray's dry English tones imbue the song with a longing, and leave the listener in no doubt that the one thing anyone could say with certainty about the next Martin Stephenson move would be that it would defy easy prediction.

On its release on 27 February 1995 *Yogi In My House*, perhaps unsurprisingly given Martin's relatively low profile, received little press attention in comparison with the Kitchenware/London albums. It did, however, receive the Best Folk Album award in *Folk Roots* magazine's end-of-year critics' poll.

This first Demon record greeted the world with a close up of Martin's daughter's face on the front cover. The sleeve notes attributed the title of the album to his impressions of her first three years – 'becoming less wise every day' – ruminating on the father's need simply to minister for her needs and understand that, even though she may travel with the flock, 'her core is star'.

Years later, when the album was re-released on the Barbaraville label, the photograph was reduced in size and placed amid a pile of London bricks but without the album title obscuring Phoebe's face, which Martin had never been happy with.

Martin's audience was still out there, evidenced by the good attendance at gigs, many being sold out – but record sales were no longer to be a measure of the quality of the output.

Having separated from his wife Angela a year previously, 1995 was to become a critical milestone in Martin's life, principally through meeting and falling for Karen Birrell, his partner on the next stage of the journey.

The year ended with a 'various artists' CD, appropriately entitled *Sunshine Paradise*, which contained the track 'Boat to Bolivia'.

1996 began with an affectionate trio of songs in session on Robert Elms' GLR show. In spite of a surfeit of alcohol having been consumed the previous evening (and the shakes that were testimony to the over-indulgence), Gypsy Dave and Martin produce a warm version of 'Maverick Waltz' from *Sweet Misdemeanour*, followed by 'Taker on the Globe' and 'Get Get Gone', dedicated to the recently departed Alan Hull – one of the creative forces behind Lindisfarne, the darlings of the Tyneside folk rock scene, a peer of Frankie Gibbon and someone whose oeuvre is attracting more attention now than it seemed to when he was with us.

Both Robert Elms and Phill Jupitus clearly enjoy the sessions over which they preside and Martin and Gypsy Dave find it easy to transfer the craic from live performance to the intimacy of the studio, in spite of the occasionally hungover state of the artists. The banter is as good as ever, as the between-song craic starts to appear mid-song as spoken raps. When the two re-visit Elms' studio three years later, listeners are treated to musings on the soul, as well as the latest traffic forecast and Newcastle United's latest result.

It's clear that the live music experience can capture something

denied to the recording studio atmosphere. Witness The Who's
Live at Leeds, Neil Young's *Live Rust* or any number of the myri-
ad of Jeff Buckley's live recordings. Sometimes the moment matters more than the correct tuning, the right chord or the fact that
the singer's rapping about Elizabeth Taylor and Madonna having
a fag at the back. Who would have thought Young's 'Cortez the
Killer' would sound better via a cod-reggae backing? Perish the
thought.

As 1996 arrives the band of gypsies accompanying our newly
focused hero are Joe Guillan, Gypsy Dave Smith and Graham
'Shipcote' Anderson on double bass. Gig notices promise 'early-
day numbers, busked tunes, rockabilly covers and guitar rags'.
Looking back, the message that my fellow author words so well,
is starting to ring out a little clearer: *a belief in music as a healing device, as a power for good and as a tonic for emotional trauma.*

I met Graham 'Shipcote' Anderson on a misty morning in
Saltwell Park, one of Gateshead's most enduring icons. It was as
if I'd met Martin, the similarity in outlook, affection, positivity
and, curiously, physicality. They look alike. At first he found it difficult to pin specific anecdotes to our historical sequence of musical outputs, but one by one, they emerged regardless. Like
Frankie before him, the recollections were not those of a weath-
er-beaten career musician, but a companion on a journey.

If there's a musical form that can be borrowed, then so be it. If
there's a time, an epoch that can be re-created, then that's all
right. If the ear-curdling scream from a Dick Dale record does it
for me, then that's OK too. Martin was walking away from the
well-ploughed, *original material only* track.

Some would argue at the time that this hid a failing on the
part of his muse. Some argued that his own material no longer
came up to the mark and some accused him of simply amplifying
his song range to attract a wider fan base, as if wanting to please
everyone in the working men's club.

Those prepared to listen were quickly captured by the
message, recognising the first faint but unmistakeable tones of
an artist realising his purpose: to hand on musical styles, to
teach the past to the present to protect the future, to hand
down the tradition and to keep the flame burning. And,

curiously enough, the medium itself would soon reap the benefits of its own muse.

Martin's move to Scotland came next, and was movingly recalled in a piece Martin wrote for the *Sunday Times* in May 2006. Beginning with the revelation that he had always entertained the notion of holding a gig on the Isle of Eigg in front of 50 people, with whom he would eat rainbow trout afterwards, Martin describes the circumstances that took him to the Highlands. 'I wanted to be a minstrel,' he declared, 'which is the last thing the music business wants of you when you're in a successful band. Rob Ellen (promoter with Medicine Music) looked after us back then – he used to put music on in the Phoenix in Inverness, and he was living in Nairn at the time, so I stayed with him at first. After that, Rob was really my main connection with the Highlands. He's a leftfield character, and really good-hearted. I've seen him struggle to get money for food and all that. He'd invest his money into doing some posters and putting a band on instead! That's what attracted me to Rob: he was nothing like the rest of the music industry; he was like a wild man who lived up in the hills, and I love that about him.'

Carefully articulating his initial fury at – then increasing tolerance of – the industry he goes on to explain how the move to Scotland prompted his 'becoming clean': 'I recognised where the alcoholism was coming from. I recognised an element of low self-esteem and I made a choice to work hard to stop.'

Martin's performance at one gig in particular made him realise his drinking was getting out of hand. He was booked to play in a club in the Highlands owned by Gavin Sutherland, formerly of the Sutherland Brothers and Quiver; famous for their 1970s hit single 'Lying in the Arms of Mary' and more so for writing the million-selling hit 'Sailing' for Rod Stewart.

On this particular night Martin was a little more wired than normal having downed the best part of a bottle of whisky and, uncharacteristically, he had also had a toot of the Colombian marching powder. In this state he arrived on stage in front of 75 nice, quiet Highland folk-music fans. He gradually started playing in a somewhat distracted fashion.

Part way through, he regains his focus as to where he is and remembers it's Gavin Sutherland's club and shouts out, 'where's

Gavin?' A nervous Gavin in the audience makes himself known to Martin, who starts very slowly and gradually singing 'I am Sailing' – stomping, growing louder. He then gets down off the stage and starts walking towards Mr Sutherland still singing and getting more and more aggressive – 'I'm fuckin' sailin' / home again / across the bastard sea,' freaking everyone out to such an extent that the poor target of his ire has to run away and hide in the cloakroom.

'The next day I phoned Alcoholics Anonymous. It really scared me because I had never been violent or confrontational before.' Again, Martin speaks of a spiritual journey, but is quick to explain what he means by this. 'I've not had a drink in 10 years. When I talk about *spiritual journey*, I don't mean religion, but simply connecting with people.'

While there would be no album releases in 1996, February and March that year saw what could then be labelled a gruelling tour, containing many consecutive nights' performances and covering a great deal of the UK. Demon continued to back their new favourite half-heartedly, apparently accepting of the diminishing 'popular music' appeal of their artist but ensuring publicity for the dates, especially as there were two albums to promote.

As the year wore on Martin, Gypsy Dave and Joe would re-appear at many of the same venues, returning to the Jazz Café for another sold-out night in October. For once, it seemed that there was a clear path forward, combining Martin's own spiritual compositions with accompanied tours of a range of musical styles, mostly US-founded. Of the many roads travelled so far, this one seemed to hold meaning. It seemed to be the right one.

Taking a break from touring the UK, Martin and some of his immediate cohorts decided, on a whim, to drive around Ireland in a Vauxhall Chevette (although some of the travellers recall it as being a Fiat Uno – the make and model are not really the point). Less credibly, they also decided to tie some moose antlers to the bonnet (or at least that's what Martin told an interviewer that year). I recall a Woody Allen story in which his friend (the unlikely named) Guy de Maupassant Rabinowitz and his wife took a bullet-stunned moose to a fancy dress party. On this occasion, the moose woke up (and won second prize), while the full horror of Martin's antler adventures has yet to be revealed.

The recollection reads like a self-deprecating Geordie take on the famed first chance meeting of Neil Young and the other future members of Buffalo Springfield in the California of the early sixties, except Neil had driven a hearse from Canada rather than a Chevette from Belfast. No doubt he would have appreciated the moose antlers though. *American Stars and Bars*-era Young doesn't seem too far removed from the Martin Stephenson of this period – alcohol still to the fore. Travelling along the ditch with interesting people, maybe, but less safe.

Further south our merry band happen upon the town of Leap, to the west of Cork, and the notorious hook of the Irish folk community immediately enchained the Tyneside heart. In Leap, with its strong musical traditions and belief in spontaneity and the craic, Martin met up with Emmet Tinley (of Prayer Boat fame), members of The Devlins and The McCluskey Brothers (who formerly shared a gig with The Daintees as The Bluebells). Along for the ride came Brendan O'Regan, whom Martin had met several years earlier when touring Ireland with the Daintees. Brendan takes up the story: 'I always liked the Daintees and knew their stuff. I had seen them live a few times. We used to have sessions in all-night *shebeens* after their gigs. Much fun was had then and I always remember that it was the beginning, I think, of Martin's fascination with the acoustic flat-picking thing. I suggested a way of working gig-wise with real low, almost ambient monitor and PA settings, thus drawing the audience in, as opposed to the then mandatory hit-them-over-the-head volume thing which was apparently the norm in the venues we played in. I think Martin was real pleased with that. We discovered a whole different set of dynamics – it was high on subtlety which made it even more special.'

The Leap troupe immediately convened and recorded *Beyond the Leap, Beyond the Law* at Connolly's studios. Rather than paying heed to the counsel of recent music critics and abandoning the twee spontaneity (as they saw it) of recent recordings, Martin's third offering since coming under the wings of Demon was even more skewed towards the 'moment'.

Martin explained as much to an interviewer at the time: 'It was exciting. I think I'm just a little tiny part of the healing process. I know I'm not going to sell millions of albums or have a high profile but what I have to do is be social with the music and release good, organic albums. Making the record was the most important thing I've ever done, bringing those people together. It's like when you meet some people and you just know them and trust them. The first time I met Mark Dignam was at four in the morning just outside Bewley's. I can't explain it but I just knew him straight away. We arrived in the Chevette – it's a very special place to me.'

In a separate interview Martin explained how it all came together.

I was in Dublin in 1996 with Glen Hansard (of The Frames); we did some acoustic gigs together. He invited me to his girlfriend's party at a pub called the International Bar. We went upstairs and there was a folk singers' night on. This old guy had a clipboard and he was going round collecting names; he said to me, 'What's your name?' I said, 'Martin.' He said, 'right, you're on at 8 o'clock; you've got two songs – no more.' So I went up, no PA, just a little wooden plinth. Emmet Tinley out of The Prayer Boat was there, I remember he had a big white shirt on, and when he sang he just connected with me. Hazel O'Connor was there, Christy Moore's brother too – it was a lovely night, everyone was just sharing – no egos.

Afterwards we all went for breakfast in Bewley's café on Grafton Street. There I put the concept of making an album to Emmet and the rest of the guys. He got The Devlins involved – he was calling The Prayer Boat 'the Rapid Response Group'! We ended up singing 'Rain' outside Bewley's at four in the morning.

The next day, we all went down to Connolly's in Leap. A lot of the songs weren't written, like I had the words to 'Indian Summer' in my pocket, I didn't even have any chords for it. So we just plonked the bits of songs down on the table with the Guinness and took it from there.

There was about fourteen of us together in a little farmhouse. It cost £80 to put us all up for eight days! One of the Prayer Boat's crew Paddy was really small, so he slept in a cot – someone put a bottle in his cot with him! They were all really nice blokes and everyone found their role.

Emmet became the boss as he's just a natural leader – he was kicking my arse all the time, organising everybody. Gypsy Dave was just looking for the Guinness!

Later Mick McNeil (the keyboards player from Simple Minds) gave me some studio time in Glasgow. That's how I got the McCluskeys to play.

I promised everyone that any money I got from it, I would share out between us all. But I've never seen a penny. I'm hoping one day Demon will give me the rights to the album and I can put it out again and hopefully pay those guys a few quid.

The outcome of those sessions was Martin's best album yet – to many, the spiritual follow-up to *Gladsome, Humour and Blue* and proof that his vision and his songwriting skills were undiminished. The laid-back, organic feel of the album is what makes it so inherently listenable. It is a bunch of like-minded souls sitting around playing – but, in another way, it is far more than that as subtleties and nuances come out of the songs the like of which no ordinary bunch of musos having a jam session could possibly hope to produce.

Even more incredibly, the sheer quality of the material and the playing is maintained over all sixteen songs (including the four throwaway, unlisted tracks at the end) to provide an album of rare beauty.

Opening with 'Losing All Part of the Dream' (another of Martin's grammatically-challenging song titles) the intent is set out early. Feeling edges out production clarity and the 'moment' but the song shines through in the end, being one of the more memorable tunes on the record. Also the opener has an ambitious lyric, the like of which exceeds anything Martin has attempted so far, from a call for humility ...

I want to travel with no procession,
Live a life of few possessions.
I want to be my children's friend
Instead of Victorian born again.

... to his warning to those who populate the soulless world of *Hello* magazine (watch out!), those who've lost the dream completely. Finishing with a rap featuring Madonna, Liz Taylor and the Woolworth's girl, the reference points find their mark.

Things calm down a little with the acoustic picking and Gypsy

Dave slide-accompanied 'Testing Time' (co-written with Paul Handyside), a song about belief in the face of adversity.

The mandolin-playing of that great Irish musician Brendan O'Regan leads into 'Great Star of Fraternity', written for spiritual healer Barbara Anne Brennan, who has a significant influence on Stephenson in recent years. Emmet Tinley takes the lead vocal on another epic that sums up the whole concept behind *Beyond The Leap...* :

> There are healers, there are dreamers, listeners, observers,
> In the great star of fraternity,
> Everyone has a role to play.

I understand that the next song was recorded around twenty times, but not because no one could get it right – simply because everyone had such a great time playing it. And you only need a cursory listen to the 'Irish version' of 'Wholly Humble Heart' to know that must be true. The feel is celebratory and raucous at the same time – every time I listen to it I hear a different guitar part. The mic is shared around through the verses with everyone and his brother joining in on the chorus. It's a great version of a great song (and any similarity with Lynyrd Skynyrd's 'Sweet Home Alabama' is entirely coincidental). The looseness, the rapture and camaraderie evident on this latest recording is a moment in time that will long provide positive memories for everyone involved.

'Carry My Friend' (a cover of an obscure 1993 song by Massachusetts-based collegiate folk-rock quintet Leticia) is a beautiful pure ballad with a sensitivity rare in modern music. It opens up like Springsteen's 'The River' before settling on a familiar theme of support and love. Louise Reid adds backing vocals to heighten the maternal, nurturing feel of the song.

'The Crying' is about a child finding her father crying. A delicate ballad in every sense of the word, it is as much about the father getting to grips with the situation as it is the child. The lyric is arguing that the pressure to appear strong to our children is unfair to both parties as the adult denies their emotions and the child thinks that outward emotion is a weakness. Whatever, it is a touching song and one that is supported perfectly by the playing, making a memorable entrance with zither and harmonica shimmering behind Martin's voice, right up into the mix. There's a subtlety to the recording that recalls Brendan O'Regan's earlier comments about creating a subdued set of dynamics to draw the audience ever closer.

'Song of Love and Desertion' (dedicated to Martin's partner Karen) exhibits a definite Latin influence in the music (it would later be performed live in a ska style).

Bob Neuwirth is a former compadre of Bob Dylan and toured with him regularly in the '60s. A singer-songwriter himself, his 'Great Spirit' (from his *99 Monkeys* album of 1990) provides Martin with arguably his best cover version yet. Accompanied only by percussive acoustic guitar (taking a Native American Indian rhythm) and harmonica, Martin gives forth on the concepts of freedom and humility whilst avoiding sounding clichéd.

'Out of Communion' places Martin's words in a cowboy lament, just short of breaking into 'The Streets of Laredo'.

'The Waves' features partner and teacher Karen Birrell quoting verses from Leonard Cohen's 'Teachers' including the observation 'follow me, the wise man said, but he walked behind', reminding us of the unifying potential of music and the need for one to express oneself, while the Crosby, Stills and Nash-like 'Hollow Days' leads us to the official album closer, the tea dance-paced 'Indian Summer'.

I say 'official album closer' as the four unlisted tracks remain. The Brazilian samba appeal of 'A Thing Of It' stands out and 'Don't Go Home' places Martin's pleas against a backdrop of *Lost Highway*.

The outstanding unlisted track, though, is undoubtedly 'Long Forgotten in This World' which grieves for the children massacred in Dunblane and soldiers fighting in pointless wars around the world – instigated by 'ye men of power'. The sadness to the lyric is balanced by one of Stephenson's most beautiful melodies and, combined, they create an incredibly powerful, evocative song which would feature in Martin's live sets, in various forms, for many years to come.

Beyond the Leap, Beyond the Law is a rootsy affair, but even then the touches that appeal immediately come to the fore. The bass guitar soothes the other instruments and voices interchange as different guests take the microphone.

Back in the UK music industry, though, the same criticisms were flying in Martin's direction. Looking back now, we could draw some consolation from the fact that Martin's albums were reviewed at all in the likes of *Q*. Nowadays the sighting of a Martin album review in a major music magazine would have members of his passionate E-group rubbing their eyes in disbelief. But back in 1997, critics were still in awe of that original Daintees sound and the promise of a modern ragtime star with a whole new sound.

Now, it was the other 'old' sounds that were bothering them. *Q* itself gave *Beyond the Leap, Beyond the Law* three stars. This time the reviewer abandons the direct criticism received by *Sweet Misdemeanour* and *Yogi in My House* and offers some consoling words, after placing Martin 'somewhere between Prefab Sprout and a whispering Nick Drake'.

Acknowledging his abandoning of all things commercial, the reviewer appears to get the message. 'His third solo outing is quiet, acoustic, deeply introspective and imbued with such olde worlde [sic] romance and gentle humour that one can only admire his understated talent.' And then came the damning with faint praise. 'It has no place amid all this modern music, of course, but for the kind of concert hall that still scatters sawdust across its floor, this is the perfect soundtrack.'

In a rare *Mojo* review the by now usual criticisms are trotted out. 'There's a looseness to the playing,' the review beings promisingly, but 'unfortunately there's also large amount of looseness to some of the writing.' 'Great Star of Fraternity', a clear tribute to the gathering of musical souls, is picked out as a high point, as is 'A Life of Her Own', but many are described as 'throwaway' – an adjective that's easy to find when ones like 'spontaneous' elude the lazy reviewer. And that's not to take the easy road and declare that everything Martin records is genius. It's just that the music business had begun to despair at what it saw as self-indulgence. To be fair to *Mojo*, the reviewer concluded positively: 'Overall though, this is a very pleasing spontaneous affair, and while it's scarcely *The Basement Tapes*, those who are still mourning the passing of Ronnie Lane could do a lot worse than check it out.' Praise indeed.

On re-appraising the album ten years after its release, one has sympathies with the *Mojo* reviewer. The spontaneity is there, but perhaps it would have been better served by an actual live recording. One senses an audience present would have gold-plated the obvious comradeship in the studio. But throwaway? The words are meant to convey a lack of depth, a compromise or filler. They express an artist's derision for his or her audience, accusing them of complacency, simply fulfilling the contract.

And yet, when Johnny Cash recruited Rick Rubin for his *American Man* suite of albums, he wanted everything pared down to just Cash and his foreboding voice. Some of the work on these albums is immensely moving, cutting out, as it does, the 'icing on the cake' and concentrating on the pure emotion of the song – in this case, the last redemptive words of a much troubled soul, finally at ease with his Saviour.

Throwaway? Maybe not. The song cycle chosen is inspirational, whether in choosing Trent Reznor's 'Hurt' or Ewan MacColl's trembling 'First Time Ever I Saw Your Face' but the production is minimal. When it suits, it's throw away, but not in Cash's case. No, cry the critics, we mean half-baked, not properly finished.

Enter Roger Keith 'Syd' Barrett, who passed away in 2006. He may have been struggling with his own demons when he released *The Madcap Laughs* and *Barrett* in 1970 and 1971, but some of the songs were not even finished. David Gilmour, who'd been brought in to help his old friend complete the recording task, ended up hesitantly committing to tape some songs that are so unflinchingly bare, that they are almost unlistenable. But Barrett is especially quoted as the archetypal English songwriter, themes founded on fairy tales and gobbledegook. Martin Stephenson is among the many who saw the diamond in the rust of those two solo albums. *Throwaway* can be so dreadfully misconstrued.

Some critics could make out a leap forward with the new album, with one declaring it 'warm, rousing and life-affirming; a mix of country sensibilities with the very best of pop catchiness', but these comments were more than likely to occur in specialist and/or local music publications. Not a failure of any sort, but recognition of Martin's audience in 1997.

Beyond the Leap, Beyond the Law may have confounded the

critics with its earthy spontaneity, but the messages are the same as before. Certainly unplanned, but well crafted and still a memorable title in the Stephenson canon, it offered further clues to the future.

For Dublin-based E-group member Declan McGrath it meant a great deal following a bereavement: '*Beyond the Leap, Beyond the Law* is the most perfect time ever spent behind a microphone. It has been the cornerstone for a recovery and a starting point to a second chance. Bless you, Martin.'

Sales were not strong, but touring, as ever, occupied our Tyneside troubadour throughout 1997. Later in the year, there would be an interesting opportunity for Martin when his then agents Chaz Cole and Mike Western King got him on a tour with two Grapevine Records artists: Martyn Joseph and the legendary Janis Ian, composer of a classic of the singer-songwriter genre in 'At Seventeen'. Martin was invited to complete the bill and the tour, which began at Wolverhampton Wulfrun Hall on 7 November, took in 11 more dates before closing in Belfast 17 days later.

The opportunity for Martin to interact with two established talents was too good to miss. It's also clear from their own reminiscences that the feeling was mutual. In an interview in 2001 Janis Ian explains Martin's attraction. 'One of the cool things about him was the way he'd take off when we arrived in town, showing up around five minutes before show time – always with some fabulous bit of a *bargain*. I particularly remember a duster coat he was fond of, that made him look like a private detective. His rider, such as it was, for backstage food was pretty funny too – I think it specified a bag of chips and a bottle of water. He was amazed that we'd arranged for him to have a hot dinner with us every night.'

A tour sampler emerged. *Welcome to Acoustic Ville* contained four tracks from each of the artists. Martin contributed three tracks from *Beyond the Leap, Beyond the Law*: 'The Crying', 'Song of Love and Desertion' and 'Great Spirit', with a different version of 'A Life of Her Own' completing his section.

1997 ended with a widening of the Stephenson musical family tree, with branches in southern Ireland as well as across Europe and (still) in the North East of England – but also the ending of the Demon Record deal.

Not for the first time, Martin Stephenson was at a crossroads, except this one seemed more literal than usual. Commercial success had not eluded him; he had simply chosen another path – and while critical success amongst peers and supporters was as high as ever, it was not an audience that would provide the business returns required by a large record company.

Other demons (in addition to the record company) had also been cast out. Martin's reliance on alcohol – the evidence shudders through early-period live recordings – had given way to abstinence, and a healthier outlook.

Looking back, the evolution seems natural now, almost a necessity. Martin had begun to establish a community – exactly what the internet was designed for – and was no longer a mass-market player. The internet itself would play a huge part in a re-awakening of recognition for Martin's music, but for now, word of mouth was the main medium.

Anyone resident on the Martin Stephenson fan database in autumn 1998 was rewarded with an update from Greg Drysdale, soon to be drummer of The Toe Rags, explaining what Martin was up to – namely, releasing a new record on Get Rhythm, a Tyneside-based record label, and touring the country. Far from appearing on his knees, the tour seemed to be a defiant salute to the world (if one could ever imagine Martin being so assertive).

Andy White joined Martin on three of the gigs – in London, Cambridge and Bristol – and some of the legendary busking sessions happened during this tour, with Martin asking folk to come up and say hello 'if you're getting the shopping in'.

The band comprised Joe Guillan on guitar, with Graham Anderson on double bass and Greg Drysdale on drums. On stage, Martin would begin with a solo set before the band joined him.

Like many others, one member of the audience had found the gig advertised in the *Hull Daily Mail*. He'd thought, 'Martin Stephenson ... whatever happened to him?' before quickly retrieving his copies of *Gladsome, Humour and Blue* and *Boat to Bolivia*. His recollection somehow captures the appeal of Martin and his band at that time. 'I certainly wasn't disappointed. Martin has a voice to die for. He also has a great sense of humour and now appears to be the incarnation of George Formby. No, I'm not joking. He IS George Formby. The cheeky grin, the endless banter. Martin Stephenson is George Formby.'

The music is described as 'country skiffle' and this was very much the template for the new release *When It's Gone, It's Gone* – a re-affirmation of Martin's past musical bias. For this limited-edition release the familiar names supporting became The Toe Rags.

While not signifying a departure of the profundity of Bowie's *Tin Machine*, it did lead to one further recording, *Red Man's In Town*, which was to follow in 1999 and which we cover in more detail in the next chapter.

For those acquainted with Martin's live performances throughout 1997 and 1998, *When It's Gone, It's Gone* was an accurate meter-reading of where he was 'at'. Selected from three impromptu recording sessions at Moody Studios in Shepherd's Bush, Connolly's in Leap and, in this co-author's home town, Stanley, County Durham (in that order) over the summer of 1998, it showcased a set of tunes that could have formed the backdrop to Saturday evening listening at any Midwest station from the thirties to the fifties. There are echoes of everyone from Buddy Holly to the Carter Family in there. One can accuse the album of being dated – but rather than setting it squarely on a late 90s shelf, it's way over the Atlantic and some way back.

Most of the songs are group compositions, with five re-arranged traditional tunes bolstering the album. Helpfully the sleeve notes provide the answers to questions prompted by any listen to the album (especially pinning down the pub in Tain, on the Cromarty Firth, where it was the barman's birthday).

Re-visiting what would be his first truly independent release nearly a decade on, reveals a sprightly collection of numbers performed by real enthusiasts, and what it loses in some of the basic recording it makes up for in heart – a redeeming statement potentially applicable to all post-Daintees Martin albums.

Beginning with 'That'll Be the Day' – or at least the opening guitar line – we actually begin with 'Wide-Eyed and Sleepy', a relaxing mid-paced number, before Dick Dale wakes Martin up in the middle of the night with a piercing scream to bring us 'Barbarville' [sic], curiously mis-spelt on the CD cover. This song, a playful lyric concerning weird shenanigans in a village on the Cromarty Firth, opens with a bizarre jest on one of the BBC's mainstay seventies children's programmes, *Play School*, and fair rattles along after that.

Dave Brewis of the Kane Gang, producer of three of the tracks on *Gladsome, Humour and Blue*, produced the Stanley, County Durham sessions: 'I often could understand what Martin wanted in a recording, even if everyone else thought he was just mad, and even though I usually wasn't the right man for the job. But we got some progress, and I helped in a small way to contribute to Martin realising his own art, although to me his best venue is a concert of any kind. The studio is just too forced and artificial for him. An audience can be a plus, along with the knowledge that you do it just once and move on, instead of re-takes etc. Small errors and creaky chairs are actually OK, as long as the song sounds good. Something like Chip Taylor's *Living Room Tapes* was the way to record him from day one. They wouldn't let you do that in the 80s but they do now. In fact we did it eventually in the late 90s, at my old house Tanfield Hall, when Martin was self-financed. I had a vintage Studer 8-track tape recorder then, like they used in the early 1970s and Martin brought some rockabilly mates around for a couple of days to record a few numbers. It went well, but Martin's studio phobia returned a little on seeing microphones all over the room. If I could have hidden them it would have worked better.

'The two days did provide some candid performances, marred only by Martin's occasional mic-nutting (an old favourite routine) and last-minute changing of guitars or musicians or songs after lengthy set-ups and sound checks, which renders them pointless. I couldn't run a studio – it would drive me insane.'

'Cromarty Rag' provides a jaunty if inconsequential listen, while 'Through the Mist' evokes an eerie story of Martin meeting his Mum in the afterlife, before a light touch on 'Gettin' Tired' has Martin's voice back in the mix, almost akin to the thirties 'in a box' singing style that any episode of *Poirot* would evoke.

The one non-Stephenson composition is one of the weakest. 'Bullshit' at least occupies a couple of minutes until 'Johnny Guitar' brings back the finger pickin' and 'Grafters' (allegedly a failed theme tune attempt for a Robson Green and Stephen Tompkinson TV series of the same name) brings us the Everly Brothers singing 'Three Steps To Heaven'!

The light-hearted 'Barman's Birthday' dresses up another homespun Martin rap in jaunty clothing while the happy pickin' of 'Papa's Going Crazy' almost defies the unhappy message of the lyrics.

'Perkulatin'' offers another taste of Martin's finger-pickin' talent, if not his spelling, while 'Big Bills' gives freedom to Joe Guillan's shiny guitar runs.

'Keep on the Sunniside' may be a traditional number, but is respelt to evoke the small North East England town. You might think this had emerged from the Stanley sessions just a couple of miles away but bizarrely it comes from the Leap recordings. Things are never straightforward in the Stephenson composition canon.

'Ramblin' On' and 'Deep Elm Blues', two other Irish recordings, bring the album to a close.

On reflection, a decade later, the album is everything a record company would not like. Thematically placed somewhere in the American past, it's simply a gathering of friends playing music they love; and while Martin felt the need to 'hand down' musical styles – his much loved 'oral tradition' – this was a record whose appeal would not stretch beyond the band of faithful followers who'd invested in *Beyond the Leap, Beyond the Law*. The limited-edition nature of the recording, if anything, deprived the greater audience of an opportunity to listen to it anyway.

Martin regularly returns to The Toe Rags, when ex-Daintee Graham 'Shipcote' Anderson can find time away from the award-winning Hot Licks Cookies and Joe Guillan can escape the Sureshots.

The Toe Rags have a natural affinity with rockabilly, ragtime, finger-pickin' and skiffle. They belong to the fifties and one wonders, mischievously, what might have happened if they had been teleported to the *Eddy Arnold Show* in Memphis in 1954.

At the end of the recording of 'Peace in the Valley', it's recorded that a young, quietly courteous man with combed-back hair approached the house band and said, 'If I ever get a recording contract with a major company, I want you guys to back me up.' Forget The Jordanaires – or Scotty and Bill. Elvis and The Toe Rags. Wouldn't have to struggle for a record deal, would they?

1998 became 1999 with Martin, true to his musical roots,

searching out new ways to follow his muse and bring the music to the people and the people closer to the music.

Brendan O'Regan recognised the talent as soon as he met Martin. In 2001 he shared his opinion of Martin with my co-author. 'As regards my estimation of him in musical terms: he has what to me is the most brilliant gift, the ability to tell his stories fluently and with such ease, as well as his great playing, his emotive use of language and music, his willingness to go anywhere musically, which are highly admirable traits in these days of corporate muzak. He had been there and seen the light; he learned a lot, as I did.'

O'Regan pins down the Stephenson appeal in a few well-chosen phrases. 'He has a lot of great qualities as a musician, most importantly spontaneity, which is not very common with a lot of performers. He does not employ that defence mechanism that a lot of performers do nowadays, which, to me, tends to isolate either the performer or the audience. He is in there with his audience from the start; there are no rules.'

And the future, seen from O'Regan's perspective? 'He has a long, great road to travel, a lot of strength and a brilliant musicality to carry him. He has achieved the greatest desire a musician could have – freedom. Bless him!'

In Janis Ian's opinion, Martin is 'a true balladeer, a real folk singer and strikingly funny when he wants to be.'

The period 1994-98 also saw the further flowering of Martin's poetry, drawings and writings. A 1997 spring trip to Portugal allowed him the freedom to explore a new country and the time spent in Lisbon produced an affectionate short collection of work entitled *Bairro Alto* (literally: the Upper Quarter). Featuring spontaneous sketches, photographs, poems and written 'raps' such as the one describing how he and a Hendrix fan bored everyone else senseless with their reminiscing, this tiny little archive denotes a readiness to play with form and defy tradition.

Bairro Alto has the feel of the poetry originally issued with *Gladsome, Humour and Blue*: warm and affectionate, yet short of whimsical – a unique travelogue of where he was at the time. Unfortunately it would be three years, and would involve the emergence of a collective force of fans, before these poems were able to see the light of day.

In late 1998 the traditional sequential approach to releasing albums had been broken and Martin was now spreading his wings, exploring different channels of communication and reaching out to a level of intimacy with fans that would only grow stronger as the turn of the century approached. As an almost unreachable, untouchable icon on an indie stage, Martin began this period like many of his peers. He was ending it, however, free from the conveyor belt world of mass musical production and closer to the communion he sought.

By 1998 he'd almost completed the transformation. Having found a road back to the power of the impromptu – the joy of the moment – he'd found a new means of communication rooted in intimacy. He had the freedom to call in his trusty sidekicks – Messrs Guillan, Anderson, Dunn, Gibbon and Smith et al as Crazy Horse?

Once he was the man on the bedroom wall poster, communicating through his records, concerts, radio and the music press. Now charming the stars from the skies with a choice turn of words, a rhythmical lick and an enduring vibe, he'd become the man standing right next to you.

What a wonderful world it could be, as Sam Cooke put it.

Chapter 5

Go Tell Your Friends
(1999 to 2001)

The first months of 1999 saw Martin Stephenson ploughing a fertile furrow around the smaller venues of the UK in a number of different guises. As well as serving up a diverse selection of songs old and new in his solo shows, there were a bunch of storming live dates with The Toe Rags that allowed this occasional band to develop its own persona further. Ably supported by Greg Drysdale on drums, Joe and Shippy gave Martin the freedom to delve into the vast canon of rockabilly, country blues and reworked originals that formed their ever-changing repertoire, a zydeco-esque version of 'Little Red Bottle' being a particular highlight.

Additionally Martin formed a collaboration informally known as the Martin Stephenson Band (MSB) featuring young Glaswegian blues prodigy Andy Gunn on guitar, former Yes collaborator (and writer of 'Time and a Word') and Highland neighbour Dave Foster on bass, with Greg Drysdale again filling the drum stool. MSB gigs would usually see Martin playing a short solo set first, including covers of Merle Travis's 'Dark as the Dungeon' and Leonard Cohen's 'Suzanne' before the band would kick into the main event, applying a somewhat 'heavier' style of instrumentation to the songs than previously heard. As ever the mix of songs was varied, not to say completely unpredictable, throwing in old Daintees classics next to some of Martin's Demon Records output and also a cover of new US folkie Tom Ovans' 'The Folksinger'. Occasionally Martin's old buddy Frankie Gibbon would step in on bass, and indeed it was this line-up with Frankie that would feature on the next Martin Stephenson album.

In autumn 1998, being without a record deal and yet to harness the power of the internet to distribute his music, Martin had become part of new independent label Floating World's roster of artists – including the aforementioned Tom Ovans and UK singer-songwriter Curtis E Johnson. Set up by Jonathan Beckitt,

Floating World was named after Japanese writer Asai Ryoi's work *Tales of the Floating World*, which discussed the Buddhist principle of Ukiyo – the concept that life is transitory and nothing worldly lasts forever. Martin's relationship with Floating World was definitely transitory – but more of that later.

The initial result of the Floating World link-up was the *Martin Stephenson* album. It was recorded during September 1998 in Scotland in former old folks' home Dalmore House, Ross-shire, which had been taken over by the Cerebral Palsy Action Trust. Martin with Andy Gunn, Frankie and Greg as the core of the band and working with producer and engineer Gerry O'Riordan, used a mobile studio they'd taken up from London for five days. Martin took the opportunity to involve some of the Highland-based musicians he had met since his move to Scotland, including singer-songwriter Dave Fleming, singer Maria Lark, percussionist Henry Fosebrooke and 'Mr chocolateness in ragtime', guitarist, singer and general master of Astral Funk: Jeep Solid (a candidate for a future biography if ever there was one). Overdubs were added later at Snake Ranch studio, Chelsea.

Like the MSB live repertoire, the album was an interesting if not essential re-run of some Daintees songs and solo tunes mostly from *Yogi In My House*. A version of 'Little Red Bottle' that really brought out the song's flamenco tendencies courtesy of Dave Fleming's classical guitar work and an extended version of 'The Wait', featuring Irish guitarist Peter Byrne's excellent acoustic guitar-playing – as well as taking in a rap from an old Strange Relations song 'Subterranean Rhythm' – were among the highlights.

Most importantly, though, this album set a precedent for most of Martin's output over the next ten years: the concept of the album as a 'new performance' as opposed to a 'new album'. In other words traditional music-industry values such as ensuring the new album was all new material to add to the artist's body of work – just so much more 'product' in many cases – would be given second ranking to the quality, originality and joy of the performances therein. This was just another way for Martin to free himself from the constraints of the industry and, most importantly, to enjoy what he was doing. If people chose to buy these recordings then so much the better.

However, this approach would cause tension between Martin and his independent record label collaborators, both in 1999 and onwards to a greater or lesser degree. The issue with Floating World that would gradually raise its head over the next year or so was based around the ability of artist and label to recoup the recording costs for their projects. Using Gerry O'Riordan and Snake Ranch studios is not the usual way of recording for an artist selling the number of albums Martin was capable of in the late 90s. O'Riordan's track record included working with classical and MOR artists such as Elmer Bernstein, Johnny Mathis, Michel Legrand and Tony Bennett, and Snake Ranch had seen the likes of Bill Wyman's Rhythm Kings, Mari Wilson and Michael Nyman record there recently. If anything it brought back memories of Martin's major label concerns from the 80s.

On its release in May 1999, *Martin Stephenson* received relatively positive reviews in the likes of *Mojo* and *Q* magazines, both recognising the quality of the performances whilst questioning the 'need' for the release in traditional industry terms.

What wasn't clear at this point, given the two-year hiatus since the lapse of Martin's Demon Records deal, was just how many people would be likely to buy the album. How many Martin Stephenson fans were lurking out there? How many had followed his journey all the way through the Daintees years and onwards through the 90s, and how many had lost touch, instead focusing their energies on families and careers etc and hence needing their musical entertainment delivered in as convenient and comfortable a fashion as possible?

For this writer the story is quite simple. After hearing *Boat to Bolivia* and *Gladsome, Humour and Blue* on a C90 cassette, taped for me by a workmate and friend in 1988, I went out and immediately bought these albums on vinyl. It would be ten years before I bought another Martin Stephenson album. The fact is that as much as I loved those two albums I don't recall hearing about any future album until *Beyond the Leap, Beyond the Law*. Having children and buying houses and thus having less disposable income is probably part of the reason, but for long periods of time I don't think I even knew that Martin was still playing music. I guess I assumed he had packed it in at some point in the early 90s and taken up the carpet-fitting professionally. That was until one week in November 1996 when my wife Tracy was glancing through the *What's On* guide in the *Hull Daily Mail* and noticed he was due to be playing at a venue in Hull called The Room – predominantly a dance music venue – on my birthday. It seemed like a decent idea for a night out ... that little gig advert has subsequently had a lot to answer for. People have moved house from one end of the UK to the other because of that gig advert – indirectly.

Including Tracy, myself and the bar staff there were about 25 people in The Room that November night. Martin was up with Gypsy Dave Smith and for around three hours at least two of the 25 people were absolutely rooted to the spot by what was happening on the small stage. MGS and GDS played a mix of old Daintees numbers, some traditional tunes and some new songs that they mentioned they had just recorded in Ireland. The songs, old and new, were amazing, the onstage banter was hilarious and it suddenly struck me that I was listening to an artist like no other I had ever heard. Beautiful melodies and heart-rending lyrics, mixed with the rootsiest of guitar- and dobro-playing – it simply made me wonder what the hell had I been missing.

Over the next couple of years Tracy and I would endeavour to get to as many gigs as we could within our geographical reach. Fibbers in York was our favourite. I bought *Beyond the Leap, Beyond the Law* (at a gig, I think) and was enthralled by what I heard. It was just like that gig at The Room, but with more musicians. I still wasn't quite sure I knew what the whole picture was, though, in terms of Martin's musical history. Details on the internet were few and far between and Martin's recollections when I got the chance to chat to him were shaky to say the least. Mostly I was just amazed at the lack of attention for an artist so talented, compared to the masses of pages, both web- and paper-based, for some incredibly ordinary musicians. There was an imbalance. It wasn't fair.

Fast-forward to June 1999 and it gradually became apparent that I wasn't the only person on whom Martin Stephenson's music was having a significant effect, but who was struggling to catch up with the albums and gigs. Jane Cooper decided to set up an 'E-group', or internet/email discussion group, to enable likeminded souls to discuss Martin and his music and ensure that the blank back pages could be filled in, as well as being the first stop on the internet for finding out what Martin was doing now. In some ways Jane's reasons for setting up the E-group were very similar to why I would immediately join it as soon as I found it. Martin's music had recently had a profound effect on us and we wanted to find out more. However, Jane's motives were based on a much more powerful experience than mine.

Jane's story

It was a Friday evening in February 1996 and I was living in Aberdeen when I was attacked. The attack was more than brutal and the man that did this to me was my best friend's brother.

My flatmates were the first to find me after it happened. I was rocking backwards and forwards in a corner, curled up in a ball with my arms around my knees making little whimpering noises and unable to speak. They tried to get me to go to the police but I refused. I grew hysterical just at the thought of it. If I did this, I would have to confront my best friend with what her brother had done. I couldn't do that. I didn't have the strength. I was feeling totally crushed as it was. I just couldn't face it. For the next couple of days I hid in the house and howled to myself and hoped it would all go away.

Then he phoned. I didn't want to talk to anyone and so I let the answer-phone take the call. When I heard his voice I thought I was going to faint. He wanted to speak to me and could I call him back? I couldn't believe what I was hearing. I deleted the message immediately. He rang again a couple of hours later. This time one of my flat mates answered and hung up on him as soon as she heard his voice. But this was just the beginning. He rang every day, several times a day. Still I refused to go to the police. I didn't feel I could live with the pain it would cause my friend to know what her brother was capable of. Instead I lived in terror. Then he started calling at the house. We refused to answer the door to him and so he would hang around outside. I was terrified of being left alone in the house and equally frightened to leave the house. I had to start going to and from work at different times of the day from normal and using different bus routes to get there after he started waiting for me at bus stops. The man was not taking no for an answer. He refused to leave me alone and I was terrified that he would get me again. I hated leaving the house but I was scared to stay indoors in case he called or the phone rang. I felt like I was losing my mind. My fear occupied every waking moment and invaded my sleep, too.

About two weeks after that awful night, a dear friend travelled to see me from Birmingham to lend some support. We'd known each other intimately for years and years and we'd both been fans of the Daintees whilst at college. I was still in a terrible state but my friend suggested that a night out would do me a world of good. It just so happened that Martin Stephenson was playing that evening at the Lemon Tree, the local arts centre. I'd not heard anything of Martin for years and to be honest, the last thing I wanted to do was go to a gig. I just wanted to stay indoors, where it was safe, and stare at the wall and think about killing myself. However, my friend was having none of it and insisted that a night out would help me take my mind off things. I doubted this but reluctantly I agreed to go along.

I was so nervous on the walk to the venue. I must have checked over my shoulder a hundred times. My stomach was in my mouth and my pulse was racing. I could feel the adrenaline rushing round my body and every instinct was telling me to get back indoors where it was safer. However we arrived at the venue safely and found a candle-lit table. I was still very, very nervous. We listened to a number of support acts – I can't recall exactly who played as my concentration was all over the place. I was so jumpy. I just couldn't relax and was really thinking that it had all been a big mistake when Martin took to the stage, sat on a stool and started to play.

I can't describe what happened then, only that for the next three hours I completely forgot that I was living in a nightmare. The feelings of fear and panic completely dissolved away and I sat dumbfounded with the biggest grin in the whole wide world on my face. I was mesmerised. For the rest of that evening all my troubles were forgotten and replaced by feelings of genuine happiness. That evening was a tonic for my soul. I'd heard people talk about gigs that were a life-changing experience and never thought such a thing was possible. I was wrong. For a few hours I was able to escape the horrors and relax whilst my ears were bathed. The sense of relief at being able to escape from it all, even just for a short time, is something that I will always remember. I felt so totally grateful to the man that had done this that I felt I owed him one. I felt that one day I would have to return the favour.

After that night I felt so much more in control of my situation.

Although I didn't feel ready to deal with all my feelings, I knew that I couldn't carry on the same way and that I had to do something about the situation I was in.

Two weeks later I was living in Birmingham. I had decided that the best thing I could do, rightly or wrongly, was to vanish from Aberdeen without trace and never return. The same friend that had persuaded me to go to the gig found me a bedsit in Brum. From then on, I took the opportunity to go to as many of Martin's gigs as I could. For a long time, I still carried a lot of troubles in my head, but the gigs helped banish the demons for a couple of hours at a time. The problem was, I never knew when Martin was playing in my area. Gigs didn't seem to be advertised in the press and it was often through accident rather than by design that I stumbled across them. I think a classic example of this was finding a flyer for a gig pinned to the community announcements board at my local swimming baths. What was the most frustrating thing about it all was the way that often I'd find out about gigs after they had actually happened and it was too late.

This pattern continued for the next couple of years or so. During this time, I'd moved away from Birmingham, found a partner that treated me like a princess, and had pulled myself back together again. The ghosts of my experience still haunted me from time to time but generally I was feeling on top of it all. I'd also subscribed to several music discussion groups via the internet and had found them a very useful way of finding up-to-date information on artists and bands I was interested in – except Martin Stephenson. While the internet yielded information on just about anyone you could think of, information relating to Martin was conspicuous by its absence. Then it dawned on me that this might be my opportunity to return the favour that I felt I owed. I decided to set up an email discussion group to allow the exchange of news and information related to Martin's gigs and releases, etc. In doing so, not only would I be returning the favour but I'd be providing an information service for anyone that wanted to participate. And so the Martin Stephenson E-group was born. At the time I could never have imagined what a powerful force the E-group would become.

The growth of the E-group is a marvellous tale in itself. It's a story of an incredible community and something I feel incredibly proud to be part of. It's a tale I'm not about to start telling here. I'll leave that to someone else. I guess that my tale is one of those 'every cloud has a silver lining' stories. The E-group came into existence as a result of a terrible thing that happened to me that I could never wish on anyone. However, something marvellous came out of it. It gives so much to so many. On a personal level, I believe that the E-group has had a massive role in my recovery. Before the existence of the E-group I was living with my past and trying to deal with it. Now I've done more than that, I've conquered it. I left Aberdeen swearing that I would never return and at the time I meant it. However, the journey to the Martin Stephenson Gathering in Portmahomack in 2000 saw me fly willingly into Aberdeen airport. Not only that, but I took great delight in swanning round the city centre, rediscovering all my old haunts. Even passing the house where it had all happened could not faze me. I simply gave it a two-fingered salute. That chapter of my life was well and truly over.

Indeed the growth of the E-group was something quite extraordinary. Not just because of the many hundreds of people who would join it over the next couple of years. I am sure many musicians can boast considerably greater numbers on equivalent discussion groups. What was unique about the Martin Stephenson E-group was the level of involvement with the artist that the members had. In the coming months many people who had previously never had any contact with Martin aside from enjoying his music would come to work directly with him in some capacity or other. Rob Hurst would develop Martin's first proper website; Andy Cairns would become his manager; John Ewing would record Martin and the Daintees live and have input into the reissued Daintees albums; Kieran Fitzpatrick would create the artwork for many of Martin's future albums. All of these collaborations, and more, only came about because of the E-group and the resulting direct interaction with the artist.

Meanwhile back in the summer of 1999 Martin and The Toe Rags released their second album – *Red Man's In Town* (total budget £1,235). Recorded in the South Gosforth loft of Joe Guillan's mate Howard Rickard in late April and early May, it captured The Toe Rags in fine form.

It kicks off with 'Duck Bill Blues', a hilarious tale of hotel-based shenanigans featuring Donald Duck and Minnie Mouse, set to a traditional country hoedown-style tune. The lyric was written by retired art teacher Geoff Marston, who insisted the band record it as payment for him providing the front-cover artwork. A great business deal for both sides.

The remaining songs, all originals barring the odd 'trad arr.', combine to make a much stronger and more varied album than *When It's Gone, It's Gone*. The most significant thing about the album, though, is the authenticity of the recording. Recorded live, Joe Guillan – with his producer's hat on – captures a sound that could have come straight out of Memphis in 1952. Greg Drysdale is once again on drums, steel guitarist Jim Hornsby makes his first appearance on a Martin Stephenson album (more of Jim later) and members of North East legends Deacon Jones and The Sinners contribute: Deacon Jones on saxophone and Blind Brother Hetherington on piano.

One of Martin's finest ballads, 'Highland Afternoon', written for Karen Birrell, is a delightful tune in waltz-time capturing the headiness of finding new love set against the background of the Easter Ross area, which Martin had now very much made his home.

Next up – 'The Ballad of Joe McCue' – couldn't be more different. It's a desperately sad story about a young man who can't cope with his depression and ends up setting fire to himself using petrol and a match. After all these years, Stephenson still has that ability to shock and make you sit up and listen to his lyrics.

The title track is a romp about a legendary North East lothario called Joe Watson, 'a real character'. The instrumental 'Ballintrad Tickle' is played with suitable élan and again great attention to detail in the recording.

Greg Drysdale takes the lead vocal on 'Crazy Times' – Graham 'Shippy' Anderson's lament for the cult of celebrity; Zoe Ball must feel suitably chastised.

'Alabama Man' is next up: a real rocker that features blistering lead guitar from Joe as Martin tells the story of a meeting with the ghost of Roy Buchanan in North Shields, 'playing the guitar with a Hendrix hand'.

'Play It Straight' dispenses sound advice about avoiding a life of crime while 'Why Buy' is a great close harmony tune written by Joe and Sureshots drummer Mark Coppin.

'High 7 Moon 5' and the just-over-a-minute-long 'Follow That Dream' are new MGS songs that introduce a more spiritual element to The Toe Rags that is usually found more on Martin's solo albums.

'Way Down Town' and 'Turn Me Loose' close the album in typical rip-roaring style. Deacon Jones stars on sax on the latter and helps the band take the album to a suitable climax. There are a number of hidden tracks that kick in after a few minutes of silence including a Deacon Jones song entitled 'Repent' which frankly lowers the tone of this album in a way you will just have to imagine if you don't own it.

Issued on independent label Real To Reel in limited quantities, this fine album soon became very hard to get hold of and subsequently has been known to sell on eBay for upwards of £60.

In typically perverse fashion, no Toe Rags gigs were lined up to support the release. Instead Martin set out on a solo tour that autumn including gigs at Manchester's Band on the Wall and the Hebden Bridge Trades Club. Already E-group members were arranging to meet at gigs and audience numbers were steadily increasing.

In November Martin also made a low key announcement via the E-group and his website that The Daintees would be reforming for some gigs in 2000. This announcement precipitated a huge amount of discussion on the E-group – flyers Martin handed out at solo gigs had the E-group address on as well, so new members were joining every week, most of whom had been Daintees fans back in the day, many when students.

In a completely unrelated, but helpful twist that autumn a Kitchenware best-of compilation was released, entitled *Happy Ever After*. Martin and The Daintees were featured with 'Crocodile Cryer' and 'Wholly Humble Heart' alongside the expected classics from Prefab Sprout ('When Love Breaks Down') and The Kane Gang ('Closest Thing to Heaven') et al.

1999 finished with Martin and Gypsy Dave playing a session live on air for Robert Elms' GLR radio show ahead of a heavily advertised gig at Biagio's restaurant, Piccadilly on 18 December. The session featured the old Merle Travis song 'No Vacancy' and a new MGS song that he had apparently written on the plane flying down from Scotland that morning, called 'My Time Has Come'.

In early 2000 Martin had good reason to call on the direct support of the E-group. He had a passionate belief that the batch of new songs he had ready for release were as strong as any he had written for several years and very much wanted to make a top-quality 'album' in the traditional sense of the word. His issues with Floating World had escalated, with no chance of a resolution, and hence he returned to Frankie Gibbon's Wildtrax studio in Durham to make what would be one of the finest albums of his career.

The problem was that with the Floating World impasse Martin had no means of getting the album pressed and distributed. Hence a call went out to the E-group to ask individuals to pay for their copy ahead of it being made. Sufficient funds were raised to provide a limited-edition release of 1,000. During April 2000, E-group members received their copies of *Lilac Tree* signed and with a hidden track 'dedication' featuring Martin, hilariously at points, attempting to fit everyone's names and messages into a version of 'Deep River Blues'.

On playing the album for the first time it was clear that Martin had served up something a little special. On a par with the first two Daintees albums and *Beyond the Leap, Beyond the Law*, *Lilac Tree* was in essence a bunch of new, predominantly original songs, played by Martin and his collaborators and recorded with great empathy and attention to detail by Frankie Gibbon. Backed by Frankie on bass and keyboards, Paul Smith on drums and experienced picker Jim Hornsby on guitar, dobro and pedal steel, Martin had never sounded as assured and at home in a studio setting.

The album kicks off with the title track, a song of great spirituality that sees Townes Van Zandt, Julius Caesar and the man who sweeps the road all equal in the eyes of whichever greater being they believe in, be it Jesus or Buddah. Martin had been playing the song live for a couple of years and would often turn it into an extended rap, calling in all manner of diverse subjects and bits of other tunes. But here on the album he plays it straight for once and the result is outstanding, aided by Paul Fisher's soaring backing vocals. Martin recalls: 'With the song "Lilac

Tree", I took an Fm7 tuning from a new age guitarist called Alex De Grassi. Lyrically I wanted to put Jesus and Buddha together – a mental image, like I'm a painter but I can't paint so I translate them into songs. Jesus and Buddha with their arms around each other like they'd just being playing football with headbands on, like Rodney Marsh and George Best.' (Dear reader: this will be the only reference, veiled or unveiled, to Fulham Football Club in this book.)

Next up is 'Orange' – a 'new hippy' song for a very different age. The lyric was inspired by spiritual healer Barbara Anne Brennan (for whom Martin had earlier written 'Great Star of Fraternity'). Speaking in 2001, Martin explained the philosophy behind the song:

> She works with colour and teaches colour awareness. I was inspired by her and dedicated this song to her. Take the spectrum of white light split into a rainbow, i.e. Newton's prism. Just like music, colour has a basic scale with a myriad of subtleties the further in you go. The basic colour scale is what we know as a rainbow:

Red	Drive/sexual
Orange	Joy
Yellow	Peace/study
Green	Calm/healing
Blue	The song of the soul
Indigo or magenta	Cornucopia
Violet	Cosmic consciousness
Rose	Love
Gold	Protection
Silver	The healer's hand

> As in musical notes C, D, E, F, G, A, B, then octave C.

On the body we have chakras which are kind of energy vents. Healers work these vents and can channel colour in many ways. Your body has seven main chakras and each chakra is connected to a colour, i.e. base chakra which is at the bottom of the torso is red; sacral chakra is between groin and belly button and is yellow, and so on. There is also a hara line connected to the centre of the Earth coming straight through our base chakra and out of our crown chakra and straight through the vortex and into the Godhead. Barbara teaches corestar meditation along the hara line. The hara line is very common in acupuncture and is the main energy line that is used.

On a lighter note orange is a good colour for hosting. Restaurants use orange to great success, a very joyous colour.

On an even lighter note this song was responsible for a very minor increase in the number of orange t-shirts sold across the UK during 2000, as E-groupers came up with a way of identifying their internet friends at gigs.

'Rainbow', written by Highland poet Gary McCourt, follows 'Orange' thematically with its use of colours and the concept of healing features again. Clearly Martin's move to the Highlands and the simultaneous freeing himself of alcohol addiction and the chains of the music industry were still a big influence in his choice of subject matter.

'2 Sorrows' brings Jim Hornsby's masterful playing to the fore as he weaves his Telecaster around Martin's voice. Martin recalls: 'The big thing for me is to *play* the guitar. I'd say to Jim, "look, just have fun!" A lot of the stuff Jim did was first take. He was asking me if he could do it again but I feel it's about getting the magic. If you play it again and play it again something gets lost. I hear records on the radio and it's like listening to tech drawing, all prepared and planned, with an agenda that is purely to make money and I can smell it.'

'Every Step' was co-written by Martin and Karel Fialka, another musician resident in the Highlands. Born in India to a Czechoslovakian father and a Scottish mother, singer and multi-instrumentalist Karel had a minor hit in 1980 with 'The Eyes Have It' before hitting the number nine spot with 'Hey Matthew' in 1987 on Miles Copeland's IRS label. He had long since set up home in the Highlands and become something of a mentor to younger musicians in the vicinity. 'Every Step' has an African high-life feel to it enhanced by Jim Hornsby's pedal steel.

Next up is 'The Folksinger', as mentioned previously, written by Floating World singer-songwriter Tom Ovans. Ovans had released it when signed to Demon Records on his *Dead South* album in 1997. The lyric portrays the main character as a determined but predominantly ignored troubadour tramping the boards 'on the streets of Babylon' – a lyric which Martin clearly identified with deeply. Martin added the chorus lyric himself – 'Said the folksinger to the king, if Jesus is from Nashville then Tom Ovans is him' – as a dedication to the composer. Musically it is a highpoint of the album as it builds from Frankie Gibbon's muted piano and Martin's acoustic guitar backing to a climactic ending featuring Jim Hornsby on searing lead guitar as the lonesome folk singer has the phone put down on him by his ex, before taking the stage in 'some foreign country'.

'On the Brae' uses a traditional Scottish musical backing as Martin sings a simple love song about meeting one's intended on an idyllic Highland evening after being freed from 'work's dull cage'.

'Country Shuffle' sees Martin and the band picking out a song celebrating the joys of playing old-timey bluegrass music. Martin's continued discovery of the various strands of American music, and in particular his passionate obsession with the guitar-playing of Doc Watson and Merle Travis, would develop even further throughout 2000 and beyond.

'Peculiar Man', featuring another reunion with ex-Hurrah! guitarist Paul Handyside on 12-string Rickenbacker, tells the sad but intriguing tale of Martin's old friend Michael Hedley (the guy who had suggested the name The Daintees back in 1981), by all accounts a very shy, tortured soul who couldn't cope with the social mores required in modern life. It also features the delightful lyric, 'He would never ransack the graceful church of a woman / Merely light a candle within her that would shine on forever'. The song draws considerably on Simon and Garfunkel's 'A Most Peculiar Man' from *The Sound Of Silence* album, a fact that freaked Martin out completely when I pointed it out a few months after the album's release, thus showing how the subconscious can play tricks on a musician.

'Rowan Berries' is a love ballad with one of the most memorable melodies that Martin has ever written. Gypsy Dave Smith described it to me as being as good as any classic folk song. A simple picked acoustic guitar and piano backing supports another of Martin's tales about finding love in the Highlands (and being married by a bird!) – and again is dedicated to Karen Birrell.

'Posey Rorer' is a key song on the album and again a key song in Martin's repertoire of the time. As part of Martin's discovery of old-time American music he had come across legendary 1930s band Charlie Poole and his North Carolina Ramblers. This had partly come about via the E-group spreading its wings across to the USA where one Dolphus Ramseur, former tennis player and musicologist, as well as a huge Daintees fan, had picked up on Martin's interest in thumb-pick, 'Travis'-style guitar-playing and invited him over to North Carolina to dig down to the roots of this relatively ignored music (more of which later). This connection resonated with Martin as he had originally heard about Charlie Poole several years before via a book he had been lent by Graham Anderson. Posey Rorer was the fiddle player in the North Carolina Ramblers and the song tells the tale of him having to sell his fiddle to a taxi driver for whiskey as the band's famous hard drinking gradually became an addiction. Martin so got down to the roots of this music that he would later link up with Rorer's descendants in both the USA and the UK.

The next song, 'New Found Light', sees Martin back to more traditional English folk music in another love song for Karen, backed only by acoustic guitar and Paul Fisher's harmony vocals.

The final song, 'O So Far Removed', is Martin's dedication to Nick Drake. Piano and acoustic guitar provide a suitable backing for a delicate, mournful snippet of a song sung by Paul Fisher about the enigmatic Drake, who was 'stolen by the moon'. Martin is clear in his praise of the dedicatee: 'Nick Drake was mentioned in a review of *Boat to Bolivia* but I'd never heard him. A year later a guy turned up at a gig and handed me a Nick Drake tape but I never listened to it. Then a few years after that someone played me some Nick Drake and I loved it, and around that time my ex-wife Angela bought me a boxed set of his work as a gift. I think he was a great artist – so aware of his limitations as well as his powers for such a young head.'

On its release the album was hailed as a triumph by those able to obtain a copy. And whilst an element of bias could be attributed, as many E-groupers had an interest in its production and release, listening to it several years later it is clear that *Lilac Tree* is as strong a collection of songs and performances as any Martin has produced. It would later be re-released by Voiceprint, albeit with different artwork.

Speaking about the E-group and his musical approach in 2000, Martin noted: 'The choice I've made to work on a less materialistic level is because I want to break down the artist/audience barrier. The E-group is a revolutionary way of doing that. And it's about sustainability, something I've learned from my friend Henry Fosebrooke. The last thing I want to be bogged down with is too much material and money; that might distract me from my path. If I can sustain myself by selling, say, 500 copies of an album then that's all I need.'

Floating World, in a bid to recoup as much as they could, released the Redwood demos in May under the same title, thus causing potential confusion for cursory buyers/non-E-groupers. The Floating World *Lilac Tree* was actually an interesting document in terms of tracing the studio development of some of the songs, but nothing more than that. What most annoyed Martin was the tagging on to the end of the album of unauthorised live versions of two of his oldest songs – 'Rain' and 'Boat to Bolivia'.

Following a bunch of solo gigs in March and April, Martin reconvened with Gary and Anth Dunn, along with Mark Coppin from the Sureshots on the drum stool, for rehearsals in Newcastle, ahead of the first Daintees gigs for eight years. Ahead of the tour, a Martin quip turned into a gloriously apt piece of publicity material: 'A long time ago in *The Last Waltz*, Robbie Robertson, young and stoned said, "I phoned up The Hawk. We're putting The Band back together. You'll not get much money but you'll never run short of pussy." Eight weeks ago Martin Stephenson rang up Anth Dunn and said, "Anth – we're putting the band back together. Now as usual you won't get much money and you'll never get any pussy." Daintees are from the planet Love and are back again to play their part in the next phase of healing. Love's coming in!'

And thus The Daintees' reunion tour commenced at Blackheath Concert Hall on 4 May and continued through to the beginning of June. I think a fair description of the gigs would be 'joyous' with a touch of 'celebratory' thrown in for good measure. Certainly at the gigs I saw at Morecambe The Platform, York Fibbers and Sheffield The Boardwalk, Martin and the band were in stunningly good form. Usually opening with 'Crocodile Cryer', they worked their way through a couple of hours' worth of songs from the four Daintees albums as well as picking up on some of Martin's solo songs including 'Solomon' and 'Always Us'. The most significant thing, though, was the obvious respect and affection these guys had for each other, as if the stresses and pressures of the late 80s/early 90s had never happened.

To give a feel for the atmosphere at these reunion gigs I've taken the liberty to include below some reviews that I posted on the E-group at the time.

Rich's review of The Daintees, Morecambe The Platform – 9/5/00

I decided to drive from Washington (where I was working) to Morecambe – journey time one hour 45 minutes. There is only one band I would do this for – well maybe Orange Juice as well. Met them (and Andy Semple) in the pub next door to the gig – main topic of conversation: the Floating World version of *Lilac Tree*. Martin is not happy and is 'taking advice'.

An old mate of Joe Guillan's called Terry is with us. Martin points out his uncanny resemblance to Leonard Cohen – cue a major wind-up of the audience later as Martin introduces 'Leonard'!

Went through into the gig and watched the support band Equation who were OK but I'm afraid I wasn't really there for them.

Martin Stephenson and The Daintees: only their fourth gig of the reunion tour – the first dates since 1992. Martin, Gary and Anth Dunn and Mark (out of the Sureshots) on drums. They open with 'Crocodile Cryer', taken slower than the recorded version – almost as if to milk it for every drop of nostalgia, and a shiver went down my spine. The sound quality in The Platform was very average, due to its surprising similarity to a railway station! It was all glass and concrete, very high and wide, meaning that the sound went floating off in a somewhat tinny fashion.

The receptive audience, of around 120, didn't seem unduly worried by the dodgy sound as The Daintees (yes, it's really them!) followed with a stunning 'Always Us' – Anth Dunn with a grin on his face that doesn't shift all night.

Martin tests the band with an obviously unrehearsed, but somehow all the better for it, 'Losing All Part of the Dream'. 'Little Red Bottle', 'Coleen' and the title track are all played from the first album; 'Slaughterman' and 'Nancy' are classics from the second.

Gary Dunn comes into his own on a version of 'Goodbye John' that was worth it for the devastating intro alone. In line with Martin's recent solo gigs, bits of songs are interwoven into other songs to create an ethereal, timeless quality – the 'Orange is the colour of joy' motif features heavily.

The band leave the stage after half a dozen songs and Martin plays a trio of acoustic numbers: 'Posey Rorer', 'Folksinger' and 'Rain' – the latter punctuated by Martin's comment of 'you put me off' to a poor toilet-bound member of the audience.

The sheer power of the band comes through on 'Better Plan' and 'Big Sky New Light' before they lift themselves onto a higher plane altogether with dynamic versions of 'Running Water' and 'Look Down, Look Down'.

Only one encore of 'There Comes a Time' is allowed with the fascists in charge of the venue insisting that the boys are off by 11.00pm (here's hoping that York, Fibbers on Saturday is somewhat more easy-going).

Quick chat with everyone afterwards – the band had thoroughly enjoyed it but were disappointed with the sound. Then a two-hour drive back to Washington – fell asleep knackered but happy at 2.00am.

Bluffed my way through work the next day and collapsed into bed around 9.00pm, only to be woken by my mobile ringing at 11.05pm. I could hear 'Nancy' (?) – Andy Semple had rung me on his mobile from the Ashton gig! 'Here's a treat for you, mate,' he shouted. Or did I dream it?

Rich's review of The Daintees, York Fibbers – 13/5/00
Arrived in York about 2.00pm and very soon made contact with Helen & Andy and Rob & Karen who were all staying in our B&B. No sign of Andy Semple, though. Mark Thompson had mailed and phoned me and said he would be arriving later in the day with his friends Jim & Bev – they had all had a great time at the Whitley Bay gig the previous night.

The six of us walked into the centre of York and ended up in The Golden Fleece for lunch before laying into some serious alcohol – primarily vodka and Red Bull. Mark, Bev & Jim turned up and I could sense that a major evening lay ahead! The Daintees (minus Martin) came into the pub for some pre-gig food, and I decided that the atmosphere could not get any better – except for the fact that Andy S was still missing. Managed to raise him on the phone to find that he was 'dying' with asthma-related problems – poor kid.

Went across to the gig just after 8.00pm and quickly remembered why Fibbers is my favourite venue ever. Small with a low ceiling, and very soon came some loud music provided by the excellent support band The Halcyons – sort of a cross between The Only Ones and The Ramones (but not really). Martin watched them and seemed very impressed.

About 9.15pm Martin and The Daintees took the stage starting with a stunning version of 'Slaughterman'. A similar set list to Morecambe but with an atmosphere ten times as good. Community singing featured heavily during 'Rain', huge smiles during everything else and I seem to recall pogoing to 'Running Water' and 'Look Down, Look Down'. The band had to be off by 11.00pm which meant a somewhat curtailed performance by Martin's standards but it was still one of the best gigs I have ever been to. Energy, love and wonderful songs – it doesn't get much better.

The nine of us left Fibbers after big hugs with Martin and co, clutching or wearing our *Lilac Tree* T-shirts. I seem to recall a Chinese restaurant but it was all very, very vague by this stage.

A brilliant day that I will remember (well, most of it!) for a long, long time.

Rich's review of The Daintees, Sheffield Boardwalk – 20/5/00

Arrived at very dodgy B&B about 5.00pm. Andy Semple rang to say he was in the pub down the road so we got out of the smallest bedroom in the world ASAP. Food & drinks and then went to the gig about 8.00pm only to be told that Martin and The Daintees hadn't arrived yet! Went for another beer and then returned about 8.40pm to hear them finishing the obviously very brief soundcheck. No support band tonight meaning a longer show from our heroes, and what a gig it was – the best of the three I have seen.

Highlights:
- 'I Pray' – an incredible version with Gary Dunn on his best form of the tour
- 'Roll On Summertime' – yes!
- a walkabout by Martin and Gary with a guy from the audience on

bass and Anth on acoustic guitar

- loads of dancing from the audience, initiated by Tracy and Andy S along with two ladies called Janet.
- Horrendous breakfast and hangover the next day – I want to do it again!

In June Martin, rather perversely, got a support slot on the Vonda Shepard tour. Vonda was flavour of the month after her appearances in the *Ally McBeal* series. A slightly strange gig for sure as Martin picked away for half an hour in front of a bunch of mainly uninterested Vonda fans.

Later that month Martin recorded two solo albums in the space of a week. *The Disciples of Merle and Doc* was his first full-blown album covering the playing styles of the two guitarists most influencing him in recent times – Doc Watson and Merle Travis. Ably assisted by Gypsy Dave Smith, Aberdonian harmonica player Spider Mackenzie and – on five songs recorded back in March for Radio Scotland – Scottish bluegrass band The Moonshiners, Martin for the first time on record had free rein to develop the picking style that cousin Jamie Harwood had introduced him to when they were teenagers.

Highlights included Travis classics 'Sweet Temptation' and 'No Vacancy' and Doc Watson's 'Southbound' as well as a great version of Travis' arrangement of the American songbook standard 'See You in My Dreams'. A version of Doc Watson's arrangement of John D Loudermilk's 'Windy and Warm', which Martin would often weave into his own 'Posey Rorer', was recorded for the album in his hotel room in Portsmouth on the Vonda Shepard tour. It was recorded direct into a Minidisc recorder, a tool that Martin would use often, never more so than on the second album that week – *The Church and the Minidisc*.

Dedicated to 'the people of the Scottish Highlands', *The Church and the Minidisc* was recorded between 21 and 23 June in Tain Church and Croick Church in Easter Ross. With contributions from poet Gary McCourt, flautist Charlie Caruthers and Highland historian Jimmy Sutherland, the album is a piece of Scottish folk music pure and simple. Unique in its use of the modern Minidisc capturing the natural echoes and reverb produced by playing in a church, it is at heart a very serious affair. The centrepiece of the album is Gary McCourt's 'Clearing the Glen'. A song about the Highland clearances of the 18th century, it was recorded in Croick Church where in 1845 some 18 families sheltered in fear of their lives prior to being shipped off to America, cleared from homes their families had lived in for generations in order to make way for sheep.

'I love the fact that Gary, Charlie and Jimmy all know about the history and culture of where they live,' said Martin. 'But you take a Jimmy Nail album – big expensive studio, George Harrison on guitar and it doesn't mean a thing to me. There's no agenda with these guys: their talents are directed at their own community and I think it gives the album a good heart.

'When we recorded the song "Bengarrick", we'd been at Gary's house for a coffee and he had a folder of poems he'd written since he was 16. I said, "come on, grab your folder and bring it to the church." I just randomly picked out the "Bengarrick" poem, set up the microphone on the pulpit and put the poem on the music stand. I picked out a bit of music as a backdrop and cued Gary in to read part of the poem. Did it first take.'

The second key song is 'Absent Fathers', a desperately sad lyric clearly based on Martin's separation from his daughters: 'Everywhere you wander, see your children's eyes. And there's no sleeping, every night you cry.' A more positive tune dedicated to Phoebe and Esme is 'Daughters', celebrating their summer visits to Martin's home in the Highlands, where they would go out in the forest at midnight with Martin's pal Henry Fosebrooke and sit around a fire with guitars and Henry would play the digeridoo: 'Your father is a simple man who dreams his life away.'

'I consciously put the mic at the other end of the church 'cos I wanted it to sound like a spirit,' recalls Martin. 'I wasn't bothered if it didn't pick up the lyrics that well. You think of all the people that have been in and out of that building and what's trapped in the walls and the ambience of the place.

'Charlie Carruthers loves to *play* his flute and that really comes across. I said' "just walk around, have some fun, feel the room," because it was so resonant. A couple of times when we were recording we'd turn round and there would be all these people, tourists with headphones, doing the Tain Through Time tour!'

The album mixes in more poetry by Martin and Gary McCourt as well as love songs 'You Are the One' and 'Heaven' which lighten the tone, along with two covers, a version of Galway musician (and *Beyond The Leap* contributor) Brendan O'Regan's 'Autumn Child' and Virginia Astley's 'A Long Time Ago'.

The overall tone of *The Church and the Minidisc* is a sombre, melancholic one, the complete opposite of the relaxed picking of *The Disciples of Merle and Doc*. One thing the albums had in common, however, was Kieran Fitzpatrick's artwork. Kieran, who as mentioned before had made contact with Martin via the E-group, produced two very different but totally empathetic pieces of work that would have stood up to comparison with anything produced by a major label's art department, and in many ways because of not needing to pander to any 'market' were artistically far more in keeping with the spirit of music.

The whole concept of making the two albums without any traditional music industry involvement was an artistic success and financially cost a fraction of some recent projects: proof if it were needed that musicians in the new millennium were not tied to the usual constraints imposed by major (or minor) record companies. Martin effectively had the freedom to do, artistically, anything he wanted and still make a humble living out of it. 'I've seen albums made in the 80s with so much fear, so much pressure to make money. What I'm doing now is the highest level. There's no manager coming in here making us feel uncomfortable because I don't have a cocoon.'

In July 2000 Martin and Karen Birrell, at the invitation of Dolph Ramseur, flew out to North Carolina for two weeks. Dolph announced the *My Grass Is Blue* trip on the E-group in typical style and detailed the forthcoming itinerary.

Dear Group,

I just wanted to take this time to let everyone know that Martin Stephenson is coming over to North Carolina between July 5-19. Martin and Karen will be my guests as we journey around the area meeting and pickin' with some of the best musicians in the world.

After corresponding with Martin for more than a year it was evident that he was fascinated by the music from this region in which I live. Martin is a fan of Doc Watson, Charlie Poole and the North

Carolina Ramblers, Merle Travis and many more. If you have *Lilac Tree* or have seen him live in recent months you can tell that this influence has led him to perform such songs as 'Posey Rorer', 'Country Shuffle', and 'Canon Ball Rag', etc. I wrote to Rob Ellen about six months ago and told him that Martin should come over to North Carolina and record an album. Martin loved the idea and we have been working on this project ever since. The working title is *My Grass Is Blue*. Here is what we have planned:

A meeting with Sammy Walker. Sammy recorded two albums for Warner Brothers in the 70s, two for Folkways in the 70s, and two for Brambus records in the 90s. Sammy lives in the mountain region of North Carolina and is a great song-writer and finger-picker. Sammy was discovered by the late Phil Ochs. He has played with Roger McGuinn, Steve Goodman, Doc Watson, and many more. Sammy was kind enough to help with this project. With his many contacts he was able to arrange for Fiddlin' Howard Cunningham, guitarist Don Fox, banjo picker David Brose and the world famous fiddler Mr. Ross Brown to be present at this meeting, which is scheduled for 15 July. Fiddlin' Howard Cunningham is one of the best fiddle-players in the United States and ninety-year-old Ross Brown is a world famous left-handed fiddler. He is regarded as one of the best ole' timey-tradition fiddle-players that has ever lived. This session will be recorded.

A meeting with Kinney Rorer. Kinney is a relative of the late Posey Rorer and he lives in Danville, Virginia. Posey was the fiddle-player for Charlie Poole and the North Carolina Ramblers. Kinney has written a book about Charlie Poole that I highly recommend. He also has the last banjo that Charlie Poole ever owned and played and he has the last fiddle that Posey owned. Kinney is a walking diction-ary when it comes to this form of music and will really educate us on this art form. Kinney plays the banjo, his brother plays guitar in the Doc Watson style, and he has a fiddle-player that plays in the smooth Posey Rorer style. This session will be recorded.

I have booked Martin a live show at the Visulite Theater, Charlotte, North Carolina on 7 July. He will be playing with the Acoustic Syndicate. They have a following and I expect there to be 400-plus people at this show. They are from Cleveland County, North Carolina. This live show will be recorded.

A live show at Fat City, Charlotte, North Carolina. Martin will be playing with 4th Root and the Cold Mountain Rhythm Band. Both of these bands are up-and-coming in the newgrass/bluegrass movement. This show will be recorded.

In-store appearance at Mixed Media Record store, Charlotte, North Carolina. Scheduled for 8 July.

Yours in truth,

Dolph Ramseur

This initial North Carolina trip would form the basis for *The Haint of the Budded Rose*, Martin and Dolph's musicology project focusing on the much undervalued old timey bluegrass music of the area; more of which later.

Meanwhile back in the UK, members of the E-group were busy organising a 'Gathering' – which sounds incredibly hippyfied but was really just a great excuse for as many people as possible to meet up and drink and dance to Martin and his music.

As referred to in Jane's story earlier, the location for this meeting of, mostly, internet friends was a place so secret and beautiful that no map maker is allowed to show it on any map.

Portmahomack (or The Port, as those fortunate to have been there know it) sits somewhere north of Inverness and somewhere south of Wick. It is essentially a bloody long way from anywhere. People have been known to say 'it's not the end of the world, but you can see it from there.'

The reason for its choice of location for the first Martin Stephenson E-group Gathering mostly revolved around Martin living just a few miles away. Also it had a very music-friendly pub/hotel called The Caledonian. The 'Cally' had a small function room at the back, bedrooms above, and very friendly hosts Phil and Irene (unfortunately since departed for pastures new). It was here on the weekend of 25-26 August 2000 that a lot of Martin Stephenson fans met each other, and Martin, properly for the first time.

Approximately 30 E-groupers made it up to Portmahomack that weekend. Most of us had a moan about how far we had travelled, but curiously the only ones not moaning were Cyril and Nadya Povyshev, who had just popped across from Ekaterinburg, Russia; just the 2,400 miles or so as the very knackered crow flies.

Cyril had first heard Martin Stephenson's music via the *Rainbow Warriors* Greenpeace compilation back in 1989 – specifically the song 'Wholly Humble Heart'. He and Nadya had been fans ever since but often struggled to get hold of the albums. Hence the E-group was probably a resource of even greater importance than to most of us Westerners.

Our Russian friends made a proper road trip of the UK leg of their journey via London, Nottingham, Garswood and finally The Port, staying at E-group members' houses along the way and taking in a couple of gigs. I guess it must have been some sort of a culture shock for them, but probably not as shocking as having Gypsy Dave Smith drive them from Garswood (near Wigan) to Portmahomack for the Gathering weekend.

The Gathering itself was a huge success. Many great friendships were made that weekend, much food and alcohol was consumed and most importantly Martin and Gypsy Dave Smith played a helluva lot of music. The sight of my Mum dancing to 'Always Us' is one I won't forget in a hurry. Some further highlights below – again pinched from E-group posts of the time:

Chris Sellers:
It's 600 miles to Portmahomack. We've got a car full of kids, half a pack of murray mints, it's dark and we're wearing sunglasses. HIT IT!

Rich's highlights:
Meeting those of you we'd not met before.

Young lad on the beach asking Martin 'Mister – are you a cowboy?' (that hat!)

Gypsy Dave's song for Martin: 'The Dreamer's Road' – the verses mention 40+ of Martin's songs and the chorus is beautiful (such a shame we missed the recording on the beach on Sunday night – guess what: we were knackered).

Hannah (our six-year-old) so excited at prospect of hearing Martin but then falling asleep at the exact moment he plugged in and waking up immediately he finished!

My Mum dancing with Andy Cairns on her birthday – I don't need to do drugs when I can picture stuff like that for free!

A kid from Garswood, Lancs dancing with a lass from Ekaterin-burg, Asia.

Johnny Tomorrow telling the 'bounty' joke, and my kids shouting 'Dad, that's your joke!' – it being my favourite joke of all time. I told it to Martin in Fibbers, York two years ago – being a Geordie he did-n't appreciate it, muttering something about Andy Capp stereotypes!

Andy Semple and Andy Cairns doing the raffle – a meeting of minds!

Winning *The Boy's Heart* in said raffle. Not found it on CD before – result!

John Ewing's Minidisc recorder – man, you are going to be so busy.

Cripps' song 'Done & Dusted'.

*

While we all returned home to rest and recuperate from travel-ling and partying, Martin simply continued to do his stuff.

In September, *The Church and the Minidisc* and *The Disciples of Merle and Doc* albums were released. Also E-group printer Rob Hurst re-published the *Something To Carry With You* poetry book which had originally been available in limited quantities to those buying the *Gladsome, Humour and Blue* album in 1988. Rob's reprint was top-quality and even featured a bonus extra poem or two. Additionally Rob published the *Bairro Alto* poetry book, the content of which was inspired by Martin's trip to Portugal in 1997.

Rob was also responsible for developing Martin's first proper website, which complemented the E-group and became an excel-lent resource for both the dedicated fan and the newbies who would navigate there no doubt after having had their spirits raised and faces made to ache with smiling at some gig some-where in the UK or USA.

The last quarter of 2000 was taken up mostly with further gig-ging – predominantly of the solo variety but often with comedian and orator Johnny Tomorrow (aka Bob Smith-Wright) support-ing. Bob's 'Standing at the Crossroads Just Outside of Liberty' is some sort of poetic classic and should have reached a far wider audience.

The year ended triumphantly with Martin and The Daintees

(with Alex Ross filling the drum stool) playing two amazing nights at The Borderline in London's West End on 4 and 5 December. Despite being on Monday and Tuesday nights, these two gigs effectively resembled a mini-Gathering with E-groupers travelling from relatively far and wide (OK, no Cyril and Nadya this time) to behave in a pretty similar fashion to the Portmahomack weekend. Drinking beer from teapots in a Chinese restaurant after hours is one memory that lingers.

So, in summary, 2000 saw Martin Stephenson release three albums ('official' ones anyway) and two poetry books, reform with his beloved Daintees, set up a website, visit North Carolina, and convene a Gathering of fans in the North East of Scotland. Quite amazing for a musician working almost completely outside of the traditional music industry, and releasing, in *Lilac Tree*, an album as good as anything he had produced before.

*

As the first year proper of the new millennium dawned, yet again the troubadour was on the road. From February through to March 2001, Martin gigged predominantly in the North of England, this time with travelling companion, Easter Ross musician Dave Fleming.

This period also saw the introduction of yet another means of artist/audience breakdown, a.k.a. the Lounge Gig. It was an idea that Martin had picked up from North Carolina musician Michael Reno Harrell. Quite simply, on a date in between official pub/club/arts centre gigs, Martin and Dave would turn up at your house and play for as long as anyone would listen. All they asked for in return was a bed for the night if convenient.

As I was fortunate to host my very own Martin Stephenson Lounge Gig, I can bear witness that they are very special events indeed. The age of the audience ranged from five to 65 and each and every one of them loved it. I'm sure there were some people there who had never witnessed any sort of live music before, never mind an event as up close and unplugged as this one.

The kids loved the *Muppet Show* theme tune and the Scott Joplin 'Entertainer' rag; the oldies rocked to the Western Swing tunes and we more serious types stroked our chins and nodded wisely as Martin played the classic Daintees numbers. After passing the hat round the smiling audience, those staying over at ours chatted till the wee small hours before falling asleep exhausted. Knowing that the maker of some of your favourite albums of all time is kipping on a mattress downstairs is a very odd experience, I can tell you.

While all this live activity was going on, one Monsieur Laurent Bailly, French E-group member, had compiled another E-group CD entitled *B-sides Stories #1*. It collected together, quite sensibly given its title, all The Daintees singles B-sides. As was customary for these unofficial releases, all that was required was for the buyer to send a fiver to Martin's PO Box.

After digesting the news that Joey Ramone had passed away in April, The Daintees headed out on another tour in May, starting at the Penrith Playhouse and wending its way down south via Birmingham, Cambridge and London and culminating in a storming gig at the Brighton Komedia on 30 August. One memorable gig on that tour was at Liverpool's Masque Theatre on the night that Liverpool were playing Alavés in the UEFA Cup final in Dortmund. Due to a combination of Daintees fans getting caught up in heaving pubs and the fact that the match went into extra time, the gig was put back until almost 11pm. Cue the sight of Martin coming on stage wearing a Liverpool shirt: 'the club owner made me do it, honest; don't tell my Dad, will you?!'

Following the success of 2000's Gathering (G2000) a follow-up was organised by the indefatigable Jane Cooper. This time the location was a little further south at the Schooner Hotel, Alnmouth on the weekend of Friday 13 to Sunday 15 July. The timing and location caused our hero a slight issue as he had for some mental reason been booked to play in Richmond, Surrey during the daytime of the Saturday. Fortunately the UK's railway system was working at a 'good' level of service that day and Martin made it back to Alnmouth in time for that evening's entertainment.

Again I make no apologies for reverting to some original E-group postings to convey the spirit of the weekend. Firstly from John Ewing/Sonic Chronicler:

Day 1
Hi Gang, Mr Sonic Chronicler here.

Just a quick note to keep you up to date with what's going on up in the Gathering 2001.

Well, weather has been wet & dull, but spirits have not been dampened. Everybody seems to have arrived safely, with more reprobates arriving today.

Old friends and new faces, everybody fits in fine. With everybody fed and watered, the Gatherers retired to the Conservatory of the Schooner for an evening of music by The Rorers and Gypsy Dave.

Some mighty fine guitar playing was on show, all suitably sonicly chronicled for future consumption. The Rorers played a traditional old timey sort of set which went down really well, a few familiar tunes and loads of new (old) ones to digest.

Gypsy Dave followed, in fine form, starting on dobro and swapping with acoustic throughout the set. Highlights included the set-closing 'Blue World'.

After the Gypsy, we retired to the back bar where someone had conveniently left a piano. If anybody needs a recording of thirteen different versions of 'Chopsticks' then I'm your man – send cheques to the usual address.

The piano was soon given up as a bad job, but inspired versions of 'It must be Love', 'House of the Rising Sun' and the intro to 'Pretty Vacant' made it bearable.

Then the guitars came out. Axe performances from Colin Bertram, Rich Cundill, Pete Bell, Lorna Bartle and Langy showed us that, despite having a wealth of musical talent in the group, nobody knows the words to any songs. Mumble-along-a-Stephenson tunes were suitably murdered, but we almost had it with 'Rain'.

Pete Bell is this year's Michael Thewlis! (For now – The Thewlmeister arrives today).

To end the night (as far as I know, 'cos we left at 2.30) Gypsy Dave gave us another acoustic set, including the Martin tribute song 'Dreamer's Road'.

So, there you have it. I'm knackered, as I'm at work today, but ready to go for tonight's gig in Newcastle.

Keep you up to date.

John

And from Suzanne:

Day 2

Well, after we left (on Saturday morning at 2:30) some of the boys decided to have a very early morning constitutional, managed to get themselves locked out in the rain, didn't get let in until about 7am! Apparently quite a few people heard them knocking and shouting but thought they were just having a laugh!

Last night at the Live Theatre was a stormer. First Robert Smith Wright led with a bit of oratory, then Gypsy Dave with a few favourites including another rendition of 'Dreamer's Road' (with the crib sheets!).

Mr Stephenson came on next wearing what I think was a new shirt (although someone should say something about that hat). Played a few but not enough, included 'Posey Rorer' of course, which was good 'cos next came the North Carolina Ramblers with some more finger-picking tunes, including songs I knew: 'Sweet Georgia Brown' and 'Summertime', which were excellent. They were ably assisted first by Martin then by Gypsy Dave.

The night was topped off by a romping set by The Toe Rags, which led to some impromptu bopping by Jane et al, all suitably recorded for posterity! Toe Rags tunes included 'Barbaraville' and 'Little Red Bottle'.

The Alnmouth-based E-groupers were all transported away in a bus at the stroke of midnight. Not sure if they were heading for bed, though; find out later!

Cheers Suzanne xx

And finally a post from myself, summing up the weekend with a very small mention of the 'lock-out' debacle. Don't ask!

Here we go: managed to get most of my brain cells functioning again – but not enough to write a follow-up to Andy S's Sunday intro (can anybody remember the rest?!). Top highlights of the weekend for me (in no particular order):

Friday night listening to Gypsy Dave in the bar (far better than the actual gig)

The Friday night strum-alongs (Pete Bell is a star player!)

Drunken ramblings with Andy, Langy & Red Rob (but not Declan as he fell asleep on the shitter!)

I'm not saying anything about the getting-locked-out bit, 'cept

God it was cold!

Kevin Birt's laugh!

Martin playing 'Kathy' on Sunday night for Kev

Meeting Donna who used to go to college with Anth & Gary's sister Clare Dunn

The bar staff, who let us drink forever (possibly a mistake in retrospect!)

My girls being genuinely scared when The Toe Rags played 'Barbaraville' (in the UKs most haunted hotel!)

Meeting Graham 'Shippy' Anderson properly for the first time

Joe Guillan's comment about Jeep – 'this fella potted the black years ago didn't he?'

Martin playing 'We Can Roll' on Colin's Washburn for us in the bar on Sunday night

NOT getting divorced!

Finally, just the great fun and friendship continuing, all because of this funny little band I heard when my mate Boo gave me a tape in 1988 – who would have thought?

Looking back, this period from G2000 to G2001 was really the golden era of Martin Stephenson's E-group. I guess it caught the predominantly thirty/fortysomethings who were involved at a point in time when they had just started using the internet at home, and were looking for something real to grab onto in a busy world of work and/or parenting. Rediscovering that a major artist from their youth was developing a network of like-minded souls and, more importantly, was directly interacting with that network to create new music and a whole new way of working, was a tremendously healthy and vital thing. Just as important were the friendships that were made across that network, many of which I'm sure will turn out to last a lifetime.

Under the shadow of the 9/11 Twin Towers attacks, Martin snuck out another couple of albums in the autumn. *Live in the 21st Century* was a live document of the Daintees' Borderline gigs the previous December. Unfortunately the source recordings made by John Ewing had been pretty horrendously butchered by Fresh Ear Records, even to the extent of having the same snatch of audience noise between each track. That such a wonderful two nights of music was reduced to this was hugely disappointing. (If anyone needs some decent live Daintees from this period just see the Sonic Chronicler himself – he will sort you out!)

Next up was a strange release known as *The Incredible Shrinking Band*. Clad in Kieran Fitzpatrick's homage to early independent label artwork (see some of Scritti Politti's Rough Trade singles and you'll know what I mean), this was Martin's punk rock statement but via the medium of traditional pickin' songs. At the time many thought it to be some sort of piss-take, made up as it was of lo-fi versions of songs we had heard before and three consecutive versions of 'Will The Circle Be Unbroken'. But as Martin explained back then, it was simply the final stage of a very necessary move to get back to his roots and as far away from the music industry as possible:

This album is the last in a series of field recordings at the present time: 1. *Church* / 2. *Merle* / 3. *Haint* / 4. *Inc Shrink*.

I see them as photographs that can never be repeated. There is a great freedom in them and I hope they have been good concepts. I am deeply grateful to the people who have supported these expressions and hope not to have offended anyone with the so-called 'poorness of quality'. I particularly see *Church* as a beautiful watercolour attempt. Just for 'Passing By' alone makes the *Inc Shrink* worth it. I just want the group to know that I am not taking the piss and am very serious about what I do. I think Kieran's artwork is excellent. I suppose these four albums are a big fuck-off to *Salutation Road*, Kitchenware Records, Prefab Sprout consciousness.

A big hello to Hurrah! who, along with the Daintees, were the only real people on that indie label. It's also a big hello to Jonathan Richman. It's a cutting at the wire of security consciousness. It's busking when you need to and don't need to.

Today I am going to Inverness and will stand on the street for an hour. I'm gonna play 'Passing By'. Pick some rags. Be free and stand by the songs and the art.

In truth, as Dolphus Ramseur says.

Martin x

And so the circle had been made complete. The artist returning to the reasons that had made him want to play music for the first time as a 16-year-old.

As if to underline this Martin played a gig in Leeds in October 2001 with a slightly unusual Daintees line-up featuring Joe Guillan on bass, Gordon 'Jesus' Larkman on drums and a young guitar prodigy by the name of Nick Rickard. Not only did Martin play live for the first time his delightful tribute to his recently departed Mum, 'Home' ('it's two days old – it's shite'), but he also got ex-MPs guitarist Tim Reid to jam on manic versions of 'Louie, Louie' and 'Sweet Jane'. Punk rock had never sounded more real.

Chapter 6

You Go Your Way and I'll Go Mine
(2002 – Present Day)

He may have invented bifocals, the Franklin stove, the glass harmonica, the lightning rod and a carriage odometer, but Benjamin Franklin is nowadays remembered more for the wisdom of uttering the following words: *doing the same things and expecting different results is the first sign of insanity.*

It's not known whether the famous Founding Father held such views as a result of any perceived stagnation in early-18th century North American music, but it's clear he'd happened upon a truism that applies equally today as it did back in the days of *Poor Richard's Almanac* and the *Pennsylvania Gazette*.

Had Benjamin been defrosted from a cryogenic state in 2002, a cursory glance at any music band's diary would reveal a monotonous cycle of writing, recording and touring, apparently set to repeat ad infinitum. He'd have been tempted to mutter his aphorism with some passion. If the truth were told, even the indie scene of the early noughties had become, for many bands, a step towards TV-presenting rather than an end in itself.

As the late, lamented Bill Hicks might have cried: 'isn't it time we started to evolve ideas?' Stagnation did have the effect of creating the manure in which the green shoots of some new revolutionary strands of music could thrive, but it was far from the mind of Martin Stephenson, whose 2002 was as varied, journeyed and lived as a calendar year could ever be.

Ten years previously he'd been putting the finishing touches to *The Boy's Heart*, but the first release of this year would be something put together, once again, by Laurent Bailly for members of the now flourishing E-group. *Remembering Frances* was an affectionate and objective collection of Martin's music, directed towards the memory of his late mother and whose curation recognised the all-encompassing intimacy of the Stephenson canon.

With 20 tracks covering the very early days (including his very first song: 'My Girl Doesn't Want Me') to the more current finger-pickin' USA tunes ('Black Mountain Rag') the CD – in typical uncommercial style – was described as a 'friendly unofficial Martin Stephenson release'. Not to be found on the shelves of HMV or Virgin, it would, once again, be obtained by simply dispatching a fiver to Martin or members of the E-group itself.

Dolph Ramseur had been involved in the project, collating much of the content and he had the benefit of a wide palette to choose from. There were items recorded in Martin's Mum's kitchen in 1983 through to some of the first recordings he made with him in North Carolina at the turn of the century.

The CD, which enjoyed Martin's blessing, found its way quietly into the hands of a group of fans who had re-discovered him after losing touch around a decade earlier. In many ways the E-group was responsible for a continuation of more traditional products, like CDs for example, as Martin himself was more interested, by this point, in playing 'pure' – even microphones were treated with suspicion, as if somehow capable of diluting the moment. One imagined him now striding into a recording studio, tutting at all of the recording technology, dismantling it, using it to light a fire in the snug, opening the windows and ensuring that the noise of any passing vehicle could be in his new song.

And it's not as if everyone couldn't have their own slice of Stephenson. Indeed, by this point, it was possible to book Martin to appear in your very own living room. Those that did describe some wonderful evenings, a re-invigoration of their interest in live music and an 'artist as jukebox' rejuvenation of a lost musical heritage. Oh yes – and the passing-around of a pork pie hat for tips. Indeed, Martin's progress was no longer charted, like most musical icons, by his CD releases but by his live appearances. There were fewer clues on his CDs to where he was 'at' than in his increasingly engaging gigs. There might be an obvious new release that one would expect to hear at a gig, but by the time the gig came around, Martin's bus would be already collecting passengers at the next stop.

So 2002 saw a happy Stephenson, no longer conditioned by the music business, but beginning to dance to his own tune. The E-group had really raised his spirits and from a personal fulfilment perspective, he had come from playing to 20-odd people in a club in the Highlands to more and more well attended musical happenings.

Much evidence of the times is to be had by talking to John Ewing. Fans of Martin will know this gentleman as the 'sonic chronicler', someone who would regularly appear at live appearances with expensive recording equipment, top-of-the-range microphones, a neat little Minidisc machine and a penchant for the unconventional – a fact guaranteed to prick up the Stephenson ears. *Sonic* did indeed record his own version of Martin Stephenson and the Daintees' *Live in the 21st Century*, upon which we have commented in the previous chapter, producing an outstanding mix that truly conveyed the evening's craic (and which, to many, was not reflected in the official release at the time).

Andy Cairns managed Martin at this time. Andy, whom we introduced to you in the previous chapter, found Martin, like the rest of us, through the E-group. Andy did a lot of promotion and publicity – he had his own PR agency – and because of the mountain of contacts he possessed he could get gigs at a click of a finger. But he was also instrumental in laying the ground for the appearance of *Collective Force* later in the year.

But earlier in 2002 Martin had made a trip that would further establish his current strand of musical exploration. He returned to North Carolina. This time accompanied by noted poet and oil-rig worker Gary McCourt, he headed for the Ramseur homestead – a new spiritual home on a ley line from his Highland base.

Dolph Ramseur had been a correspondent and fan of Martin for some time, being a fan of British post-punk music and having been in touch with Martin since the mid-80s. To find someone deeply connected to the heart and soul of front porch music taking an interest in the industrial tones of post-punk strikes one as a little strange, while the irony is emphasised by the fact that our very own post-punk minstrel had harboured a love for all things finger-pickin' since before putting down the first Daintees album. Two separate, well-travelled roads were due to converge.

That shouldn't sound as unlikely as it does, since the more observant of you will have noticed the track 'Tribute to the Late Rev Gary Davis' on the first album *Boat to Bolivia*. I had spotted this too, but assumed it was a reference to the explosion of teeth that was the Radio One DJ of (almost) the same name.

The country swing and skiffle of 1995's *Sweet Misdemeanour* had drawn Dolph further in, but a relationship of sorts had been in place for several years beforehand. It was entirely natural that Martin would take the opportunity to go and learn something about the legacy that Dolph himself was drawing on – and that would lead to the future recording of both *The Haint of the Budded Rose* and *Hell's Half Acre*, as well as accounting for an increasing new strand in the live performances.

Like a latter-day Harry Smith, collating his own American folk music anthology, Martin was able to immerse himself in this undiscovered panoply of sound. He performed at gigs, appeared at front porch gatherings and found names from his past becoming real as the likes of Etta Baker appeared in front of him, explaining their backgrounds, their influences and appreciating Martin's infectious take on their own musical expression. Etta and others would become, for Martin, musical mentors – directional beacons if you like – allowing him to develop an even more organic approach to his own music.

In radio interviews given to North Carolina's WFAE and WNCW stations in 2002, we not only get an insight into the motivations guiding Martin at this time, but also bear witness to the power of the internet. As the presenter introduces Martin to 'Charlotte Talks', five emails arrive from Europe, requesting songs. To laughter, Martin explains that they're probably all from the same person – and later in the interview when a local namesake calls in, our minstrel asks him if he can shed any light on where his missing royalties might have gone.

Again, Martin explains the method in his madness. 'I was cocooned. I needed to break free and I did this by making all of the wrong career moves. Being from the North East of England, which has a great kinship with Scotland, it seemed the right move. Most people travel south to London to make it in the business. It felt right for me to travel in the opposite direction.'

Martin compares a former life of three articulated lorries with playing to 25 people on the Isle of Eigg, explaining to the listeners: 'I have to trust my own two feet, rather than a manager with a big business plan.'

When asked by the presenter about marketing his music, we

get a typically low-fi response from the artist: 'Just like a potter, for example, would make 20 pots and sell them, I will make 1000 albums and sell them the old way – just like the potter. It's the power of the small that interests me.'

We learn how Dolph Ramseur's first attempt to contact Martin by telephone many years previously had ended in failure: 'I didn't know it was Dolph,' claims Martin. 'There was a message from some crazy American guy on my answer phone. It was a while later that, while communicating by email, I realised that Dolph had been the scary guy on the phone!'

In returning to the theme of North Carolina's musical heritage, an evidently engaged interviewer asks Martin who his specific inspirations were. 'The old players. They're nice, relaxed people. I enjoy mixing with the older generation,' responds Martin, before identifying Ned Mullis as a particular hero. 'I was able to go into his music store and meet a man who's had a Western Swing band for more than fifty years'. It was clear that this offered a depth of learning that would propel Martin forward.

Charlie Poole, not unnaturally, also gets a mention. 'I am obsessed with him,' Martin explains. 'He was the Shane MacGowan of his day. The double bass player in The Toe Rags [Graham Anderson] turned me on to him. He would never stop talking about him.'

Among the anecdotes shared is the one concerning the story about Posey Rorer, who traded his fiddle for a bottle of whiskey at a particularly dark time. That inspired Martin's song of the same name.

Turning to how Martin first got into music throws up a few surprises for the Stateside listeners. 'I was a table tennis prodigy,' he explains to general consternation. 'All I listened to was Frank Zappa's *Hot Rats* album and both Santana's and Fleetwood Mac's *Greatest Hits*. I used to love Elvis's voice – and Diana Ross's too.'

We gain more insights into what life must be like living with Martin as he explains how his partner thought he was obsessed with a Doc Watson instruction video. 'I used to play it 24 hours a day – I revered him,' is Martin's summary of his love for all things Watson. 'It was the Doc Watson flat-pickin' and finger-pickin' course we learn. All he would say to his pupil would be: *pick it, son!*'

In amongst the reminiscences and stories of Martin's love for the sound of North Carolina, we get a few live performances. They include 'Posey Rorer', 'Rowan Berries' and a 'Piedmont Blues' tune dedicated to Etta Baker. Gary McCourt is brought out to recite (from memory) a poem and the confluence of the different voices stresses a message that echoes long after the interview ends.

As you'll read, the subject of the interview and soon to be released *The Haint of the Budded Rose* isn't the excursion that one might imagine. As Martin himself explains to the presenter, when asked about his musical journeys, 'everything is just an accent. Everything is one song.'

Hearing the mix of Highland Scots, lilting Durham and the melodious Tar Hell twang, I think he had a point.

*

It was ironic really that when Harry Smith first began to create his famous 1952 six-album, 84-track compendium of American Folk Music, he'd focused on two key points in musical history: first, 1927 when developments in electronics made the accurate recording of music possible; and second, 1932 when the Depression settled in. Put simply, improving technology had allowed Smith to develop and curate his collection, and share it with the world. In 2002 technology had progressed so far that Martin Stephenson was minded to travel backwards, to remove the reliance on technology and focus on the music itself. The man who put the 'verse' in reverse.

But one result of these musical adventures was an improving musicianship on the part of Martin himself. This natural urge to find the originators of the North Carolina sound had led to a curiosity that could only be sated by *becoming* one of them. Curiously, for one known for the warmth of his voice, Martin was to embark on singing lessons within 18 months of these travels.

This passion also helped to complete Martin's rehabilitation after abandoning alcohol several years earlier. He'd devoted himself to the Alcoholics Anonymous twelve-step programme for recovering addicts and had learned that most of the participants would complete two or three steps and then think they'd ended their personal torment.

Martin, on the other hand, was determined to go through the whole programme, which included several key stages, from admitting one's addiction through recognising a greater power to examining past errors and making amends for them. This commitment would lead eventually to work with less privileged kids in his Invergordon neighbourhood, but right now these North Carolina adventures were providing a useful context for self-realisation.

Martin's music had become the route map to completing the programme – the template not only for making amends but also for fulfilling the life that the beer would have otherwise denied him.

Around this time Andy Cairns negotiated with Kitchenware and London Records to get back the rights for Martin's first four albums. Now while it would be another year before the four would emerge (*Boat to Bolivia*; *Gladsome, Humour and Blue*; *Salutation Road* and *The Boy's Heart*), Martin had already decided that these releases would be augmented by a touch of the modern Martin, appending freer, impromptu and much more heartfelt new versions of album tracks to the end of each disk (with the unmistakeable accompaniment of a roaring fire on at least two of them).

Another change would manifest itself in the CD covers, with Kieran Fitzpatrick – creator of the cover design for this book – providing some striking artwork for the new versions, the most memorable of which adorns the 2003 release of *The Boy's Heart* (Martin never did like the original Big Top and Clown imagery).

The positive state of mind and increasing activity reflected the solid relationship with Voiceprint Music[4] that Martin had fostered with Rob Ayling. Rob's North East-based independent label to this day still majors in lovingly curated re-releases, from Hawkwind, via Gordon Giltrap, Barclay James Harvest, The Fall and Martin. From the 2003 early album re-releases to 2008's *Western Eagle*, Voiceprint has provided the backing required to allow Martin to concentrate on his muse.

And this is no insignificant observation. As Martin's friends will testify, he has often been dragged out to the desert and

---

[4] www.voiceprint.co.uk

tempted with the riches that many musical entrepreneurs would offer. 'You're not as well regarded as you should be. There's so much we could do together. You need someone with my connections behind you – so let me help you', would be the typical mantra.

What Martin needed was the support of an organisation that knew who he was, what he stood for and where his journey might lead. Because as we have observed before, the road would be *less travelled* (bringing new meaning to the phrase 'country tracks') and many 'professional' movers and shakers would be unused to some of the sharp turns and byways that would follow. Alternative roots indeed.

Rob and Voiceprint would provide this foundation – a SatNav for the soul – and it was against this background of personal contentment and realisation that Martin would embark on his next project: *Collective Force.*

The plan, as ever expressed with detail and enthusiasm by Martin, was to include collaborations with 'everyone' – or at least a wide range of musical personalities from his own recorded history, plus some new favourite pals. This new enriched musical vision had its roots in the mix of musical travellers Martin enjoyed in 2001, from touring again with the Daintees to a host of other group ventures and duets. It was also in many ways a response to the new popularity he was enjoying, thanks to a session recorded for Janice Long's Radio 2 show, featuring a track reminiscent of his earlier Daintees work called 'Orange is the Colour of Joy'.

Voiceprint provides a neat summary of the origins of this album, attributing its conception to Martin's recent 'return' or, shall we say, decision to take a path more recognisable to the commercial music fraternity.

Pete Rawson generously allowed Martin to record most of the album at his Redwood Studios in the Highlands. Given that many of Martin's current musical collaborators were also based up there, it meant he could draw on their support and time too.

Late in the previous year, the recordings had been completed in Brighton, where they were enhanced through the participation of a number of further friends, including BJ Cole (pedal steel guitarist with a session track record that would double the size of this book – let's just say Elton John and REM for now), Bobby Valentino (ex-Hank Wangford and fiddle-player on The Bluebells' 'Young at Heart'), one-time Lotus Eater and *man about Merseyside* Peter Coyle and a gospel choir from Sussex.

Voiceprint said at the time: 'The result of all this is an album of sunny, spiritually happy sounds, musically as varied as usual and successfully fusing Martin's style and the traditional types of music that inspire him.'

Listening to the album six years on, one finds it hard to disagree with this and it was no surprise that the music media rediscovered their affection for Martin and his music at this time. In fact, once they had him in their presence (sessions were recorded for Radio Scotland and for BBC6's Gideon Coe) they were all swept away by the charm of the man. Janice Long would repeatedly play the opening track 'Orange is the Colour of Joy' and Rob Ayling will confirm interest at the time from the likes of Bob Harris, Mike Harding, Johnny Walker, Terry Wogan and the Kershaw siblings. Given Wogan's liking of all things Country & Western (albeit with washed and combed hair and 'Still the One'-type happy outcomes – no *Lost Highway* for our Tel) any number of interesting futures could be contemplated.

Revisiting the album, you get an immediate sense of the fun that was had during the recording, with Martin the master of ceremonies, guiding us through an encyclopaedia of music dear to him, like a repentant Pied Piper leading the children from the brink back to the Promised Land – or at least a welcoming hostel.

Having rooted through the reviews at the time and re-listened to the tracks one by one, with growing affection for what is a riotously joyful affair, we find Gordon Baxter's review of the album in *Blues on Stage* appropriate for inclusion here. 'Stephenson has always had a knack for producing highly infectious pop tunes, one of which, "Orange is the Colour of Joy", opens the album. In its earlier incarnation it was a simple yet effective tune. Here it takes on new life with the soul/gospel-inflected backing vocals.

'The album has a few bluesy moments, most notably on "The Sun's Coming Out" and "Blind Man's Blues". The former has shades of Reverend Gary Davis with a 12-string guitar laid over a half-speed bad rave beat/sample. The end result is a Piedmont-meets-Club sound, if you can imagine such a thing! "Blind Man's Blues" is much more straightforward: Stephenson sings and demonstrates his finger-picking skills while Australian exile Gypsy Dave Smith adds the fine slide guitar.'

Baxter identifies Bossa Nova, Western Swing and some natural Harry Smith-style field recordings, summarising: 'There is not really a British equivalent of Americana, but if there was, Martin Stephenson would exemplify the whole genre. Folk, pop, blues, gospel and much, much more, yet nearly all instantly recognisable as Martin Stephenson. The addition of the various elements brought by The Force adds an extra dimension that makes Stephenson's songs sound even better. Albums like *Collective Force* help to lift the spirits and makes [sic] the world seem a better place. Immensely enjoyable.'

Listening again, one has to agree with Baxter's sentiments, regardless of how objective this co-author is trying to be. The album fair pings along with a freshness of spirit and a richness of feel that deserves repeated plays.

'Every Step of the Way' and 'Long Forgotten' stand out for me, one with its gentle African influence and memorable Andrea Mackie backing vocal and the other representing an official release for what dedicated fans know as a Martin Stephenson classic. Elsewhere, there were treasures a-plenty, culminating in 'Spirit Song', a track that seems to sum up everything the artist stands for. 'From the past to the future' – it's life-affirming and spiritual at the same time.

The album was warmly welcomed by the music press, perhaps reflecting a wider period of reawakened media interest. David Roberts, writing in *Q* magazine, praises this 'busker supreme'. He appreciates the return to a more rounded, full band sound. 'They play everything from pedal steel guitar to didgeridoo to steel drums, replacing the low-fi meanderings of late with a big fat smile of a record.'

The success of the album must be, in great part, down to the atmosphere that accompanied the recordings, for these were people who knew that Martin was unlikely to respond to a schedule or a project plan. So it was through serendipity that Patrick Cleasby mentioned Dallas Simpson to Martin. Martin had heard that name before – from the lips of Dolph Ramseur, who, from afar, was still aware of Dallas's reputation as the UK's best 'binaural' guy. Martin and Dolph had already planned to approach Dallas, so this further mention sealed the idea and Martin's next album entered the planning stage.

But before this, there was a short trip to North Carolina, from 5 to 24 March, accompanied by Gary McCourt and, of course, Dolphus Ramseur. Dolph kept the E-group informed:

> Hello Group. Martin is without a hat on this tour of North Carolina. He has tried to find one but has not been able to locate a hat that has that special 'vibe'.
>
> I sense that describing Dallas as a *binaural soundwork performer and recorder* may not immediately ring bells for the reader, so best use the words of the man himself from his website to paint a clearer picture[5].
>
> 'Binaural sound art is both a particular style of recording and a particular approach. By inserting very high quality sub-miniature microphones into his ears, Dallas is able to sample his own human hearing and record what is known as *binaural sound* to conventional two-channel stereo, with all the potency of a three-dimensional surround sound experience when replayed on headphones.

Effectively, Dallas would walk around the performer to re-create the aural experience as near to the human template as possible. The emphasis here is on natural recreation of sound, and it was this that took Martin's interest. Martin was intrigued at the possibility of not just placing the listener in the same room, but having the listener walk around the artist, getting different sound perspectives.

In order to pursue this growing curiosity, Martin and Patrick looked to Jim Hornsby. Jim had worked on *Lilac Tree* with Martin and had remained a close colleague. Martin had held Jim in awe for some time. A master of the pickin' sound, Jim is still regarded as one of the best in the British Isles. In the sleeve notes to the impending album, Martin says: 'I have never met a guitarist who is such a master for getting inside the song or the music.'

---

[5] www.dallassimpson.com

The resulting album, *Down to the Wood* (or *Martin and Jim Go Binaural*), emerged on Voiceprint's new Martin-only Barbaraville label in the late summer of 2002.

The simple facts are plain enough. The album was recorded, Dallas Simpson-style, in a wood near Ambergate in Derbyshire. It featured fourteen songs, none of which appeared to be new, but that only tells half the story.

There were four 'crew' members: Martin, Jim, Dallas and Patrick Cleasby, who videoed the event. Imagine a Derbyshire-based *I'm a Celebrity, Leave me in Here*. The crew rose early and scaled the heights to arrive at a hillock opposite some dramatic cliffs. Here the first part of the album was recorded, with Patrick trying to manage the video equipment while not falling over the edge, Dallas walking around Martin and Jim and a small fleet of recalcitrant midges providing background vocals. The midges decided they liked the look and smell of Jim Hornsby, who must have been wondering if Clarence White or Chet Atkins ever had to put up with this. They spent most of this part of the recording trying to put him off. The sleeve notes explain that Jim was such a professional that he would let the sustain die away naturally before freeing his hands and slapping the midge against his neck.

Following a repast of reviving Golden Syrup cakes, the crew made it down to the streamside, where the remaining part of the album was recorded.

A collection of a variety of styles and tunes, some familiar and some less so, the results may not be everyone's cup of tea, but you cannot deny the relevance of this process to Martin's general direction of travel. In fact, Dallas's website unwittingly appears to underline exactly why Martin Stephenson should be interested in his work. It is described as: 'an open invitation for each of us to establish a new and sensitive relationship with our environment, for it is only when we fully appreciate its worth that we will strive at all costs to preserve it.'

Patrick Cleasby's memories of the recording share something of the spirit of the endeavour and the destiny of the connection between Ramseur and Simpson. 'Sometimes something as wonderful as this can be hard won. And as we dragged recording gear, chairs, amps and guitars up to the Shining Cliffs in the morning, the vibe was good, but a little out of breath. The location for Part

San Sebastian 1994

The Toe Rags, Bigg Market, Newcastle 1999

...with Henry Fosebrook, Easter Ross 1999

Rich interviewing Martin while Dave Fleming plays for Rob Hurst and daughter

...in the bar of the Caledonian Hotel, Portmahomack 2001

Gypsy Dave Smith

...with Robert Smith Wright, poet extraordinaire

The Toe Rags kick ass in Newcastle

group gathering, Alnmouth 2001

...with Gary Dunn, Anth Dunn and Jesus, Sheffield 2001

North Carolina 2002

Anth Dunn

...with Finn McArdle, Bute 2004

...with Jim Hornsby, Soundfield Sessions, North Carolina 2004

Martin and Helen, North Carolina 2007

1 [of the album – from 'In the Woods' to 'Home'] is on the brow of a hillock facing the Shining Cliffs and it had an inspirational effect on the artists. The flies were less charming, although Martin loves the binaural buzzing and the rest of the guys were amazed that I didn't end my day in the bottom of the gully as I messed around with my video cameras perched on the edge of a precipice.'

In summarising his memories of the day Patrick hits the bull's-eye. 'A day to remember for all concerned. You can't repeat or edit or rehash these events. You just have to make them happen once. Once is enough.'

A sentiment wholeheartedly in tune with this Song of the Soul.

*

Having emerged from the woods in early 2002, it took until November that year for the appearance of *Down to the Wood (Martin and Jim Go Binaural)* on the Barbaraville label – created by Voiceprint and devoted purely to Martin's own releases. A new listen to the album reveals some hidden treasures as well as a feeling that the familiarity of many of the tracks and the unique recording style might lead to extended bouts of obscurity in one's CD racks. Described as 'an exquisite dynamic sonic ballet', a recent listen (with the stream audible in the background) sparked a smile, as did the appearance of 'Home' – recently bulked up with Hammond organ and rhapsodic backing vocals on the *Western Eagle* release (and going under the soubriquet of 'Track 13', as if to persuade the listener that this wasn't the same track).

Having reached a stage where simultaneous releases were the rule rather than the exception, it was *Collective Force* whose impact had propelled Martin's star upwards in the early part of 2002. There was the Radio 2 Janice Long session, a live broadcast Belfast show and launch party at the 12 Bar club in London in August, featuring a cast of thousands – or, for those familiar with the venue, a cast not quite capable of swinging a cat (but mostly the likes of Andrea Mackie and other members of the E-group and their friends).

The confident times led to a bout of Daintees touring – typi-

cally informal, ad-hoc and unpredictable, perhaps characterised
by a memorable evening at the Verge in London on 28 May, witnessed by co-author Rich Cundill, long-time supporter Jane
Cooper, Michael Thewlis and company. But it wasn't a purely
Daintees summer. Martin was also engaged in solo touring – his
own particular brand of the Bob Dylan non-stop, forever
approach – and this continued, at least from the perspective of
the audience, to provide peace of mind and connection. Not for the
last time would the phrase 'the power of the small' ring true.

These gigs, no two the same, helped Martin get by. *Collective
Force* may have pushed our troubadour into the limelight temporarily, but it was no commercial success (and there was no
advance behind him). The reality of having to make a living
meant that fans could be guaranteed at least an annual visit from
Martin to the local venue. And, as if this wasn't enough, there
was an opportunity to make a purchase from Martin's mobile
shop: a suitcase full of recordings, poetry books and keepsakes.

I recently participated in a meeting of Newcastle United football fans in the North East of England, at which one of the gathered clan explained his opposition to being referred to as a 'customer' of his beloved football club. 'We're not customers,' he
explained. 'We're part of a movement.' It was a brutally concise
but eloquent description of a relationship that eludes most
attempts to nail it down, and it also applied to the career and
community of Martin at this time.

In an industry where the most conventional interpretation of
something shocking and new was someone not miming on *Top of
the Pops*, a man prepared to re-release tracks embellished by the
sound of the Derbyshire Dales, provide impromptu bus stop gigs
and 'rap' against a finger-picking rhythm, was so far *out there* he
was beginning to lap his peers, like an acoustic guitar-wielding
Chris Hoy.

The modern music industry was no longer the context for
Martin Stephenson. The longed-for aim of commodity-based
music production – being *everywhere all of the time* – was, curiously enough, within reach. Martin's music was effectively everywhere, all of the time. But unlike the one-dimensional synthetic
reach of mass-produced chart music, Martin was actually there
playing it.

One E-group member swears to this day that it wasn't the beer that caused him to recall Martin playing two gigs in two different parts of the country in the same evening.

So the connection had been strengthened with only the curvature of the Earth obscuring what the future had to bring, while Joe Strummer's star suddenly fell from the firmament in December 2002.

*

2003 began with a tour of Germany – in itself an indication of an increasingly co-ordinated management approach, featuring three key figures. Bob Lyng handled the German side of things with Iain Strefford looking after the UK and Dolph Ramseur in the USA. John Meadows – a long-standing member of the E-group – worked with Bob, setting up tours and gigs in Germany, courtesy of a move provoked by his German-born wife. The band contained Jim Hornsby with Dave Foster ('Time and a Word') on bass, and *Jesus* on drums.

Now, I say 'increasingly co-ordinated' as if that indicated some vast period of calm on the organisational side. Of course, I would be wrong, since chaos was already planning to step in. It seemed as if the devolution of management from the artist to a team did not work. E-group members talk of the falling-out, the arguments, the disagreements and the pulling in different directions. The New Christy Minstrels might agree, as three wheels on Martin's wagon were way too many in 2003.

So Stephenson-watchers continued to expect the unexpected and they weren't disappointed. What would come next? A live solo recording? A new Daintees album? An attempt to record Martin underwater?

One jests of course, but the diverse canon of artistry was about to be enhanced once more. As a result of a collaboration with Duncan Kennedy, *The Well of Harmony* appeared in early 2003. This was something new: a music book – with tabs, chords and arrangements for people to follow – accompanied by a CD, some elaborate packaging, poetry and a collection of Scottish folk music.

The CD contains a traditional collection of tunes, from Ross-shire and other places; waltzes, rags and simple melodies. Lovingly presented, the origins of each song are described in detail and the book also contains, via extracts of emails between Duncan Kennedy and Dolph Ramseur, an initial pitch of an idea that would eventually evolve into *The Well of Harmony*. Listening again, the album feels close up and personal, almost reverential in its wonder of the old songs: respectful of the need to convey the magic of the small, again.

There is much to behold in the music from 'The Ball of Torridon' (to re-appear on *Wheel of Fortune*), with a strident *The Good, the Bad and the Ugly* feeling and 'Fenderango', shiny shimmering arpeggios grabbing the attention.

In April, Voiceprint reissued the first four Daintees albums, all with extra tracks and adorned with new artwork by Kieran Fitzpatrick. For those who like detail, the dedication accompanying '8.30 Mowbray Morning' on the reissued *The Boy's Heart* is to Rich Cundill, rapidly emerging as an archivist of some diligence. One of the (many) excuses for the delay in getting this book out has been the fear that we might have left something important out. Then again, had we left everything in, you'd need heavy lifting gear to finish it.

Rich has the ability to draw out some interesting facts from Martin's discography, such as this little gem. On two of the reissued Daintees albums there were extra tracks where Henry Fosebrooke accompanied Martin beside the aforementioned roaring fire. Fosebrooke (or 'footbrake', as my spellchecker suggests), made a living making drum skins out of animal pelts and building incredibly detailed tree houses. Or at least that's what Rich tells me.

The re-release of the first four albums had, like *Collective Force*, found its way into the music press. *Q* magazine again had kind words for their 'busker supreme'. Nick Duerden summarised Martin's non-traditional career path succinctly: 'he has gained a loyal following but notched up few album sales,' but went on to acknowledge the uniqueness of the artiste. 'Still, he remains an affecting songwriter, with *Salutation Road*, in particular, retaining a sunshine charm that's hard not to warm to.'

And just as the four albums were beginning to provoke a reappraisal of the Stephenson genre in the music press – there were encouraging reviews – Martin headed off into the woods again, metaphorically as well as literally (he had Jim Hornsby with him). The gigging continued. Hornsby, with whom Martin has had the occasional falling-out, was not the only regular collaborator in 2003. Kieran Fitzpatrick, illustrator and artist of some note, was also kept busy. September finally saw the release of *The Haint of the Budded Rose*. This wonderful collection of front porch ballads, which accompanies a sunny Sunday morning better than a full English, had been delayed by complications brought on by the complexity of the artwork: a standard-sized CD with contributions from a range of new North Carolina friends (as well as Martin himself) accompanied by a CD-sized book of related writings, lyrics and stories.

The Haint provides enjoyment and education in equal measure – a feat not always capable of being pulled off without patronising the listener big-style. Martin uses the album to link the past to the present, enjoying the moment with players who are able to pass on the songs, help the tunes live on and share something of their origins.

Like Harry Smith's famous *Anthology of American Folk Music* reduced to a North Carolina bandwidth, the work resists overcomplication, mixing old standards with Martin's unique take on the genre. It's the sound of an enthusiast, and as such is something you can dip in and out of, even if this co-author sees its rightful place as playing in the kitchen on Sunday mornings. I think the reverence therein deserves regular airing on the day of the Lord.

But Martin is also following a path laid down by friends closer to home – and re-igniting a passion that continues to feed the hearts of many of his North East England country folk: the love of America and the desire spiritually, if not physically, to seek communion with the Far West.

From Jeremiah Dixon to Eric Burdon and a million frustrated miners, truck drivers and shipyard workers in between, America has held great attraction. From the Irish immigrants whose initial fear of the coffin boats led to a shorter journey east and who dreamed of swapping the coal mine for the dust bowl, to the 'beat groups' of the sixties who swapped Newcastle City Hall for Madison Square Garden, Brown Ale for dope, and chips for tacos, there's always been an affinity between the North East of England and North America.

A drive out along the A68 from Corbridge southwards takes you past Castleside, Tow Law and Crook and deposits you in the Wear Valley, west of Bishop Auckland, amidst some of the most attractive countryside in Western Europe. But take your time when you're next out here and look out for the Stetson-wearing cowboy, the lone horseman and the tall rider looking for his own Blue Moon of Tantobie. Fellow County Durham songwriter Paddy McAloon's last apparition as Prefab Sprout was to bring together a selection of Country Music, some of which had been written for Jimmy Nail, another North Easterner who could not get the itch out of his system until 'Crocodile Shoes' became the lotion.

When last seen, McAloon was sporting a beard that made the Dubliners' recently departed Ronnie Drew look like he wore a permanent five o'clock shadow, but the point is made. There is an almost obligatory sense of fellowship between North Easterners and New Frontiersmen, and Martin Stephenson is the latest in a long line of explorers who is bringing it back home.

The Haint of the Budded Rose would not be the number one recommendation for anyone new to his particular canon, but for those interested in understanding the roots of popular western music, the album's charm is in the way it steps back to go forward. The Band's particular historical palette was no doubt wider than the chimes of old Carolina, but in essence, Robbie Robertson and his pals were still drawing on the past in a similar way.

'To travel to a foreign country by the power of its music is an exciting and helpless must,' Martin writes in the accompanying booklet. 'To be greeted with such warmth and visionary guides was truly a gift from God.' The love invested in the booklet is apparent and the detail awe-inspiring. One imagines it could be set as an A-Level text in future years and you wouldn't need to look anywhere else to find the answers.

The 46 tracks that journey over two disks don't take you on any unexpected diversions, but ramble from porch to porch and front room to front room, introducing you to voices from the near and far past – and some, like Jeremy Stephens, from the future.

Starting with a track recorded back in the Highlands, 'Oral Tradition' features a short introduction from Dolph and a gift back to the people of North Carolina from Martin – and all the way through to 'New Five Cent Piece', 46 songs later, there's affection, education and the joy of opening up the music of the Tar Heel State.

With a modicum of commercial success Martin would no doubt be producing, directing and starring in a TV documentary about the roots of modern music, like BBC2's *Coast* set to banjos. But that wouldn't be right. In actual fact *The Haint* is more than this. It's the homework you leave until last because it's the most fun to do.

But the urge to explore and re-present the past did not leave him. He'd soon co-write a play with scriptwriter Graham Rhodes entitled *Ramblin' Boys*, which was videoed and which told the story of Charlie Poole and the North Carolina Ramblers. *The Haint* contributed a large part of the soundtrack – it was evident that this exercise had stirred something deep inside – and Martin called upon a host of actors and musicians from the North East, as if aware of the psychological link. Graham 'Shippy' Anderson, Ray Burns, Gypsy Dave Smith, Jim Hornsby, Stephen Foster-Pilkington and Peter McCormick formed the 'orchestra pit' while local actors Margaret Cowan, Crystal Millard, Alun Gunter, Chris Parrinder and Jonathan Ashton brought the story to life. There were only two performances (22 and 23 June 2003) of a work that surely deserves a new airing, as a companion piece to *The Haint*.

But if there's one element of *The Haint* that engages the casual listener it's the sense of communion between the protagonists. Martin has used the phrase 'the power of the small' as representing a kind of guiding philosophy for him, and the uniqueness of the North Carolina gathering ended up re-invigorating a need to engage with people not just from a stage, albeit a small one, but from within. So, on the weekend of 27 and 28 September 2003, Martin's first ever guitar weekend took place.

The venue? The Howood Inn just outside Glasgow. If attendance was any indication of success then it was unlikely to be repeated, as apparently very few people turned up. The idea was sound though: to have fun playing guitar, to learn a few new picks and patterns and to make friends.

Inevitably, the call went out and within a short while the idea had been refined by one Andrew Bailey and the annual Martin Stephenson Guitar Weekend was born, shortly to be augmented in 2005 by a Songwriters' Weekend, which again has developed into an annual event.

With Martin having somehow sated the need to travel in any number of directions simultaneously, the final few weeks of 2003 saw the recording of the *Airdrie* album which, like the football team bearing the same name, was going to find it difficult to emerge into the light. While Airdrieonians capitulated at around this time (to be replaced eventually by Airdrie United), Martin's album only exists in the hands of those few trusting folk prepared to part with their cash the minute it appeared, for a disagreement with Blooming Generation records would lead to its immediate withdrawal from sale.

One might ask why Martin would abandon the reliable and supportive Voiceprint to test the waters with another company – albeit as an agreed one-off. But then again, you don't make omelettes without breaking eggs and Martin doesn't make records without someone losing their temper.

It will come as no surprise to learn that my co-author was one of the first to obtain *Airdrie* and while many Martin fans will have heard some of the songs courtesy of their appearance on his MySpace site, a full listen to the album reveals (typically) one of the finer works in the Stephenson discography.

This well-rounded, painstakingly produced album manages to combine Martin's love of the moment with a desire to provide a rich, melodious listen. The playing and singing is strong throughout and songs such as 'Mountainous Spring' and 'Nairn Beach' convey the peace endowed by a long Scottish sojourn. There's even a kids' song on the album – a genre that Stephenson could develop further if he wished, such is his facility with a younger audience. If there's one group of people that respond to Martin's wide-eyed innocence, it's the wide-eyed and innocent. The fact is, an accidental harmonic in a live set might produce a grimace from the mixing desk, but not when our man is playing. I've witnessed a group of previously hyperactive under-tens sit in a worshipful silence as Martin uses this technique to conjure up the sound of stars and raindrops.

The *Airdrie* incident, as it's come to be known, also produced the latest in a line of fall-outs. On this occasion it was the end of the relationship between Martin and Iain Strefford, who first became involved during the previous year's tour of Germany. Strefford had lost money in the *Airdrie* venture, but like many had probably overestimated Martin Stephenson's interest in the commercial aspects of recording. As even-handed as an author tries to be, it's not difficult to understand why the commercial world has found it difficult to lure our man back into the tent.

And while we're defending the authors of this book, we don't want to be associated with the promotion of unofficial or illegal recordings. But if you must hear *Airdrie* in its entirety, join the E-group. Someone there will be able to help, I promise you.

People don't evolve in neat annual cycles and it's a curious human artifice that requires such a summary when reviewing the works of another, but in trying to reconcile the multiple journeys taken this year, it's tempting to see them as an English summer. As I sit and complete this chapter, it's late August. We've had several consecutive days' rain, but also splashes of tremendous sunlight and refreshing gusts of wind. We've heard about hailstones on the M56 and floods in Northern Ireland and this meteorological review only takes us to the start of the week.

Such was Martin's 2003. From the nod to commerciality that aspects of the German tour invoked to the bright sunshine of *The Well of Harmony*; from the re-release of the first four albums with their celebratory but familiar air to *The Haint of the Budded Rose* with its North Carolina musical history tour; from *Ramblin' Boys* on a tiny Tyneside stage to one of his best but least known albums and another fall-out, we had all four seasons in rapid succession.

We watch the weather broadcast on TV, even though we know they'll be wrong. But half the fun is in not knowing. When your driver is without a conventional map, you go to the less visited places.

*

Like the *Fast Show* version of Barbara Cartland whose only task is to fill the pages, it would be easy for Rich and me to produce our very own Mountainous Spring of Martin Material. We'd simply do this by listing out every gig played, since this was now the 'day job'. Martin was continuing his personal journey, cropping up in the most unusual and least remarkable places. But 2004 would see him further flung than ever. Any other touring musician would need an army of logistics experts, accountants and deal-makers to complete an Australian tour successfully. For Martin, however, all that was required were a few phone calls to a bunch of mates and a trip to Trailfinders.

If anyone loves the Buddy Holly song 'True Love Ways' as much as I do, they'll share my admiration of the opening to the song. I'm not referring to the wonderful opening refrain but to the few almost inaudible words that precede it. You're hearing the directions from the producer and co-writer Norman Petty. The assembled cast of musical pioneers were using Petty's studio in Clovis, New Mexico and had happened upon the observation that the use of orchestration somehow magnified Holly's voice.

It occurs to you that this is a live take! There's something magical about a song that would require several thousand overdubs these days were it to be placed in the hands of Ronan Keating or some such. But even though orchestration was required, it's the sound of a band at the top of their game, standing to attention, buttoned up to the collar and respecting their more experienced forebear by producing a perfect take that to this day must still provide a great deal of succour to Maria Elena Santiago. *Just you know why.*

About 1600 miles north east from the scene of this glorious recorded moment (and around 46 years later), Martin Stephenson now re-appeared in North Carolina to record the sessions that would make up the new *Hell's Half Acre* album. Like Holly, Martin and Dolph Ramseur were after the 'moment' but unlike Holly, the occasional bum note or backfire would not spoil the session but authenticate it. For *Hell's Half Acre* would be a return to the backyards of *The Haint*, but this time, straight down the middle pickin' style rather than a storytelling experience.

By simply erecting a series of microphones around the very same front porches of the previous year's journeys, Martin and Dolph were able to commit to disk the real North Carolina sound.

Having spent the first part of the year in Australia and North America it was time to come back to Scotland, increasingly the spiritual home. August saw the sessions for the next album, *Wheel of Fortune*. This album was recorded with a father/son duo from the Highlands called John and Isaac Sutherland.

There's nothing spectacular about such a collaboration, but it wouldn't be part of the Stephenson folklore had it been a straightforward, conventional recording. Martin was again interested in the moment and the sonic possibilities of getting closer to nature. On this occasion he was straying as close to the sea as is generally advisable and recording in a lighthouse.

Martin had met John and his son Isaac through the Scottish music scene and had spent time with them in their Highland home smoking dope and looking out to the North Sea. The trio had been playing in and around Tain, Portmahomack and Invergordon, developing a facility with the Stephenson musical compendium to the point that the resulting album, recorded at Sandstorm Promontory in a lighthouse built in 1831, would feature old songs such as 'Alabama Man' (from *Red Man's In Town*) as well as new numbers like the title track. The last track, 'Worried Man', had originally been planned as part of *The Boy's Heart* some 12 years previously, but appears here rejuvenated by Isaac's remarkable musicianship. His regular appearance as a Daintees stand-in drummer is testimony to the impression created.

Second cousin to Dire Straits' 'Twisting by the Pool', 'Long Way To Go' opens the album with a mid-paced afternoon dance number, quickly followed by 'Stone Broke Stone Cold Sober', making its first appearance in the Stephenson canon (and to re-appear three years later on *Western Eagle*). Reminiscent of Dr Feelgood's 'Milk and Alcohol', one can imagine the customers of the bar rooms of Easter Ross getting incredibly sweaty to this one.

The third track, 'The Fool', even nods towards gothic/progressive rock music, recreating the Psychedelic Furs, and 'Happiness Cloud' takes as its starting point *Sandinista*-period Clash reggae, adds a dash of ska and provides us with our first Andrea Mackie moment on the album.

Having stepped away from the more conventional genres (if that's not a contradiction in terms when contemplating the Stephenson back catalogue) the next track 'Stone Wall Jackson' evokes a Toe Rags hoedown with a rousing harmonica line.

More bar-room boogie with 'Alabama Man' and an excerpt from *The Well of Harmony* follows. 'The Ball of Torridon' takes us (not for the first time) back to The Shadows and the Gateshead twang of Mr Marvin while the title track finds Martin comfortably sat within the country vibe.

'Around With You' and 'The Age of Meditation' continue the uptempo vibe with the latter finding us thinking the Sutherland Brothers and Stephenson combination might one day revisit *Collective Force* – they seemed to be really enjoying themselves during this recording.

The upbeat acoustic waltz 'Hangman' runs away from home and tries to join the North Carolina Ramblers while 'Bad4U' and 'Worried Man' bring the album to a close: one a country-esque twang of a ditty and the other creating a 'Sunday Halo' feel.

It was at this point that the E-group tracked Martin down to a pub on the Isle of Bute for another gathering of the clan. Among the notable guests were Bap Kennedy, brother of the better known Irish singer Brian Kennedy; and irascible singer/musician Baz Warne – ex-Toy Doll and now front man of the Hugh Cornwell-free Stranglers, guitarist of some note and owner of the fantastically named alter ego Robot Elvis. One E-group member recalls a 'hard-looking bald-headed man who could kick off at any moment'. Then again, that could describe this writer. Hardly the circumstances for a quiet period of reflection, but remembered with affection by those who were there.

One incident recalled by many featured Finn McArdle, the noted percussionist who has played with Martin on many occasions over recent years. Finn and Martin were playing in the bay window of the bar, with a sash window open behind them. Finn's mobile went off mid-song and without missing a beat he took it out of his shirt pocket and tossed it out of the window, to roars of laughter. Martin then intentionally let the song run on for ages just so Finn didn't have the chance to go out and collect the offending phone.

The latter part of 2004 saw Martin again pursuing sonic adventures and looking at capturing some of his songs in a new environment. Lincoln Cathedral was chosen for its obvious choral qualities, and the resulting album (and accompanying DVD) *Lincoln Cathedral* would follow some nine months later.

The songs on this album were all familiar to E-group members and other Martin-watchers. 'Rowan Berries', 'Solomon', 'Great Star of Fraternity' and 'Lilac Tree' all received another airing, albeit augmented by the natural echo of a building thought to have been constructed originally in 1072, placing it several centuries before the lighthouse at Sandstorm Promontory. With Martin accompanied again by John and Isaac Sutherland, E-group members were asking 'what next? Martin plays the Coliseum?'

But joking apart, the function of the cathedral is to be the heartbeat of any community and to offer a place for worship. Martin's choice of such a natural sonic chamber is understandable in pure music terms but also places his music in a new context: one of celebration and praise for creation.

When one considers that not half a dozen albums away in the artist's canon, you could hear the same songs played raucously in a bar near Cork or by a stream in Derbyshire, it's clear that the songwriter was either searching for the authentic version of these pieces or perhaps considering that in their different guises they were, in fact, different songs.

To some of the E-group, the album is for 'completists' only, but in the chronology of Lincoln Cathedral, the recording stands out spectacularly. Check it out yourself. Martin's work nestles alongside uncomfortable bedfellows such as Nigel Ogden and his church organ (and many others with their, err, church organs).

If we accept that Martin's spiritual journey is to be characterised by a need to communicate more closely with people, then *Lincoln Cathedral* is a particularly strong example of this communion.

The set of songs is familiar. Tracks like 'Solomon' have made several appearances now, but one resists the temptation to criticise the artist for repeating himself. In reality, each release is more akin to a live appearance by a career artist. But in Martin's hands, the songs are simply an update – an email from where he is today. 'Here's what I'm doing now,' it says. 'See if you like it.'

Upon opening the CD a second disk is to be found. Play this and you hear the Dallas Simpson Binaural version of the recording. Wait a few months for the DVD and you get to see Dallas walking around the artists chasing the muse in a slightly unnerving manner with his unique 'in ear' microphones. As Martin himself describes him in the sleeve notes, he's the 'Doctor Who of Binaural'.

Latterly artists such as Christian Forshaw have fused modern arrangements with choral and worship music to produce a genre that sounds at once deeply ancient and refreshingly new. Likewise Iarla Ó Lionáird takes the Sean Nós tradition – old style Gaelic a cappella singing – and places it within a context of modern ambience, folk melting into electronica, melodies disappearing, deteriorating and returning. The background gives the voice space to breathe and emphasises the spiritual nature of the message. *Lincoln Cathedral*'s touch is light and if there is a criticism of this approach it is perhaps the lack of new Martin material. But there I go again – thinking like a consumer.

*

We come to the period of writing this book. From even earlier than 2005 Rich had been discussing the idea of charting Martin's journey ('career' somehow seemed inappropriate), obtaining the 'thumbs up' from the artist but then wondering how he would complete the massive task of sifting through the archives, the personal recollections and the massive database of craic accumulated through so many E-group friendships.

Having paused to approve the idea of a book, Martin was off again: first to Australia where he repeated the adventures of the previous spring, re-engaging with old friends and attracting new ones; and then to Scotland – Dumfries specifically – where the now well organised and administered Guitar Weekend would take place in April.

Born of a lighthouse, *Wheel of Fortune* finally saw the light of day in June 2005, arriving shortly (and chronologically correctly) before *Lincoln Cathedral* (August 2005).

At the end of 2005 this co-author comes into the story. Nowhere near as qualified a 'Martin fan' as any of the E-group, I'd last listened to Martin's music in 1992 when *The Boy's Heart* became one of the first CDs I'd bought. I recall telling my wife Ana that he was the first artist whose music I owned on vinyl (*Boat to Bolivia*), cassette (*Gladsome, Humour and Blue* and *Salutation Road*) and the new CD.

It amuses me now to recall how ownership simply underlined the notion of music as a commodity – a product to be used to enrich the people with the least interest in the emotion generated.

But back in late 2005 I was planning a surprise party for Ana. The publication of the revelation that she was to complete 40 years on the planet in the late spring of 2006 will not impress her now, but it's important for it brought me into contact with Bob Paterson, who for some time now had been helping Martin with booking and organising gigs.

While messing around on the internet, I came across Martin's website, after basically asking myself the question: what is Martin Stephenson up to these days? What I discovered was that it was possible to book him to play your own gig. I acted quickly and following a couple of early email exchanges with Bob Paterson, I'd soon hear direct from Martin himself.

When, shortly into 2006, I revealed to the intended guests that I'd booked him to play, a diverse group of 40-year-old-plus ex-Sheffield University students broke into spontaneous reminiscences. I hadn't appreciated what an impact he'd had on one of his several visits to the Octagon in Sheffield in the early- to mid-eighties. There were executives from the pharmacy industry, publishing directors, journalists, teachers and (to cries of 'we're not worthy') people who were still students. The buzz ensured a 100% response to the invitation from guests, while my better half remained unaware of the 'blast from the past' that was about to remind us all that he'd never gone away in the first place.

Logistically the evening presented a couple of problems. We needed to get the guests there before Ana, and we also needed to get Martin there early enough to do a soundcheck and to settle in. A plan was drawn up. I would drive up to the venue first, ostensibly to make sure all the catering was organised. Martin would arrive next, then the guests and then Ana, who until this point knew only that there would be a reunion of some sort, unaware of the location or the schedule.

I can dimly recall the rider presented by our guest performer. Usually one might expect a crate of extra strength lager, some cigarettes and a packet of Skittles (but only the green ones). Having set aside a couple of hours to procure said items I received a call from Martin asking only for some pistachio nuts, a cheese sandwich and a bottle of water (he never did eat the sandwich). I made the assumption that my supplier – an independent organic food store in Halifax – would somehow meet with the approval of my guest. What a crazy rock 'n' roll world.

As the time approached for Martin's arrival, I was preparing the pre-gig music: a selection of songs, old and new, that would have some meaning for those gathered. From Pete Wylie's 'The Story of the Blues', via the Passions' 'I'm in Love with a German Film Star' to the Cocteau Twins' 'Heaven or Las Vegas' and from Wire's 'Outdoor Miner', via Talk Talk's 'It's My Life' to anything coming out of Sheffield in the early 80s and a basket of salsa from Juan Luis Guerra to Rubén Blades, it felt appropriate for the evening. It's worth saying that we also were forced to shoehorn Girls Aloud's 'Biology' in for the youngsters. None of the gentlemen present in the early part of the evening knew anything about Girls Aloud, but interest did increase when a photograph of said lissom pop group was presented.

My phone rang. It was Martin. 'My guitar broke so I had to divert to Newcastle to pick up a spare. I'll be with you in half an hour.' Smiling nervously, I thanked him for the call and started on the task of biting my fingernails to the bone.

The guests began to arrive and the sun obliged by warming up the late spring afternoon. The kids gathered outside on the upper deck of Cragrats Mill in Holmfirth, West Yorkshire, while the adults greeted each other and began the age-old reunion tradition of pretending that 'you haven't changed a bit'. Even if my glabrous state and more rounded figure declared the opposite, I could actually claim the statement was true. The fact is, when last seen I was probably wearing the same shirt.

At this point – and dangerously close to my wife's planned arrival time – I received a second phone call from Martin, just to clarify local directions. He was upon us.

But so were my wife, kids and parents. I stepped outside. It was still light and two cars were making their way up the hill. In the first, an old but sturdy C-series Mercedes, was Martin. In the second, my wife and kids. Although I was tempted to run out, best man-style, and instruct them to do a lap of the block, I was forced to act more reasonably, so managed, with the help of a friend, to smuggle Martin around the back while my wife, wide eyed with surprise, walked into a throng of guests. Martin never did get to do that soundcheck.

So there we were: 50-odd guests, musical reminiscences, a curry buffet and a former 80s heart throb nibbling at a pistachio in the green room.

One by one I brought various guests in to meet Martin. My sisters Catherine and Sarah, my best pal Mark and one or two others (who still had the poetry book that came originally with *Gladsome, Humour and Blue*) wandered in, starry-eyed, to come between the minstrel and his cheese sandwich.

After the food, the lights darkened and my daughter Elena took the microphone. 'Ladies and gentlemen,' she announced as my wife caught a glimpse of my own guitar resting against the back of the performance area (and probably drew a gloomy conclusion about whom she was about to hear singing). My daughter continued 'All the way from County Durham … it's Martin Stephenson!'

I can recall every detail of the evening that followed: the riotous combination of songs, from Chet Atkins via children's songs to Doc Watson, raps on encounters between Julian Cope and Gypsy Dave and an obliging 'request' section where rapt members of the audience called for their favourites.

True, there were few requests for anything chronologically placed after *The Boy's Heart*, but that mattered little. Our guest had conjured up an atmosphere that the organiser could not have dreamed of: an ability to connect with every member of the audience. At one stage my brother-in-law Martin approached the stage to offer our singer a pint of lager. It was politely declined, but rather than casting off the offer, it led to an entertaining rap on all of the demons that Martin Stephenson was trying to overcome. My brother-in-law felt less like an interloper and more like a participant in a comedy sketch.

At one stage Martin transformed the atmosphere by producing a series of harmonics and engaging all of the youngsters present by comparing them to rain drops and stars, while at the end of the show, rather than walking into the embrace of 50-odd portly ex-students (I can hear them saying: 'speak for yourself') he sat down next to my parents and spent an hour talking about common acquaintances from Stanley and Consett, County Durham.

The Stephenson travelling market stall was then produced: an old suitcase containing a miasma of material: all of the CDs, the poetry books and much more. We buzzed around him like wasps on a rare English summer's day.

To the vast majority of the people in the room, this was not a comeback, but a new beginning. There were people there who were new to his music and there were those present who were patiently waiting for either 'Running Water' or 'Crocodile Cryer', but the consensus at the end of the evening was that it was a total vindication of the decision to turn his back on the path of musical careerist, and an evening to live long in the memory.

It felt like a family gathering, a ceilidh, a celebration of the power of music to bring people together. It was authentic. There was no set list, just an invitation to make requests and challenge the minstrel to reach out to all of us.

The evening ended with guests walking back down the hill to local B&Bs, hotels and friends' houses, children laughing in the darkness and me and my publisher being told by our guest that we should speak to a friend of his called Richard Cundill. The rest, as they say, is history. Or given the time it's taken us to pull this together, maybe the rest was double Latin, because with so much happening all of the time with Martin, it hurts your head to choose those little moments that define him so richly.

He told us he was interested in the 'power of the small', not the grand gestures or the big artistic and commercial manoeuvres, and one can imagine Martin rejecting the idea of offering a new album free, on-line, in favour of turning up in your kitchen and playing the new songs live.

The next day Ana's mobile phone rang. It was Martin. He was ringing to make sure she'd enjoyed her evening. If this man were ever to issue customer feedback forms, his advocacy levels would be outstanding.

So in 2006 my second Stephenson period began. I had a lot to catch up on and after spending all of my beer money on *The Haint of the Budded Rose*, I was immediately struck by the variety of the canon post-*The Boy's Heart*. I was soon also struck by my wife, when she realised I'd spent the beer money.

Rich and I met up shortly afterwards, and through Ronan Fitzsimons' careful curation, we began to figure out a way of stepping back and recording the journey we were both witnessing from completely different perspectives. One of us, the arch-fan, the archivist, the friend and the supporter; the other, starry-eyed, discovering that one of his favourite artists had just released sixteen 'lost albums' all at once. Like having Dennis Wilson appear in your front room on Christmas Eve and play 'River Song' just for you, with an angelic chorus behind him, it's sometimes hard to be objective, but the contrasting perspectives of my distance and Rich's proximity have hopefully helped follow the clues and present an objective view of Martin's particular song.

*

2006 ended with news of the deaths of both Bob Lyng and drummer Alex Ross, friends and fellow collaborators, and while Martin's back-catalogue sales continued to rise as a result of the Holmfirth evening, the year saw no halting to the continuous travelling and performing.

A DVD version of the *Lincoln Cathedral* album was released late in 2006, while Rich caught Martin at a gig in the Highlands at the same time. Somewhere like Evanton, a large village in Easter Ross, was not only hosting a leaving do, where the beer was flowing, but also an appearance by our artiste.

Rich's memories are clear. A great atmosphere, the teetotal performer engaging a group of well-oiled audience members, but then things changed. One of the audience left, prompting a row with Martin. Not easy to reconcile with the picture of easy interaction portrayed elsewhere in this book, but a fairly common occurrence in actual fact. It seems like Martin often places himself in awkward positions – deliberately – to see how capable he is of extracting himself from such situations. That's our view, at least, but it possibly helps explain why so many people could fall out with someone ostensibly so loveable and people-oriented.

2007 saw the release of 'son of Haint': *Hell's Half Acre*. Recorded on a front porch in North Carolina with Dolph Ramseur, Jim Hornsby and friends, the record was initially unavailable in the UK until one bright E-group spark noticed that you could order direct from the States (ignoring the international restrictions on the Ramseur Records website) and enjoy what is a real shit-kicker of an album back in Blighty.

Originally recorded in the summer of 2004, the record was mostly put to tape in the place named Hell's Half Acre (Midland,

North Carolina). It was subsequently enhanced by the addition of three extra tracks: 'Solomon', 'Time with Jesus' and 'You Become the Wind and I Become the Mountain'.

Again the track listing would not have surprised E-group members and other Martin-watchers. Opening with 'Salutation Road', the set includes old favourites such as 'Big Sky New Light' (albeit in a new North Carolina Ramblers setting), 'Lilac Tree' and 'Blind Man Blues'.

However, it was the appearance of some of the Daintees' originals from the early- to mid-eighties that caught the ear of the listener. 'In the Heal of the Night' and, especially, 'Rain', seemed to sit uncomfortably in the company of so many more recent songs, but the context and the striking production, which puts you on the porch, serving the artists lemonade, brings out the depth of the originals.

'Big Sky New Light' starts off like one of George Harrison's post-*Revolver* meditational adventures, until that familiar warm winter's coat of a voice takes you back to roads better remembered. Elsewhere 'Steel String' and 'Nairn Beach', both of which appear on *Airdrie*, create the impression that Martin – and his 'curvaceous Momma' – are in the room next door.

Everything is conducted through Martin's voice. 'Take a left turn, baby. No comebacks!' he chirps during 'Steel String' as Jim Hornsby produces a wolf whistle on the steel guitar. And on the title track, one cannot help but imagine oneself riding the back of a truck watching the trees roll by. Listen close enough and the truck turns up half way through the song!

And while *Hell's Half Acre* strode back several decades, 2007's most notable event took place at the Jazz Café in August, when Martin and his Daintees travelled back a mere 20 years to acknowledge a current trend in live music and re-visit a former glory. They were to play the *Boat to Bolivia* album in its entirety. The first night sold out and the second night fell only slightly short of full capacity. Those present were treated to a night of celebration, of reunion with old friends and no little humour too.

This and the appearance of a newly designed Daintees website led to a period of re-discovering past paths trodden. The Daintees were back in town, with the line-up of Anth and Gary Dunn, John Steel, his wife Kate Stephenson on drums, and Andrea Mackie on backing vocals. Late 2006 saw the re-invigorated band of friends alight at Stuart McLeod's studio in Scotland to record *Western Eagle*: Martin Stephenson and The Daintees' first studio album for 16 years.

But even while the band was pulling the songs together, another had already sneaked out. *High 7 Moon 5* was released in 2007. Like many of the more recent albums, this was not a set of new material but a revisiting of songs like 'Mountainous Spring' and 'Solomon' (again, albeit it trying to disguise itself under a different spelling) with a bunch of friends whom Martin had met at the Kalamazoo Club in London and over recent years' touring.

The album, with a cover that looked like a birthday card you would send to your Grandma, drew the attention, as did 'Teardrops In My Tequila', 'Ballad of the English Rose', 'Once I Loved a Sailor' and 'Tynemouth Sands', which sneaked out via Martin's MySpace page before the album arrived – a habit that has not gone unnoticed by the E-group.

The group supporting Martin on this outing was new. Chris Clarke engineered the record, played bass and, according to Martin, was 'the driving force behind this record in all aspects and areas, from engineering to playing with the lightest of touches.' BJ Cole supplied pedal steel, which does indeed add an extra dimension to 'Soloman' (as it's called here), and is joined by Sean Reid's keyboards and backing vocals. Trevor Smith plays drums.

This able backing crew helped support the three principal collaborators on the record: first, Brian Younger, a North East contemporary of Martin, who supplied guitars and banjo; next, Fiddling Jim Morrison, a name that conjures up a new career for the Lizard King on a front porch in North Carolina; and finally a name that had never been far from Martin over the years – Helen McCookerybook.

By this time Martin was, as often as not, to be seen performing with the assistance of Ms McCookerybook. As mentioned way back at the start of this book, he'd been a fan of Helen's band The Chefs, while she'd been a fan of The Daintees in the early 80s.

Over time, communication began, initially by email and then through the medium of live performance. *High 7 Moon 5* sees their first official collaboration and the results are solid. 'Once I Loved a Sailor' reveals a ripple of humour in Helen's bright and infectious tones and 'Hungry Hash House', a solid hoedown, opens up with a 'Steve, Andy, uh-huh, we're The Sweet' – which I'm embarrassed to say I recognise from my own collection of the great works of Messrs Connolly, Tucker, Scott and Priest.

Humour abounds, as it often does, but comes much nearer the surface on this sprightly collection of tunes, but there are also moments of pure emotion. The opening few bars of 'Mountainous Spring' propel it forward gracefully and Martin's singing, which has, if anything, grown stronger over the years, is confident.

Departing again from Voiceprint records, but this time more successfully than with the fated *Airdrie* outing, the album was put out by Stove Pony Records – another example of the benefit of not being tied to anyone at any particular time.

But it's *Western Eagle* that has grabbed the attention in 2008. Hearing a refreshed band putting so much passion and skill into what are mostly new songs has seen an increase in interest in Martin Stephenson and the complexities of his back catalogue.

What's more, reviewers and fans alike can see an upping of quality in some of the songs – in the production, the 'feel' and the need to hear them again. 'God is in the detail,' as they say, and the rich production values of the album, most evident in the twin bookends of 'Western Eagle' (Parts One and Two) themselves, underpin a new confidence that this is music that should be shared with the masses again.

Whether this will come to pass is probably irrelevant. Much as we fans would like to see a critical reappraisal of Martin's music, the reality is that he himself would prefer to focus on the small. There once was a feature in the *Sunday Times* and we all felt justified – proud, even – of our connection, but any sight of a promoter or record company executive approaching him is still likely to result in the sight of a man in dungarees and a small jovial hat running for the hills and laughing hysterically.

And yet the album deserves a wider listen. It's the sound of a man at peace with his surroundings, ready to draw conclusions at this stage of the journey and happy to pass on every tiny piece of wisdom: the microcosmic entertainer indeed.

It opens with the expansive and atmospheric 'Western Eagle (Part One)', a simple piano motif echoing against a wide symphonic backdrop. No lyrics, just a vibe that announces something special and 'We Are One' delivers straightaway. This second track has a circular melody that engages upon the first listen and a swirling Hammond organ intro that tells you something good is coming along. What is striking to this listener is the warmth and the age in Martin's voice. It sounds lived-in, relaxed and confident in its advice. The tune is rounded and memorable and it augurs well for The Daintees' first outing in many years. More than that, it's a new song and one of several on the new album.

'Right By You' follows with its claps and its Smiths-like changes and twists: it could even be Johnny Marr on that shiny guitar. Reminiscent of mid-period Squeeze ('Some Fantastic Place') the backing vocals are harmonious and rousing.

But an engaging little folk ditty is never far away and 'Shadow of the Sun' – a delightful story song – starts off as if there's only Martin in the room. But the rest of the band is not far away and the song fair rattles along with harmonica and brushed drum skins.

'Stone Broke Stone Cold Sober' is little more than a call and response but 'Change My Music' does exactly what the title says. Again, the Smiths are not far away and for some curious reason the 'ba ba ba' backing vocals evoke Teardrop Explodes' Julian Cope – 'Passionate Friend' perhaps – a man whose later musical journeys would challenge Martin's for their unexpected directions.

'I Cannot Run' is, in the context of Martin's current music, the opposite. A simple tune, it reduces the pace before 'Open Road' opens with an angelic chorus and introduces us to Paris, New York, London and the Mississippi. In many ways this song, with its smiley words and upward melody, is what The Daintees should sound like in 2008, but the delight in this new album is the diversity and the ability of the group to turn their hands to a much more varied set of musical styles.

'Indian Summer' provides a quiet respite before 'Cherryade and Rock 'n' Roll', dedicated to 'Syd – Barrett not Vicious'. A simple Western Swing number, it evokes an afternoon at Coney Island in the 50s. Not that I've ever been there. Martin wrote this song when he was 15 – one of the first he ever did.

'The Bubble' starts up like closing time at a nightclub. Distant tinkling piano and Tom Waits sax help him tell a seemingly sad tale, but the song is lifted by the 'higher calling' of the chorus. The quality and diversity of the record has been maintained easily, even if Martin's voice is sometimes low in the mix, allowing the band's virtuosity to shine through – like the wonderful guitar solo here. There are onion layers of magic within *Western Eagle*.

But the best is still to come. 'Western Eagle (Part 2)' may start out like a trippy cousin of Double's 'Captain of Her Heart' – Kurt Maloo and Felix Haug's little piece of pop perfection in 1986 – but it has the confidence to grow, the acoustic guitar solo grounding the final track of the album in tradition: leaving us truly unplugged and standing next to the artist in a pub in a small village in North West Durham.

Initially well received by the critics (at a time when any appearance of a review would have raised an eyebrow) it's proved to be a real grower, with many of the E-group members initially not excited but over time displaying more and more affection for the work.

The release of *Western Eagle* might have merited a grand affair in other commercial music environments, but it more or less sneaked out, initially into the hands of E-group members and then, following a much later official release date, into the hands of initially grateful reviewers.

The echoing piano motif of the opening version of 'Western Eagle' on the album will forever remind this co-author of the cornfields of Northern Indiana, as I took a train journey from Chicago to New York in the summer of 2008. I'd had little sleep; even more frustrating as my 12-year-old son dozed peacefully above me in our little roomette. I awoke at 5am to see the golden fields passing by. I picked up the iPod and pressed play and the song etched itself effortlessly into my subconscious, forever to be associated with that magical morning … and the sound of a young voice above me: *can we go for breakfast, Dad?*

The smiles on the faces of the crowd at the Jazz Café gig in August testified to a million other subconscious connections, some of which began face to face in a small hostelry in the Highlands and some, like Jane Cooper's E-group, further south.

Jane's painful past had produced a permanent community of Martin's friends. They'd served to help him through some difficult times (helping stave off financial disaster at the time of *Lilac*

Tree) and also been there during the many moments of glory. They would put the word out on new releases faster than any corporate machine and ensure new listeners had their very own induction course. Jane's crew have provided a protective shawl around Martin Stephenson without being defensive. They've created friendships and rekindled musical flames that people thought had died out long ago. And all of this from pain, extinguished by 'love and light' – a favourite invocation of Martin's.

*

Martin Stephenson's long journey began with a 'small step' as the old aphorism goes, but it's the multitude of other small, decisive ones that have defined his 30-year ego-free walking tour. From thrashing along with The Next and Strange Relations back in the late 70s to carrying recording equipment down a steep bank in the Derbyshire Dales, sitting in a cathedral in front of a bemused church cleaner and tuning up while peering out of a lighthouse window in the wilds of Scotland, the journey has taken him further than any commercial aspiration painted by the corporate guardians of his beloved Daintees.

One imagines that there are a lot of 'former pop stars' earning their dinner by sharing stories of how they turned their back on the business to pursue their inner goals, but in most examples, the likelihood is that the muse departed them and the world turned its back.

The fact that Martin Stephenson chose to abandon ship at the precise moment where LA-based session musicians were queuing up behind that familiar pork-pie-hatted figure has always tipped the scales in his favour, but it's his own reminiscences that turn the misted perception into stark reality. One in particular, culled from Martin's MySpace page, does the trick: 'There have been some memorable gigs up in the Highlands over the years. Once, Rob Ellen and I were broke and we needed ten pounds to get petrol to get to a gig at the Crask Inn in Sutherland. So Rob said, "my daughter's got twenty pounds in her TSB account. We'll hang around the school and see if she'll lend us it, you know!"

'So we were unshaven and hanging around the school. Anyway, she came out and she was really sharp – she wanted to charge us interest! It cost us twelve pounds fifty to get the tenner off her to get the juice to get up to Crask! And when we got up to Crask we got paid in venison pie and whisky. Just things like that really stand out from my time up here!'

And in case you thought I'd missed something, there's the final hidden track on the *Western Eagle* album. As is always the case with Martin, nothing is ever what it seems and he reaches back into his catalogue for a song that here becomes 'Track 13'.

The song 'Home' has not only appeared before (like several of its cousins) but also once appeared twice on the same record (*Martin and Jim Go Binaural*). It is a song of yearning with an uplifting response. In many ways it brings the story to a close, shuts the field gates for the night, puts out the fire, checks the kids are sleeping peacefully and takes you in its arms and hugs you. 'Home isn't always that house where you were born / It's just a light where love is strong / Every wayfaring stranger always winds up home.'

As this book prepares to go to press, Martin is due to release a new album called *California Star* (with a title track dedicated to Mickey Rourke) and also a collaboration with Helen McCookerybook entitled *Hamilton Square*. As ever, we are intrigued by the eclectic possibilities of what lies ahead.

Like the heroes from the past that showed him the way forward, Martin Stephenson has never faltered from his goal of closing the distance between people and flexing his well travelled muse to bring folk together. He's been travelling for a long, long time but in spite of the many miles wandered, he's never really been too far away.

Check him out at a gig in your town soon. Let that infectious smile etch itself indelibly into your memory – and tell him that Rich and Mark sent you.

Martin Stephenson – Discography

SINGLES

1982

Roll On Summertime/Involved With Love
Kitchenware SK3 (7" P/S)
The Daintees / Produced by Brad Grisdale / Reissued 1989

1984

Trouble Town/Better Plan
Kitchenware SK13 (7" P/S – glossy sleeve/paper label – with
London Records press handout) Also 2 other versions – matt
sleeve/plastic label & 'Crocodile Cryer' sleeve

Trouble Town/Jealous Mind (live)/Better Plan
Kitchenware SKX13 (12" P/S) – also promo version with same
tracks – London SKX13

**Trouble Town/Crocodile Cryer (Paddy McAloon
remix)/Jealous Mind (live)/Better Plan***
Kitchenware SKXR13 (12" P/S) / The Daintees / Produced by
Robin Millar (TT)/High Times Inc (BP) / Reissued 1986*

1986

**Inferno EP – Running Water/Look Down, Look Down
(live for Capitol Radio)/Synergy**
Kitchenware SKEP1 (7" P/S) / Martin Stephenson and The

Daintees
Produced by High Times Inc / Etched in side 1 run-off grooves
'DAINTIES EAT SMALL BOYS'

Crocodile Cryer (Edit)/Louis (Acoustic Version)
Kitchenware SK25 (7" P/S)

Crocodile Cryer (Full Version)/Louis (X-Mix)
Kitchenware SKX25 (12" P/S) – also promo version with same
tracks – London SKX25 / Etched in run-off grooves 'A F'N
CLASSIC' & 'DIVUUNT HIRRUS'
Produced by Gil Norton (CC)/Kenny McDonald (L)

Crocodile Cryer (Alternate take)/*3 tracks by other artists*
Record Mirror RM4 (12") / Martin Stephenson and The Daintees

Slow Lovin'/A Tribute to the Late Rev. Gary Davis
Kitchenware SK26 (7" P/S)
Martin Stephenson and The Daintees / Produced by Gil Norton
Etched in run-off grooves 'SLOW SENSUAL SEX SUPPLY' &
'THANKS TO KERSHAW AND CROWLEY'

Boat to Bolivia/Slaughterman
Kitchenware SK27 (7" P/S) & SKDP27 (7" P/S – double pack
with free copy of SK25)

**Boat to Bolivia (Extended Riverboat
Mix)/Slaughterman/Wholly Humble Heart**
Kitchenware SKX27 (12" P/S) & SKXDP27 (12" P/S – double
pack with free copy of SKX25)
Martin Stephenson and The Daintees
Produced by Paul Hardiman (BTB)/David Brewis (S & WHH)
also promo version with same tracks – Kitchenware SKXDJ27
also German version with same tracks – London/Metronome
886096-1

1988

There Comes a Time/Running Water
Kitchenware SK34 (7" P/S)

**There Comes a Time/Running Water/Little Red Bottle
(live)/Coleen (live)**
Kitchenware SKX34 (12" P/S)

There Comes a Time/Running Water (listed as 'Crocodile
Cryer')**/Little Red Bottle (live)/Coleen (live)**
Kitchenware SKXDJ34 (12") – promo

**There Comes a Time/Crocodile Cryer/ Coleen
(live)/Running Water**
Kitchenware SKCD34 (CDS)

There Comes a Time/Me and Mathew/The Wait (listed as 'I
Can See')
Kitchenware SKT34 (10" Album sampler) / Martin Stephenson
and The Daintees
Produced by Warne Livesey (TCAT)/Dave Brewis (TCAT
10")/High Times Inc (RW)/Paul Samwell-Smith (M&M/TW)

Wholly Humble Heart/Get Get Gone
Kitchenware SK36 (7" P/S) – 2 versions: paper sleeve/black label
& card sleeve/white label; also Dutch promo with same tracks –
London 886312 7

**Wholly Humble Heart (L.A.X.)/Get Get Gone/Come Back
To Me** (sleeve originally incorrectly lists 'I Can See (Live)'/
'Slow Lovin' (Live)' with correction sticker for 'Come Back To
Me')
Kitchenware SKX36 (12" P/S) also promo version with same
tracks – Kitchenware SKXDJ36

**Wholly Humble Heart (L.A.X.)/Get Get Gone/I Can See
(live)/Slow Lovin' (live)**
Kitchenware SKCD36 (CDS)

Wholly Humble Heart (L.A.X.)/Get Get Gone/ I Can See (live)/Slow Lovin' (live)
Kitchenware SKXR36 (12" P/S) / Also USA promo version with same tracks but censored 'gay boy' edit Capitol SPRO-79523 / Martin Stephenson and The Daintees / Produced by Russ Kunkel (WHH)/Paul Samwell-Smith (GGG)/Warne Livesey (CBTM)

Interview/Wholly Humble Heart/Migrants (live)/Let the Man (live)
Kitchenware SKF36
7" flexi – Interview with Deirdre O'Donahue on KCRW Radio Santa Monica
Martin Stephenson and The Daintees, 1988

1990

Left Us To Burn/Big North Lights/Eyot
Kitchenware SK44 (7" P/S) & SKTC44 (CASS)

Left Us to Burn/Big North Lights/Eyot/Kathy
Kitchenware SKX44 (12" P/S) also promo version with same tracks and press release
Kitchenware SKCD44 (CDS)
Martin Stephenson and The Daintees / Produced by Pete Anderson

Endurance/Men Can Be Flung
Kitchenware SK46 (7" P/S)

Endurance/Men Can Be Flung/Release the First
Kitchenware SKX46 (12" P/S) also promo version with same tracks and press release
Kitchenware SKCD46 (CD) & SKTC46 (CASS)
Martin Stephenson and The Daintees
Produced by Pete Anderson (E)/Dave Brewis (MCBF & RTF)

Let's Call the Whole Thing Off/Let's Call the Whole Thing Off
Kitchenware SK49 (7") / A-side – Martin Stephenson with Cathal Coughlan / AA-side – Cathal Coughlan with Martin Stephenson / Produced by Mickey Watson & Martin Stephenson (A-side)/Satan O'Sullivan (AA-side)

1992

Big Sky New Light/Song About the Member/Wake Me in the Morning
Kitchenware SK57 (7" P/S) & SKC57 (CASS)

Big Sky New Light/You Really Had a Heart/Looking For Some Peace of Mind/Let's Call the Whole Thing Off (with Cathal Coughlan)
Kitchenware SKCD57 Volume one (CDS)

Big Sky New Light/Far Away Meadows/Should My Friends Be Gone/Every Night
Kitchenware SKKCD57 Volume two (CDS) / Martin Stephenson and The Daintees
Produced by Lenny Kaye (BSNL)/Mickey Watson & Martin Stephenson (the rest)

2000

Lilac Tree (piano version)
MP3 single / Martin Stephenson / 2000

ALBUMS

1986

Boat to Bolivia
Kitchenware KWLP5 (LP) & KWC5 (CASS) – 11-track & 12-track*
Kitchenware KWCD5 (CD) – 12-track*
Martin Stephenson and The Daintees / Produced by Gil Norton
Crocodile Cryer/Coleen/Little Red Bottle/Tribute To the Late Reverend Gary Davis/Running Water/Candle in the Middle/Piece of the Cake/Look Down, Look Down/Slow Lovin'/Caroline/Rain/(Boat to Bolivia*)
Promo/foreign versions
Kitchenware KWLP5 – 11 tracks
London SAMP2 – BTB side 1//*Bronski Beat – Truth Dare Double Dare side 1*
London DJL223 – BTB (Riverboat mix)/BTB (single mix)//BTB side 1 – with insert*
Metronome 828045-1 (LP) (CD –2, CASS –4) – German release*
Barclay 828 012 1(LP) – French release
Released 1987*

1988

Gladsome, Humour and Blue
Kitchenware KWLP8 (LP – originally in gatefold sleeve; later version in single sleeve) & KWCD8 – 828091-2 (CD) & KWC8 (CASS)
Martin Stephenson and The Daintees / Produced by Paul Samwell-Smith/Dave Brewis
There Comes a Time/Slaughterman/The Wait/I Can See/The Old Church is Still Standing/Even the Night/Wholly Humble Heart/Me & Matthew/Nancy/Goodbye John/I Pray
Promo/foreign versions
Kitchenware cassette – with alternate take of Nancy
Capitol C1-91751 – double LP/CD USA version with some BTB tracks

Metronome 828091–1 (LP) (CD –2, CASS –4) – German release
Barclay 828 091-1 (LP) – French release (with translation – I
Can See is not listed on back sleeve)

1990

Salutation Road
Kitchenware 828198-1 (LP) & 828198-2 (CD)
Martin Stephenson and The Daintees / Produced by Pete
Anderson
Left Us To Burn/Endurance/In the Heal of the Night/Big North
Lights/Long Hard Road/Spoke in the Wheel/Heart of the
City/Too Much In Love/We Are Storm/Migrants/Morning
Time/Salutation Road
Promo/foreign versions
Kitchenware PKWLP12 & PKWC12 – LP & cassette promos –
Left Us To Burn/Endurance/We Are Storm/Salutation
Road//same on side 2
Capitol CDP794638 2 – USA CD version in long cardboard box
Metronome 828 198-1 (LP) (CD –2, CASS –4) – German release
Barclay – 828 198-1 (LP) – French release

1992

The Boy's Heart
Kitchenware 828324-1 aka KWLP19 (LP) & 828324-2 (CD)
Martin Stephenson and The Daintees / Produced by Lenny Kaye
Big Sky New Light/The Boy's Heart/We Can Roll/Ballad of the
English Rose/Neon Skies/Hollywood Fields/Sentimental
Journey/Sunday Halo/8.30 Mowbray Morning/(Least We've a)
Map in the World/Him, Her and the Moon/Cab Attack
Promo versions
Townhouse 328324-1 – promo cassette version
London – promo cassette version as above
Townhouse 328324-1 – promo cassette version with 4 tracks –
Big Sky New Light/Sunday Halo/The Boy's Heart/(Least We've
a) Map in the World

1993

High Bells Ring Thin
Kitchenware KWCD23 (CD)
Martin Stephenson / Produced by Martin Stephenson & Mickey Watson
You Really Had a Heart/Looking For Some Peace of Mind/Song About the Member/Should My Friends Be Gone/Don't Be Afraid of the Night/Far Away Meadows/Synergy/Wake Me in the Morning/I Live in the East/Him, Her and The Moon/Every Night/Music and Life/Let's Call the Whole Thing Off

There Comes a Time – The Best of Martin Stephenson and The Daintees
Kitchenware 828398-2 (CD)
Martin Stephenson and The Daintees
Little Red Bottle/Crocodile Cryer/Wholly Humble Heart/Spoke in the Wheel/Big Sky New Light/Me & Matthew/Running Water/There Comes a Time/Left Us To Burn/Nancy/You Really Had a Heart/Rain/We Are Storm/Hollywood Fields/Salutation Road/Look Down, Look Down/Candle in the Middle/Don't Be Afraid Of The Night

1995

Yogi In My House
Demon FIENDCD 762 (later Barbaraville BVCD007) (CD)
Demon FIEND 762 (LP – existence unproven)
Martin Stephenson / Produced by Martin Stephenson & Graham Henderson
Solomon/In Fire/Taker on the Globe/Think Only of the Child/New Wave/Spirit Child/Bridge of Nae Hope/Fair Company/Gone the Gypsy Davey/Always Us/Dance the Last Goodbye
Promo versions
Demon MSPROMO1 – 3 track CD – Bridge of Nae Hope/Always Us/Spirit Child

Sweet Misdemeanour
Demon FIENDCD 770 (CD)
Martin Stephenson featuring Joe Guillan on guitar / Produced
by Frank Gibbon
Maverick Waltz/Can't Find the Doorknob/Sweet
Misdemeanour/Candyman/I Could Never Be Happy/Rag Time
Groove/All I Do Is Dream/South Wind/Tremelo Men/Talking to
the Child/Keep This Time/Ball of Fire/Hold Me Love Me/Smokey
Mokes

1997

Beyond the Leap, Beyond the Law
Demon FIENDCD 938 (CD)
Martin Stephenson / Produced by Martin Stephenson & Emmet
Tinley
Losing All Part of the Dream/Testing Time/Great Star of
Fraternity/Wholly Humble Heart (Irish version)/Carry My
Friend/The Crying/Song of Love And Desertion/Great Spirit/Out
of Communion/The Waves/Hollow Days/Indian Summer/A Life
of Her Own/A Thing of It/Long Forgotten in This World/Don't Go
Home – last 4 tracks not listed

1998

When It's Gone, It's Gone
Get Rhythm GR/LE CD002 (CD)
Martin Stephenson & The Toe Rags / Produced by Joe Guillan
Wide Eyed and Sleepy/Barbarville/Cromarty Rag/Through the
Mist/Gettin' Tired/Bullshit/Johnny Guitar/Grafters/Barman's
Birthday/Papa's Going Crazy/Perkulatin'/Big Bill/Keep on the
Sunniside/Ramblin' On/Deep Elm Blues/Grafters (ver-
sion)/Barbarville (version)/Wide Eyed and Sleepy (ver-
sion)/Papa's Going Crazy (version)/Bullshit (version) – last 5
tracks not listed

1999

Martin Stephenson
Floating World FW002 (CD)
Martin Stephenson / Produced by Martin Stephenson & Gerry O'Riordan
Look Down, Look Down/Slaughterman/Better Plan/Always Us/Song of Love and Desertion/Sweet Misdemeanour/Little Red Bottle/Coleen/Bridge of Nae Hope/Running Water/Taker on the Globe/New Wave/The Wait

Red Man's in Town
Real To Reel 001 (CD)
Martin Stephenson & The Toe Rags / Produced by Joe Guillan
Duck Bill Blues/Rifleshot Blues/Highland Afternoon/The Ballad of Joe McCue/Red Man's in Town/Ballintrad Tickle/Crazy Times/Alabama Man/Play It Straight/Why Buy/High 7 Moon 5/Way Down Town/Follow the Dream/Turn Me Loose/Repent (by Deacon Jones and the Sinners)/Alabama Man (Version)/The Ballad of Joe McCue (Version)/Red Man's in Town (Outro) – last 4 tracks not listed

2000

Lilac Tree
Tree 001 (later Barbaraville BVCD010) (CD)
Martin Stephenson / Produced by Martin Stephenson & Frank Gibbon
Lilac Tree/Orange/Rainbow/2 Sorrows/Every Step/Folksinger/On the Brae/Country Shuffle/Peculiar Man/Rowan Berries/Posey Rorer/New Found Light/O So Far Removed

The Church and the Minidisc
No label (later Barbaraville BVCD008) (CD)
Martin Stephenson / Produced by Martin Stephenson & Pete Rawson
Bengarrick/You Are the One/Jane Bird Bell/When You Become the Wind and I Become the Mountain/Charlies's Flute –

Wounded Bird/The North Sea – Thatcher Is My
Shepherd/Absent Fathers/Intro Rowan Berries – Poor Boy –
Butterfly Winged Rag/Davey Crichton's Bow/Autumn
Child/Clearing the Glen/Jimmy Sutherland on The Highland
Clearances at Croick/Tain's Big Ramsay/Daughters/Heaven/A
Long Time Ago

The Disciples of Merle and Doc
No label (later Barbaraville BVCD011) (CD)
Martin Stephenson / Produced by Martin Stephenson & Pete
Rawson
Introduction to Douggie Young/They Say It's a Crime/Creole
Belle/Spider Doing a Sonny Terry & Brownie Mcgee
Instrumental/Midnight Special/Windy and Warm/Pearly
Gates/Bluesman's Attempt/Southbound/See You in my
Dreams/Chat – Runtown Rag Instrumental/Kentucky
Shuffle/Sweet Temptation/No Vacancy/Cash on the Barrelhead

2001

Live In The 21st Century
Fresh Ear CD101 (CD)
Martin Stephenson & The Daintees
Wholly Humble Heart/Left Us To Burn/Orange (Is The Colour
Of Joy)/Always Us/Little Red Bottle/Solomon/Bye Bye
Bluebell/You Are The One/We Are Storm/Goodbye John/Me &
Mathew/Involved In Love/Running Water/I Pray

The Incredible Shrinking Band
Barbaraville BVCD001 (CD)
Martin Stephenson
Intro – Pearly Gates/Dialog – Sound Of The WEM – The Rock &
Roll Hall Of Fame/Windy And Warm/Phonecall Shippy –
Feedback/Passing Bye/Will The Circle Be Unbroken (Takes One
& Two)/Will The Circle Be Unbroken (Take 379)/When I Grow
Up I Wanna Play Guitar Like A Woman/True Lord, Show Me
The Way/The Cinema Of My Head/Absent Fathers/Every Step
Of The Way

2002

Collective Force
Voiceprint FORCECD001 (CD)
Martin Stephenson
Produced by Martin Stephenson & Pete Rawson
Orange Is The Colour Of Joy/The Sun's Coming Out/All Ways
Us/Highland Bossa Nova/Home/Walking In The Dark/Summer's
Gone/Orange Is The Colour Of Joy (Backini Remix)/Blind Man's
Blues/Time For Jesus/Robert Smith Wright In Person/Toodle
Oodle Ooh/Every Step Of The Way/Collective Force/Long
Forgotten/Sounds Of The Garden/Baba Num Sana/Spirit
Song/Rowan Berries/Henry Fosebrook And The Woodland
Orchestra

Down To The Wood
Barbaraville BVCD002 (CD)
Martin Stephenson & Jim Hornsby / Produced by Dallas
Simpson
The South Wind/Testing Time/Great Spirit/Flop Eared
Mule/Black Mountain Rag/Cromarty Rag/All Men
Condemned/Jim's Mellow Blue/Home/And We Danced/Home
version 2/Maverick Waltz/Cannonball Rag/Hungry Hash House

2003

The Well Of Harmony
Barbaraville (CD & Music Book)
Martin Stephenson & Duncan Kennedy
The Well/The Ball Of Torridon/Fenderango/Duncan's C6
Blues/Rowan Berries/Highland Afternoon/On The Brae/I Love
Portmahomack/The Road Less Travelled/Barbaraville/Davey
Crichton's Bow/The Eaglesham Boys/The Barman's
Birthday/Tain's Big Ramsay/Clearing The Glen/When You
Become The Wind & I Become The Mountain/The Cromarty
Rag/The Wessington Rag/The Freeway Rag/The Balintraid
Tickle/Martin's Waltz/The Macbeath Waltz/Tam Balloch/The
Glaswegian/Lee's Gallant General

Boat to Bolivia (remastered)
Barbaraville BVCD005 (CD)
Martin Stephenson and The Daintees / Produced by Gil Norton
Crocodile Cryer/Coleen/Little Red Bottle/Tribute To the Late
Reverend Gary Davis/Running Water/Candle In The
Middle/Piece Of The Cake/Look Down, Look Down/Slow
Lovin'/Caroline/Rain/Boat to Bolivia/Roll On Summertime* (Nov
'83 version)/Trouble Town* (Nov '83 version) Slow Lovin'* (Alt
take March '84 version)
* – extra tracks

Gladsome, Humour And Blue (remastered)
Barbaraville BVCD003 (CD)
Martin Stephenson and The Daintees / Produced by Paul
Samwell-Smith/Dave Brewis
There Comes a Time/Slaughterman/The Wait/I Can See/The Old
Church Is Still Standing/Even the Night/Wholly Humble
Heart/Me & Matthew/Nancy/Goodbye John/I Pray/Get Get
Gone*/I Can See*/Me & Matthew*/Goodbye John*/Wholly
Humble Heart*
* – extra tracks. Track 7 is replaced by the single version with
track 16 being the original album version

Salutation Road (remastered)
Barbaraville BVCD004 (CD)
Martin Stephenson and The Daintees / Produced by Pete
Anderson
Left Us To Burn/Endurance/In the Heal of the Night/Big North
Lights/Long Hard Road/Spoke in the Wheel/Heart of the
City/Too Much in Love/We Are Storm/Migrants/Morning
Time/Salutation Road/Left Us To Burn*/In the Heal of the
Night*/Endurance*/We Are Storm*/Big North Lights*/Spoke In
The Wheel*
* – extra tracks, from the Calrossie Midnight Sessions

The Boy's Heart (remastered)
Barbaraville BVCD006 (CD)
Martin Stephenson and The Daintees / Produced by Lenny Kaye
Big Sky New Light/The Boy's Heart/We Can Roll/Ballad of the

English Rose/Neon Skies/Hollywood Fields/Sentimental
Journey/Sunday Halo/8.30 Mowbray Morning/(Least We've a)
Map in the World/Him, Her and The Moon/Cab
Attack/Sentimental Journey*/We Can Roll*/The Boy's Heart
(didgeridoo wig-out version)*/Hollywood Fields*/8:30 Mowbray
Morning*/Him, Her and The Moon*
* – extra tracks, from the Calrossie Midnight Sessions

The Haint of the Budded Rose
Barbaraville BVCD009 (2CD)
Martin Stephenson & Friends
CD1: The Oral Tradition/Living in the Country/Ragtime
Annie/The Old Man Died/'Charlie Poole and The Police'/Weary
Blues/Black Mountain Rag/Write a Letter to My Mother/Slide
Guitar By Etta Baker/You're a Beautiful Lady Etta/Forks of
Sandy/Wild Horse/November Fields/At Charlie Poole & Posey
Rorer's/Collie Malone/Green, Green Grass of Home/Chestnut
Waltz/Goodbye Liza Jane/'That Lonesome Sounding Fiddle'/The
Day Posey Rorer Sold His Fiddle/The Good Doctor
CD2: The Sweet Sunny South/Intro (David Childers)/Old Time
Radio Man/Chit Atkins Made Me a Star/Step Up and Go/A Dear
Old Grey Haired Mother/'Charlie Chased By Haints'/Mt. Airy
(Standing at the Crossroads)/How Great Thou Art/Jessup's
Reel/Wildwood Flower/'Posey Gave Up on the Music'/Foggy
Mountain Top/Intro (Jim Brown/Dolph Ramseur)/The
Rounds/Intro (Sammy Walker)/Some Day I'm Gonna Rock &
Roll/Police Dog Blues/Going Down the Road Feeling
Bad/Lynchburg Town/Toodle Oodle Ooh/November Fields/A Cor
Licker Still in Georgia/'Charlie Poole's Funeral'/New Five Cent
Piece
(Tracks in inverted commas are spoken stories)

2004

Airdrie
Blooming Generation BLG001 (CD)
Martin Stephenson / Produced by Stuart Mcleod
Mountainous Spring/Joy You Give/Beautiful Judas/Nairn

Beach/Daffodils/You Are Running/The Burning of
Cathaidh/Steel String/Easy Road Home/Light Step Travel/Hell's
Half Acre

2005

Wheel Of Fortune
Barbaraville BVCD012 (CD)
Martin Stephenson with John & Isaac Sutherland / Produced by
Isaac Sutherland
Long Way to Go/Stone Broke Stone Cold Sober/The
Fool/Happiness Cloud/Stone Wall Jackson/Alabama Man/The
Ball of Torridon/Around With You/The Hangman/Age of
Meditation/Got It Bad 4 U/The Worried Man

Lincoln Cathedral
Heliopause HPVP106CD   (2CD)
Martin Stephenson with John & Isaac Sutherland
Mountainous Spring/Mary's Waltz & I Will Follow You/The
Burning of Cathaidh/My Wife Went Away/Wheel of Fortune/The
Great Star of Fraternity/Solomon/The Folksinger/The Lilac
Tree/No Religion/Nairn Beach/The Hangman/Painted My Heart
Blue/The Dashing White Sergeant/Age of Meditation/Rowan
Berries/I've Got It Bad For You/Took My Gal a Walking
(CD1 is a regular recording but misses off the last 5 songs; CD2
is a binaural recording and features the full song list)

2007

Sixty Minutes with Martin Stephenson
Voiceprint VP6014CD (CD)
Martin Stephenson
Coleen/Boat to Bolivia/Me and Matthew/Goodbye John/All of
Us/Salutation Road/Endurance/Highland Bosa/Big Sky New
Light/Long Way to Go/2 Sorrows/Mowbray Morning/Dance the
Last Goodbye/Bridge of Nae Hope/Always Us/Soloman/Lilac
Tree

Hell's Half Acre – The Soundfield Sessions
Ramseur Records RR2719 (CD)
Martin Stephenson
Produced by Dolphus Ramseur, Martin Stephenson and Jim Hornsby
Salutation Road/Big Sky New Light/Hell's Half Acre/Sleepwalk/Lilac Tree/Nairn Beach/I Shall Not Be Moved/In the Heal of the Night/Steel String/Blind Man Blues/Texas Law and Justice/Rain/Solomon/Time With Jesus/You Become the Wind and I Become the Mountain

High7 Moon 5
Stove Pony WCMF004 (CD)
Martin Stephenson / Produced by Chris Clarke and Martin Stephenson
Teardrops in my Tequila/Time Changes Everything/Once I Loved a Sailor/Ballad of the English Rose/Hungry Hash House/Tynemouth Sands/Mountainous Spring/Joy That U Give/High 7 Moon 5/Soloman/The Hangman/Old and Grey

Boat to Bolivia (Kitchenware 25th Anniversary Issue)
Sony/BMG 88697145962 (2CD)
Martin Stephenson and The Daintees / Produced by Gil Norton
CD1 – Crocodile Cryer/Coleen/Little Red Bottle/Tribute to the Late Reverend Gary Davis/Running Water/Candle in the Middle/Piece Of The Cake/Look Down, Look Down/Slow Lovin'/Caroline/Rain/Boat to Bolivia
CD2 – Wholly Humble Heart/Spoke in the Wheel/Left Us To Burn/ Nancy/We Are Storm/Salutation Road/Big Sky New Light/The Boy's Heart/We Can Roll/Neon Skies/Sunday Halo/Cab Attack

2008

Western Eagle
Barbaraville BVCD014(CD)
Martin Stephenson and The Daintees / Produced by Stuart MacLeod

Western Eagle *Part 1* / We Are One/Right By You/Shadow of the Sun/Stone Broke Stone Cold Sober/Change My Music/I Cannot Run/Open Road/Indian Summer/Cherryade and Rock 'n' Roll/The Bubble/Western Eagle *Part 2* / Home – last track not listed.

VARIOUS ARTISTS COMPILATION ALBUMS

London Sampler
London LDN1 (LP)
Features – Trouble Town/Crocodile Cryer – 1985

One More For The Road
Polygram 383-2 (CD)
Features – Little Red Bottle – 1987

High Life
Polystar (Germany) 819 825-1 (LP)
Features – Boat to Bolivia – 1987

Giant
London LONLP35 (LP)
Features – There Comes A Time – 1987

Greenpeace *Rainbow Warriors*
RCA PL74065-2 (2LP) – also a Russian version with book
Features – Wholly Humble Heart – 1989

New Roots
Stylus SMDR972 (2LP) & SMDC972 (CD)/Also available on video
Features – Wholly Humble Heart – 1989

New Horizons 2
Stylus SMDR983 (LP)
Features – Wholly Humble Heart – 1989

Just Say Yes to Another Excess
Polygram (2CD)
Features – Left Us To Burn/Endurance – 1990

At Least You Know It's Mega Vols 3 & 4
Flood 2 (2LP)
Features – track(s) unknown – 1991

Pop Goes Reggae – Welcome to Paradise
?? (CD)
Features – Boat to Bolivia – 1991

The Indie Scene '84. The Story of British Independent Music
The Connoisseur Collection
Features – Roll On Summertime – 1993

Sunshine Paradise
?? (2CD)
Features – Boat to Bolivia – 1995

Doing It Right
Demon Records
Features – Sweet Misdemeanour – 1997

Happy Ever After – The Best of Kitchenware Records
EMI 7243 4 98820 2 7
Features – Crocodile Cryer/Wholly Humble Heart – 1999

A Full Head of Steam
AFHOSCD001
Features – Southbound – 1999

PUBLICATIONS

Something To Carry With You
Limited-edition poetry book (some with free flexi-single) given away to people who responded to offer on the sleeve of

Gladsome Humour and Blue for two months following its release – 1988 (reissued with extra poems & pictures 2000)

Janus
Poetry book – the collected works of Martin Stephenson & Pete McAdam – 1988

Bairro Alto
A short tour-trip of prose through Lisbon's beautiful Bairro Alto – 2000

VIDEOS/DVDS (COMMERCIALLY AVAILABLE ONLY, I.E. NOT PROMOS)

A One-Way Ticket to Palookasville
Kitchenware SK1 (VHS)
Features – Trouble Town/Poor Angel
1985 – repackaged in 1988 as *Hits From The Kitchen*, Channel 5 (CFV 00252)

Hits On Video 1
Polygram Germany (VHS)
Features – Boat to Bolivia promo video – 1987

Salutation Road Electronic Press Kit
1990 (VHS)
Features – interview with Martin and excerpts from album tracks

Martin Stephenson and The Daintees
E-group compilation (VHS) – Compiled by Andy Cairns – 2000
Trouble Town/Poor Angel/Crocodile Cryer/Wholly Humble Heart/There Comes a Time/Look Down, Look Down/Endurance/We Are Storm/Wholly Humble Heart/The Wait & Interview/Salutation Road Promo/Heart Of The City/I Can See/Left Us To Burn/In the Heal of the Night/Spoke in the Wheel/We Are Storm/Migrants/Endurance/Too Much in

Love/Wholly Humble Heart/Salutation Road/Running
Water/Goodbye John

Martin & Gypsy @ The 12 Bar Club 19/9/96
E-group release (VHS) – Compiled by Kevin Birt – 2000

**Now That's What I Call Martin Stephenson On Video Vol
2**
E-group compilation (VHS) – Compiled by Kevin Birt – 2000
Look Down, Look Down/Tribute to the Late Rev Gary
Davis/Crocodile Cryer/Running Water/Me & Mathew/Wholly
Humble Heart/The Wait/Rain/Martin Live at the Bridge
Hotel/Martin & his Dad Interviewing Newcastle United
Players/Hot Licks Cookies, Dirty River Band, The Sureshots
Live at the Bridge Hotel

**Now That's What I Call Martin Stephenson On Video Vol
3**
E-group compilation (VHS) – Compiled by Kevin Birt – 2001
Coleen (The Last Resort)/In Concert 1990/12 Bar Club – Martin
& Gypsy/The Gathering 2000/Martin & The Moonshiners,
Darlington, Sep 2000

**Now That's What I Call Martin Stephenson On Video Vol
4**
E-group compilation (VHS) – Compiled by Kevin Birt – 2001
Gilbert the Alien/Martin solo at G2001/Martin & The Toe Rags
G2001/Martin & Gypsy Dave @ 12 Bar Club 20.9.96/Martin solo
@ O'Neill's Bar 05.03.01/Wholly Humble Heart, Channel 4
1988/Martin solo @ On The Edge Festival, 15.7.01/Martin &
Gypsy Dave @ Barbican 1999/Martin and The Daintees,
Swindon 06.01/Martin & Toe Rags, Newcastle, G2001

**Now That's What I Call Martin Stephenson On Video Vol
5**
E-group compilation (VHS) – Compiled by Kevin Birt – 2002
Intro/Collective Force & Every Step/The Return of the
Incredible Dancing Man of Richmond/Jan 2001, The Caledonian
Hotel/The Wait, BBC2 slot/G2001/Martin & Joe/12 Bar Club

20.9.96/Salutation Road Promo Video/Martin and The 'New' Daintees, Sheffield 27.10.01/Suzanne/Every Step of the Way/G2001, Newcastle Live Theatre

Live at The Kalamazoo Club, Crouch End (13/3/2004)
(DVD) – Produced by Mike Wilson – 2004
Running Water/Mountainous Spring/Nancy/Oral Tradition/Little Red Bottle/Light Step Travel/Solomon/Crocodile Cryer/Hell's Half Acre/Big Sky New Light/Old and Gray And Only in the Way/We Are Storm/Posey Rorer/Map in the World/Goodbye John/Southbound/Orange Is the Colour of Joy/Rain/Coleen/Gone The Gypsy Davey/Kathy/Slaughterman/Ballad of the English Rose/Home/Wholly Humble Heart/Big North Lights/The Entertainer

Right Back Atcha
(DVD) – Compiled by Pete Shields – 2005
Martin Stephenson & Friends
Compilation of footage from Jumpin' & Hot Club Tour 2005: Newcastle, Mansfield, Belper, Leicester.

Lincoln Cathedral
Voiceprint VPDVD13 (DVD) – 2006
Martin Stephenson with John & Isaac Sutherland
Mountainous Spring/Mary's Waltz & I Will Follow You/The Burning of Cathaidh/My Wife Went Away/Wheel of Fortune/The Great Star of Fraternity/Solomon/The Folksinger/The Lilac Tree/No Religion/Nairn Beach/The Hangman/Painted My Heart Blue/The Dashing White Sergeant/Age of Meditation/Rowan Berries/I've Got It Bad For You/Took My Gal a Walking

Live at the Roscoe
Barbaraville VPDVD19 (DVD)
Martin Stephenson – 2006
Intro/Mountainous Spring/The Burning of Cathaidh/Orange Is the Colour of Joy/Southbound/Home/The Lagoona/The Hangman/Maverick Waltz/Wheel of Fortune/Age of Meditation/Deep River Blues/Will the Circle Be Unbroken/Midnight Special/Absent Fathers/Running

Water/Gypsy Dave Calypso Style/See You in my Dreams/Time
For Jesus/The Cromarty Rag

MISCELLANEOUS

Daintees Live
SKC13 (cassette) – 1986
Running Water/Crocodile Cryer/Boat to Bolivia/Tremelo Men

The Pack Tracks
Book & tape (by 'Newcastle Light Lagered Ale') – 1985
Features – Roll On Summertime (demo)
Book has a Kitchenware history & discography; a Daintees history

Souled Out
Kitchenware promotional cassette, featuring Hurrah!, Daintees
& Prefab Sprout.
Features – Miles Away/Smile on the Sunnyside/Such a Fool Am
I/Turn Me Around/Piece of the Cake/Tremelo Men/Cecil/Strut
Your Stuff
1983

New Musical Express
Raging Spool (mail order cassette) – 1984
Features – I'm A Hypocrite (Crocodile Cryer)

Jamming **magazine**
Cover freebie (7" single) – 1985
Features – Running Water (listed as 'Watch The Running
Water')

Capitol Records New Music Sampler
Capitol (USA) 4XPRO-79526 (Cassette) – 1988
Features – Wholly Humble Heart

Welcome To Acoustic Ville

Tour CD 1 – 1997
Sampler CD sold on Acoustic Ville tour with Janis Ian &
Martyn Joseph
Features – The Crying/Song of Love and Desertion/Great
Spirit/A Life of Her Own

Chrysalis Cognosci
Prefab Sprout CD Fanzine #1 – featuring the covers & collabo-
rations of Paddy McAloon
Features – Crocodile Cryer (Paddy McAloon Mix) – 1998

Smile on the Sunnyside
E-group rarities compilation – Compiled by Laurent Bailly –
2000
Smile On The Sunnyside/I Feel Fine/I'll Give You My
Heart/Cecil/Monkey/Watch Where the Kisses Blow/Turn Me
Around/Strut Your Stuff/Let's Make a Day Together/Round &
Round/Miles Away/Poor Angel/Take This Rose/Let the
Man/Think Tank/Old Black Jerome #1/Long Last Goodbye/More
Lonely Hearts/Borders/Being You the One/Wild Sex & Drug
Party/Old Black Jerome #2/Hop Down in E minor/Louis/The
Wait/I Live in the East/Hollow Days/Talking to the Child/The
Waves

B-sides Stories #1
E-group rarities compilation – Compiled by Laurent Bailly –
2001
Roll On Summertime/Involved With Love/Look Down, Look
Down (Live – Capital Radio 1)/Louis (Acoustic Version)/Trouble
Town/Jealous Mind (Live)/Boat to Bolivia (Extended River Boat
mix)/Wholly Humble Heart (alternative version)/Little Red
Bottle (Live at Manchester International)/Coleen (Live at
Manchester International)/Get Get Gone/I Can See (Live at
Manchester International)/Men Can Be Flung/Release the
First/Eyot/Kathy (Live – Bridge Hotel, Newcastle)/Wholly
Humble Heart (Re-mix)

Remembering Frances E-group compilation – Compiled by
Laurent Bailly – 2002 Running Water/Look Down/Ball of

Fire/Roll On Summertime/Watch Where the Kisses Blow/
Slaughterman/Submission/Smile on the Sunny Side/Tremolo
Men/Trouble Town (acoustic)/Midnight Special/Boat to
Bolivia/Coleen/Black Mountain Rag / Morning Time/True
Lord/Petticoat Fever/Whitehouse Blues/My Girl Doesn't Want
Me (Martin's 1st song)/Solomon (Symphony of crickets ver-
sion)/Medley for Doc

Acknowledgements

I would like to thank the following good people – with humble apologies to those I have forgotten:

Mark Bradley for his excellent writing, musical knowledge, energy and ability to talk the hind legs off any nearby donkeys.

Ronan Fitzsimons of Ardra Press for his faith in publishing this book, his love of music and all those coffees and muffins in the Waterstone's, Hull branch of Costa.

The musicians for their time and memories (even if some of them contradicted each other!): Martin, Anth Dunn, Gary Dunn, John Steel, Marty Yule, Dave Brewis, Gypsy Dave Smith, Tim Reid, Helen McCookerybook, Janis Ian, Graham Anderson, Joe Guillan, Frankie Gibbon, Pete Anderson, Dusty Wakeman, Lenny Kaye, Dave Fleming, Brendan O'Regan.

For digging out priceless information, photos and music – Mike Chavez, Robert Brown, Andy Cairns, Colin Bloor, Pete Shields, John Ewing, Daniel Coston.

To Jane Cooper for the E-group – and all who were involved in that amazing period from 1999 to 2004. You know who you are.

Mick and June Whitfield – true fans.

Not forgetting Dave Driscoll and Stephen Harris – two early sonic chroniclers.

And most importantly Tracy, Madi and Hannah for not getting too annoyed or embarrassed at their resident musical trainspotter.

RC – January 2009.

Index